once a·day

DEVOTIONAL
{ for men }

The Livingstone Corporation

ZONDERVAN®

We want to hear from you. Please send your comments about this book to us in care of zreview@zondervan.com. Thank you.

ZONDERVAN

Once-A-Day Devotional for Men
Copyright © 2012 by The Livingstone Corporation

This title is also available as a Zondervan ebook.
Visit www.zondervan.com/ebooks.

Requests for information should be addressed to:

Zondervan, *Grand Rapids, Michigan 49530*

Library of Congress Cataloging-in-Publication Data

Once-a-day devotional for men.
        p. cm. — (Once-a-day devotional books)
    Includes indexes.
    ISBN 978-0-310-44074-1 (softcover)
    1. Christian men — Prayers and devotions. 2. Christian men — Religious life. 3. Devotional calendars.
    BV4843.O53   2012
    242'.642 — dc23   2011050040

Cover design: *Faceout Studio and Jamie DeBruyn*
Interior design: *Sherri Hoffman and Jamie DeBruyn*
Livingstone project staff: *Dave Veerman, Linda Taylor, Linda Washingtom*

Printed in the United States of America

12 13 14 15 16 17 /DCI/ 20 19 18 17 16 15 14 13 12 11 10 9 8 7 6 5 4 3 2 1

CONTRIBUTORS

Rick Ezell
Dave Veerman
Bruce Fielding
Mark Jackson
Dave Tieche
Dave Jorgensen
Tom Taylor

introduction

CONNECT WITH GOD

He has shown you, O mortal, what is good. And what does the LORD *require of you? To act justly and to love mercy and to walk humbly with your God.*

MICAH 6:8

Let's be honest. Men—all across the board—are struggling. We know a good bit about "making a living," but when it comes to this business of "making a life," we've got way more questions than answers. We aren't exactly sure how to connect deeply with our wives or kids. Something in us resists opening up to other men about our real struggles. We have many acquaintances but very few deep friendships. We work hard and for long hours, but often come away unfulfilled. *Surely I've been put here on earth for some purpose bigger than this job or this hobby*, our hearts tell us. We acquire a lot of stuff and enjoy a myriad of experiences—and still our souls are restless and unsatisfied. As the years pass, we find ourselves further down whatever road we happen to be on. All the while, we keep our fingers crossed, hoping—and perhaps even praying—that we're not screwing up.

The *Once-A-Day Devotional for Men* is a way for you to find answers, to connect with the God who created you and cares about you, to depend on him and the strength he offers. The readings in this book were written by men for men and deal with a wide range of issues unique to men. Each day's reading features a key passage from the Bible, a short meditation on that passage that will help focus your thoughts, and then a sentence you can use to start your own prayer. Although these daily readings begin with January 1, you can begin exploring the Bible's prayers on today's date.

The *Once-A-Day Devotional for Men* can be used individually or for small group study. No matter how you choose to use this book, we hope it will help you develop the character God wants to create in you.

IS GOD YOUR HUB?

Let the heavens rejoice, let the earth be glad; let the sea resound, and all that is in it. Let the fields be jubilant, and everything in them; let all the trees of the forest sing for joy. Let all creation rejoice before the LORD.

PSALM 96:11–13

There's this idea floating around that God, church, and other spiritual matters are spokes in the wheel of a person's busy life. People say things like, "Oh, yeah, I go to church" in the same way they'd say, "Oh, yeah, I go to that gym" or "Oh, yeah, I'm on that committee."

But the Bible makes it quite clear that God's desire—and the best way to live life—is not to have God as one spoke on the wheel of your life, but to have him as the hub. Sometimes people compartmentalize their spiritual life, like one of those TV dinners. Your job is in one aluminum compartment, your family in another, and your spiritual life—God—in another.

But life works best when you bring God into every area of your life. He can bring change, health, and growth to every aspect of your life—from your job, to your social life, to all your relationships.

In the passage above, the psalmist charges everything to praise God. The earth. The sea. The land. The stars. Trees. Forests. Fields. Everything. All of God's creation—including us—has reason to be joyful because of how good God is.

Take a moment to consider the whole of your life. Does it all belong to God? And more importantly, does it all reflect praise to God? Chances are, you're going to say no. That's OK. Today you can invite God in. Tell him about an area you're having problems with or are worried about. Watch what a difference it makes when God is your hub and not just a spoke on your wheel. ♦

PRAYER

As I consider my life, Lord, I note that you are . . .

LOSE THE REINS

I will instruct you and teach you in the way you should go; I will counsel you with my loving eye on you.

PSALM 32:8

One of the issues that seem to plague us men today is lack of direction. We encounter so many forks in the road that at times we become paralyzed with indecision. *If only God would tell me exactly what to do! If only he would steer me in the right direction!*

What we don't realize is that all along God has been quietly teaching us and lovingly counseling us. The problem is, we don't always hear him, and when we do hear, we don't always obey. Getting direction from God is a matter of learning to seek him and trust him in the countless "insignificant" choices of our lives. When our hearts are in the right place, the bigger decisions will not be as difficult to make.

In Psalm 32:9, God goes on to tell us not to be like a horse that can only be guided by a bit and bridle. In directing a horse, the rider must pull on the reins, putting pressure through the bit on the horse's sensitive mouth. It is only by having force applied that a horse will go in the direction the rider wants it to go.

It has been said that we need to give God the reins of our lives. But God doesn't ask us to give him the reins. He only asks that we listen to his voice and follow him in trust. ♦

PRAYER

God, let me hear your voice . . .

january3

NO CAN DO?

Jesus looked at them and said, "With man this is impossible, but with God all things are possible."

MATTHEW 19:26

"You can't do it. It's impossible." Those are words no guy wants to hear. A statement like this usually results in a rebellion of sorts: "You wanna bet?" We immediately begin to formulate ways the impossible can become possible—or we'll die trying.

Most women don't understand this mindset. Men know if we just put our minds to something, we can do anything—from fixing a leaky pipe to flying to the moon and back. And we have! Yet we sometimes fail in trying to do the impossible.

Jesus discussed an impossible situation with his disciples. A wealthy young man had approached him, eager with the desire to know how to gain eternal life. When Jesus told him to give up his wealth, the young man drifted away. It was then that Jesus came out with the statement, "It is easier for a camel to go through the eye of a needle than for someone who is rich to enter the kingdom of God" (Matthew 19:24). In other words, it was impossible.

When the disciples wondered who could possibly be saved, Jesus provided the assurance in the verse above. Only God saves. We couldn't possibly save ourselves. And there are situations in our lives for which we need the help of the God who can do the impossible.

Got an impossible situation you're still trying to accomplish on your own? Do yourself a favor—trust God to *really* do the impossible. ♦

PRAYER

God, here is the impossible situation in my life ...

THE BIG PICTURE

In the beginning God created the heavens and the earth.

GENESIS 1:1

This is the first verse in the Bible. Note the emphasis: "In the beginning God." Everything begins and ends with our creator God. All of human history and all of the future of the human race is about God and his story. It begins and ends with him.

We can easily forget this truth as we live day-to-day. Confident—and let's face it, sometimes proud—of the power and influence of our decisions, we can think we control our own destiny and can know what will happen in the future. We can forget we are finite, limited, mortal. Only God is sovereign. He alone oversees all human events.

A group of men is playing a game of poker in a restaurant back room. As one man looks at his cards, he knows he has an unbeatable hand and will be a rich man when he lays down those cards and wins the huge pot in the center of the table. Unknown to that man, however, a fighter pilot in training has just ejected from his plane, and the plane is hurtling toward that restaurant. The man will not even get to play the hand.

Like the poker player, we have the illusion of control. But our knowledge is limited, narrow. Only God has the larger perspective; only God is in control. We don't see all the scenarios; we don't understand all the factors; we don't know all the facts.

Just as in Genesis 1, true life begins when we humbly acknowledge God's sovereign place in the world and in our lives. ◆

PRAYER

Creator God, Sovereign Lord, I humbly submit myself to you . . .

KEEP KNOCKING

So I say to you: Ask and it will be given to you; seek and you will find; knock and the door will be opened to you. For everyone who asks receives; the one who seeks finds; and to the one who knocks, the door will be opened.

LUKE 11:9–10

As Jesus teaches his disciples about prayer, he drops in this marvelous nugget of truth, using a metaphor that his disciples (and we) can easily understand—the importance of seeking, asking, and knocking.

That's how the process works in everyday life. If we want something, we don't expect it to be dropped in our laps; instead we go after it. Yet in our relationship with God, we can easily become passive and passé. Here Jesus is emphasizing the fact that God is always listening and will respond to our requests and pleas—but we need to take the initiative.

Often we get too busy to pray. Sometimes we become so burdened and preoccupied with our problems that we forget to talk with our heavenly Father. We may even feel as though our needs are small and insignificant and that God would not be concerned with them. But Jesus says to persist in our prayers—asking, seeking, and knocking.

The other half of this teaching is just as exciting. Not only is God listening to our prayers, but he will answer them. If we ask, we will receive. If we seek answers to our questions, God will reveal them to us. If a door blocks our way, God will open it. Of course, God's answers won't always be what we expect—we shouldn't presume to make demands. But he will respond. He loves us that much.

Persist in prayer. Talk to your heavenly Father. He wants to hear from you. Ask, seek, and knock. ♦

PRAYER

I want to talk with you, Lord, about . . .

january6

ONE WAY OUT

Jesus answered, "I am the way and the truth and the life. No one comes to the Father except through me."

JOHN 14:6

When the disciples asked how they would get to the Father and his "house," Jesus answered that he was the *only* way.

This fact that Jesus is the only way to heaven isn't popular in our age of the "it doesn't matter what you believe as long as you're sincere" and "all faiths lead to the same destination" way of thinking. People argue that having just one way is too narrow and limiting. "How can anyone claim to be the *only* way to God?" they assert.

In reality, Jesus' way is wide enough for all who believe. Instead of arguing and worrying about how limited it sounds, people should be grateful that there actually is one way to God and eternal life.

When coming to a precipice and wishing to get to the other side of the great divide, we don't pout and demand that a bridge be in place on the exact spot where we stand. Instead, we travel to the bridge, the only bridge, a few miles away, grateful that a way across has been provided.

Jesus is the *way*—follow him. Jesus is *truth*—believe him. Jesus is *life*—live in him. Regardless of the claims of cults, pop religion, or wishful thinking, no other bridge to the Father and his house exists.

Thank God he has provided the Way! ♦

PRAYER

Jesus, you are . . .

january7

FOR YOU

What, then, shall we say in response to these things? If God is for us, who can be against us? He who did not spare his own Son, but gave him up for us all—how will he not also, along with him, graciously give us all things?

In the jam-packed chapter Romans 8, we can very easily overlook this simple statement—"God is for us"—at the beginning of Paul's "response to these things." Paul is saying that because of all the evidence he has just laid out, we can clearly see that God is for us. Unpacking the statement one word at a time, here is what it means:

God—he is the all-powerful, all-knowing, limitless, eternal One, Creator of the universe.

God *is*—he exists, has always been, and forever will be—he lives.

God is *for*—he is good, all-loving, personal, involved in his creation, and always seeking the best; he is not "against," a foe or someone we should avoid.

God is for *us*—he is on our side, cheering for us, working for us, transforming us into the image of his Son (Romans 8:29). He is ahead of us, leading the way. He is alongside us, standing with us in every situation. He is behind us, our greatest fan. He is under us, providing a sure foundation. He is above us, watching over every move. He is inside us, empowering us to live for him.

God has us surrounded! His love is personal.

And, Paul confidently asserts, because *God is for us*, no person, no power, and no problem can stand against us. You want proof? God sent his Son to die for us.

God is for you! Live confidently and courageously in the light of that truth. ♦

PRAYER

My awesome Creator, knowing you are for me enables me to . . .

TEMPTATION NATION

No temptation has overtaken you except what is common to mankind. And God is faithful; he will not let you be tempted beyond what you can bear. But when you are tempted, he will also provide a way out so that you can endure it.

1 Corinthians 10:13

Temptation comes in various forms — obvious enticements to break the law, cheat, or forsake a commitment; subtle pressure to flirt with wrong, bend the rules, or delay doing right; nearly invisible urgings to gratify self, shift values, or take the easy way. Through the constant pull of our sinful nature and the consistent attacks of our enemy, Satan, we find ourselves tempted all day, daily. Facing such powerful and continual influences, we may consider giving up and giving in.

When we give in and then are confronted with what we have done, we tend to rationalize, excusing our sinful behavior — just as when Adam and Eve succumbed to the first temptation and blamed someone else. "He made me!" "I wasn't hurting anyone." "I'm only human." "I had needs." "Everyone's doing it."

Instead, we need to resist temptation, rejecting anything that would keep us from doing what is right or push us to do what is wrong.

God is more powerful than any temptation, and he is "faithful," promising to keep temptation from overwhelming us and to provide an alternative course of action, a way of escape, a "way out."

So when you are tempted, thank God for trusting you that much — he knows you can bear it. Then ask him what you should do next — look for his way out and take it.

Take God's way through temptation. ♦

PRAYER

I'm so weak, Lord, but you . . .

GOOD WORK!

The LORD God took the man and put him in the Garden of Eden to work it and take care of it.

GENESIS 2:15

Soon after creating the first man and woman, God put them in the garden and gave them a job to do. Adam was told to "work it and take care of it." We don't know what that entailed, exactly, but it was "work."

Notice that this happened before the fall, that is, before Eve and Adam disobeyed God and sin entered the world. In fact, a chapter later we read, "To Adam [God] said, 'Because you listened to your wife and ate fruit from the tree about which I commanded you, 'You must not eat from it,' cursed is the ground because of you; through painful toil you will eat food from it all the days of your life. It will produce thorns and thistles for you, and you will eat the plants of the field" (Genesis 3:17–18). Suddenly garden work became much tougher.

Often we can see a job as a necessary evil. We need the money to support ourselves and the family, so we go to work. Or we might see it as merely a means to an end—a paycheck that allows us to buy what we need and want. And when considering our career paths, we often envision a time when we can finally (whew!) retire and enjoy a life of leisure. All these thoughts reveal an antiwork attitude. But God created the world, including Adam and Eve, gave them important tasks to do, and pronounced it "good."

Instead of dreading Monday when you have to head back to the office, shop, school, or other employment venue, thank God for giving you the opportunity to work. Try to see your job as a gift and as a calling. ♦

> **PRAYER**

Thank you, Lord, for my good job ...

ULTIMATE TRANSFORMER

But the fruit of the Spirit is love, joy, peace, forbearance, kindness, goodness, faithfulness, gentleness and self-control. Against such things there is no law.

GALATIANS 5:22–23

These qualities are priceless; they can't be bought or earned. We can't work them up emotionally by wishing, hoping, visualizing, or gritting our teeth with determination. And they certainly cannot be legislated. But they are available— free—to all who name Christ as Savior.

These qualities are by-products, not goals—"fruit" of the Holy Spirit as he changes us on the inside. That is, they happen naturally as he does his work in us. He gives us love for neighbor and enemy, joy despite circumstances and in sorrow, peace in turmoil and conflict, patient forbearance during daily aggravations and persecutions, kindness in a violent society, goodness when surrounded by corruption, faithfulness though commitment is scarce, gentleness when the prevailing mood is pushy self-centeredness, and self-control in a world of wild hedonism.

These qualities stand in direct opposition to what comes naturally to sinful human beings (as evidenced in daily news reports and entertainment offerings— check out verses 19–21) and come directly from God himself.

Do you want overflowing love, ebullient joy, deep peace, strong forbearance, tender kindness, contagious goodness, enduring faithfulness, consistent gentleness, and steady self-control? Yield your will to God and allow him to work in and through you.

God transforms lives! ♦

PRAYER

I submit to you, Holy Spirit . . .

GARBAGE!

But whatever were gains to me I now consider loss for the sake of Christ. What is more, I consider everything a loss because of the surpassing worth of knowing Christ Jesus my Lord, for whose sake I have lost all things. I consider them garbage, that I may gain Christ and be found in him, not having a righteousness of my own that comes from the law, but that which is through faith in Christ—the righteousness that comes from God on the basis of faith.

PHILIPPIANS 3:7−9

When Paul spoke of "gains," he was referring to his credentials, credits, and successes in life. Paul had been a well-educated and highly respected leader in the Jewish community. He enjoyed the support of family and friends and was secure in his position. But he left it all to follow Jesus. Then Paul had become the great missionary, teacher, and leader in the early church, enjoying prestige in this new community. Yet Paul considered all he had accomplished as "garbage" when compared with the worth of *knowing Christ.* His relationship with his Savior was more important than anything else. This was more than talk for Paul—he lived it. Paul had lost status, money, influence, freedom, and family for the gospel. Then, as a Christ-follower, he had been pelted with stones, beaten, pursued, and jailed. Still he continued to live for Christ and share the good news wherever he was.

To know Christ should be our ultimate goal as well. Nothing else should come close in value.

What is important to you? Prestige? Power? Popularity? What do you place above your relationship with Christ? A career? A relationship? Financial security? Whatever stands in the way of knowing Christ Jesus your Lord is not worth it, especially when you consider what he gave for you.

Toss out the trash! ♦

PRAYER

I admit, Father, that sometimes...

KNOWN AS ... REMEMBERED

Cush was the father of Nimrod, who became a mighty warrior on the earth. He was a mighty hunter before the LORD; that is why it is said, "Like Nimrod, a mighty hunter before the LORD."

GENESIS 10:8–9

High schools can have unique nicknames and mascots. How about the Cobden, Illinois, "Appleknockers," the Grapeland, Texas, "Sandies," or the Mandeville, Louisiana, "Skippers"? Here's another one for you: the Watersmeet, Michigan, "Nimrods."

You may have heard Nimrod used as an insult. But Nimrod is a positive Bible character mentioned in Genesis and 1 Chronicles. We don't know much about this guy except for the couple of lines quoted above. Sounds as though he was a man's man — "mighty warrior" and "hunter" and a kingdom builder (Genesis 10:9–12). That name does work pretty well for a high school mascot!

The genealogies of Scripture usually just list people by name, along with their children. Occasionally we'll learn a bit more, as with Nimrod. And in his description we also find the phrase "before the LORD," probably indicating that Nimrod used his gifts for godly purposes.

While every person would love to be remembered like Abraham, Moses, David, Elijah, Peter, or Paul, after a hundred years or so, we'll be lucky to be remembered at all, and then probably just with a name (like Cush) before the list of our kids. But what if you could have a line or two that summarizes your essence? What would you want it to say: "scratch golfer," "nice guy," or "all-American"? How about "wonderful employee," "good neighbor," or "great husband and father"?

Those would all be fine choices. But here are better ones: "committed follower of Jesus Christ"; "man of God." Of course, maybe no one on earth will remember us at all — but God will, and he's the only one who really counts. ♦

PRAYER

Lord, may others see you in me ...

GREAT FAITHFULNESS!

Because of the LORD's great love we are not consumed, for his compassions never fail. They are new every morning; great is your faithfulness.

LAMENTATIONS 3:22–23

Surely you've sung it—the beloved hymn "Great Is Thy Faithfulness," a staple of Christian worship services worldwide and used often at funerals and memorial services. The inspiration for this hymn is this passage written by the prophet Jeremiah centuries ago. We see this reflected in these familiar words of a verse and the chorus:

Thou changest not, Thy compassions, they fail not;
As Thou hast been Thou forever wilt be.
Great is Thy faithfulness! Great is Thy faithfulness!
Morning by morning new mercies I see.

Morning, noon, night—arise, work, eat, sleep—our lives are defined by daily cycles. Each day presents fresh opportunities, challenges, and dangers—and sins. But as sure as the sunrise, God's compassions are "new every morning." Every day, every moment, God is ready to forgive, heal, and restore. And, Jeremiah reminds us, God *is faithful*; that is, he is always with us, supporting, encouraging, motivating, and empowering—so "we are not consumed." God stands ready to love and guide us through the day.

Whatever you've done and whatever you face, turn to God *first*, each morning. Give him your day, and then allow him to guide each step.

Our great God never fails. ♦

PRAYER

Loving, faithful, merciful Father, I give you this day ...

january14

A NEW HEART

I will give you a new heart and put a new spirit in you; I will remove from you your heart of stone and give you a heart of flesh.

EZEKIEL 36:26

Science has produced many amazing medical advances. Arguably the most spectacular is the ability to transplant human body parts, replacing old with new from donors or with artificial ones. A few decades ago, transplants were rare, but these days everyone seems to know someone with a new hip, knee, kidney, lungs, liver, cornea, or heart.

When Ezekiel recorded this promise from God, he had no knowledge of organ and joint replacements, but he carefully recorded the message of a heart transplant—and we can relate. Although the "heart" in this passage refers to the core of a person's being—not to a physical, blood-pumping muscle—the image is the same.

The Bible often uses the image of a cold and hard stone to picture a person who is "hardened"—closed to God. Hearts become hardened through repeated sin and living only for self. Sadly, even God's people can become stonelike, choosing to live their own way rather than submit to the Lord. Some people seem so hardened, wanting nothing to do with anything remotely spiritual, that we can't imagine anything or anyone breaking through their tough veneers. But God can. In fact, he can replace their hearts of stone with hearts of "flesh"—soft, alive, vital, warm, and filled with his Spirit.

Name your hardened coworker, neighbor, friend, or relative. Ask God to perform spiritual heart surgery, transforming that person into one who loves the Lord and others. And ask God to use you in the process. ♦

PRAYER

Please keep my heart soft, Lord ...

january15

DELAYS ARE NOT DENIALS

When [Jesus] heard that Lazarus was sick, he stayed where he was two more days.

JOHN 11:6

Dads know that children rank the words *not yet* as nearly the most awful in the English language, second only to the word *no*. How children hate to hear the answer, "Not yet." When the all-knowing, all-wise, loving heavenly Father deems it best to say, "Not yet," what is our mature adult response? Often, if we are honest, we say, "But God, you don't understand. I want it now."

Imagine the great urgency with which Mary and Martha, the sisters of dying Lazarus, sent word to Jesus: "Lord, the one you love is sick" (John 11:3). But Jesus purposely delayed his coming. This was God's way of saying, "Not yet." Was he callous about their pain? Hardly. About a week later, Jesus stood at Lazarus's tomb and wept. He identified with their pain.

Mary and Martha were hurt and frustrated that Jesus had not responded to their request earlier. But Jesus wanted to do something greater than heal a sick man. He wanted to raise a dead man to life.

We catch a glimpse of Jesus' understanding of prayer in this episode of his life. When we pray according to God's Word, we are praying what Jesus would have prayed.

When we pray, usually a gap exists between our request and the answer. We must remember that God's delays are not necessarily God's denials. Timing is very important to God. A request may be in God's will but not in his timing.

God has reasons for not answering our prayers at the moment. Sometimes the best answer we can receive is, "Not yet." ♦

PRAYER

Lord, help me to accept this "not yet" in my life . . .

A FAITHFUL FRIEND

As iron sharpens iron, so one person sharpens another.

PROVERBS 27:17

Many men enjoy watching a good Western. There's nothing better than to see the good guy wearing the nice hat and riding the best-looking horse. The background music in Westerns is upbeat and memorable. Everyone in the town knows that times will get better once the good guy arrives. Life is simple—the bad guys are just as easy to spot as the good guys—but there are always some twists behind that next tree or over the next butte.

Remember when you were a kid, yelling at the screen for the hero not to go around that next corner, into that train car, or through that pass? You know what happened: the hero got jumped and tied to a tree or dropped down an abandoned mine shaft. But many heroes were spared death, thanks to having a loyal friend or sidekick.

Sometimes life plays out like an old Western. There's a circumstance around the next corner from which it seems improbable that you could ever escape, let alone create a good outcome. The last thing you want is to face it alone, and you wish someone could see ahead and shout, "Don't go there!"

Men, remember we don't have to go it alone! We always have Christ to look to in times of need, but we can also find another man to partner with in prayer. When you commit to praying with someone, to helping someone through rough patches, you in turn may be helped out of a deserted mine shaft. Thanks to your commitment to prayer, you may be the hero who helps save the day. ♦

PRAYER

Lord, help me avoid trying to go it alone . . .

january17

GIVING YOUR BEST

People were overwhelmed with amazement. "He [Jesus] has done everything well," they said. "He even makes the deaf hear and the mute speak."

MARK 7:37

People living significant lives pursue excellence. They lead their organizations, their families, their businesses, and, in fact, their very lives, striving for their best. Whether they want to win games, make an impact on their children, or win their share of the market, the thread of excellence runs through the fabric of their lives.

Jesus was committed to excellence. The New Testament gospel writer Mark reminds us that God gave his very best—his Son. And his Son gave his very best—his life. His followers should do no less. Less than our best is inadequate when we consider the fact that God has given us his very best. In view of all the Lord has done for us, less than our best is less than adequate.

Martin Luther King Jr. once said, "If a man is called to be a street sweeper, he should sweep streets even as Michelangelo painted or Beethoven composed music or Shakespeare wrote poetry." Whatever our role, our position, our organization, or our lot in life, we should strive for the best. The measure of our success should be attached not to our particular career or what we earn, but on our character and what we give.

True champions are more willing to give than to get. They go the extra mile. They move beyond expectations. They strive for higher standards.

Excellence does not mean being *the* best, but being *your* best. Understanding that distinction makes all the difference in the world. ♦

PRAYER

Jesus, help me to give my very best today . . .

january18

HE'S GOT THE POWER

That is why, for Christ's sake, I delight in weaknesses, in insults, in hardships, in persecutions, in difficulties. For when I am weak, then I am strong.

2 CORINTHIANS 12:10

Having power at your fingertips is an exhilarating experience. Whether it's a diesel pickup truck, a compound bow set to ninety pounds, or a hockey stick ready to send the puck blazing past the goalie, if there's one thing men love, it's power.

Unfortunately, sooner or later, we all experience a power failure. Maybe your child gets cancer. Maybe you lose your job. Maybe your best friend betrays you. Maybe your car dies on your way home from work to pick up your wife for your anniversary dinner. No matter what the circumstance, being powerless is a man's worst nightmare!

What do we do when we can't fix the problem? It's when we feel the weakest that God's power can be most visible. God doesn't guarantee that every tragedy will have a happy ending. But he does promise to pour his power into our lives. We may not fully understand the loss, pain, or betrayal that caused the power outage to begin with, but the unending strength of our Savior will help us endure.

The apostle Paul wrestled with a thorn in the flesh—a special weakness that drove him to his knees. His struggles show us that our reliance on God's strength is what really empowers us.

Once we own that truth, we'll survive every power failure we will ever have to face. ♦

PRAYER

Lord, be my strength today . . .

SPREADING THE WORD

Everyone who calls on the name of the LORD will be saved.

JOEL 2:32

This tremendous promise has been fulfilled in the lives of millions of people through the centuries. In this context, it refers to those who turn to God during the "day of the Lord," the future time of God's terrible judgment. God does not want to destroy but to heal and to save. Thus, even until the end of time, he allows men and women to repent from their sins and to trust in him for their salvation.

This is the good news we embrace and can proclaim to our friends, relatives, neighbors, and coworkers. They can be *saved* from sin's penalty—forgiven; from sin's power—released; and from God's judgment—delivered. What a great God we have!

In his letter to the church at Rome, the apostle Paul referenced this passage in Joel and further asked, "How, then, can they call on the one they have not believed in? And how can they believe in the one of whom they have not heard? And how can they hear without someone preaching to them?" (Romans 10:14). His point to the Roman believers and to us is that we must not keep this good news of God's amazing grace to ourselves.

So what can you do to spread the word? ♦

PRAYER

Savior, give me courage to ...

THINK ABOUT THIS

Finally, brothers and sisters, whatever is true, whatever is noble, whatever is right, whatever is pure, whatever is lovely, whatever is admirable—if anything is excellent or praiseworthy—think about such things.

Philippians 4:8

The Internet has been a great tool for many things. We can go online and find long-lost buddies from high school and college, buy and sell items through auctions, and look up instructions on how to fix just about anything. We can watch silly videos, read the news, and even play games with people on the other side of the globe!

The Internet has also been a source of destruction for many men. Look at the list above. Some of these good things can be turned upside down—can destroy us—if we take a wrong turn. Contacting long-lost friends may include an old girlfriend, jeopardizing the relationship we have right now. Attention to auctions or gaming can become addictive, causing us to spend too much time online and not enough time with family, not to mention draining the bank account. Viewing silly videos can lead us to viewing videos of questionable morals or downright profane and evil content.

How do we avoid the temptations? How do we remain pure and blameless when using technology that has become second nature?

Paul told the Philippians to fix their thoughts on "whatever is true, whatever is noble." Keeping this in mind can help us to steer clear of the things that bring us down and help us to avoid the myriad of temptations that abound. ♦

PRAYER

Lord, help me to fix my thoughts on things worthy of your praise . . .

WHAT IF?

Fear of man will prove to be a snare, but whoever trusts in the LORD is kept safe.

PROVERBS 29:25

What would your life look like if you stopped worrying about what the other guy thought? What if you decided not to spend a night drinking with your college buddies? What if you told your boss that, no, you can't work late tonight? What if you were open about your struggles instead of trying to put on a good face? What if you kept that old beater of a car and used your money to change an orphan's life? What if you made the choice to spend an evening with your family rather than take on one more responsibility at church? What if you trusted God instead of fearing man?

So many unnecessary troubles and missed opportunities can be traced to the fear of man. In contrast, a life of true peace and wonderful potential is always rooted in a firm trust in God. Jesus, of course, is the perfect example. He was completely indifferent to the opinions of others, yet captivated by the Father's will. He said things to respected religious leaders that make us cringe, yet he stopped to talk to a discarded Samaritan woman. He refused to give a miraculous sign to those who demanded it, yet he cast out a legion of demons from a man who chased everyone else away.

We need a rewiring, wouldn't you agree? Let's ask God to make us into men with backbones—men who have the courage to say no and the trust to stake our reputations on Christ and his way. ♦

PRAYER

Lord, I stake my reputation on ...

january22

THE HOLE

For when we came into Macedonia, we had no rest, but we were harassed at every turn—conflicts on the outside, fears within. But God, who comforts the downcast, comforted us by the coming of Titus.

2 CORINTHIANS 7:5–6

"The Hole" is just one of many nicknames given to what is perhaps the worst punishment a prisoner can face—solitary confinement. Solitary confinement doesn't mean spending a relaxing day alone, fly-fishing in a mountain stream or playing eighteen holes on a beautifully manicured golf course. No, it means being left by yourself for days and nights on end with no one to talk to and no one to share life with. Isolation like that can drive a man insane. Think of Tom Hanks and his volleyball "friend" Wilson in the movie *Castaway* and you get the idea!

Even the apostle Paul struggled with loneliness. In a vulnerable moment he shared with the Corinthian believers how discouraged he had felt—even in the midst of his traveling companions—until Titus met up with him in Macedonia. He writes that God comforted him through Titus's presence.

Solitary confinement doesn't just take place behind prison walls. It is present in the home of the elderly widow down the street, in the lives of the family of refugees who seem awkward and out of place, in the eyes of the teenager who feels abandoned by society and misunderstood.

God also wants to comfort others through you. Be a Titus. Allow God to use you in bringing people up out of "the hole." ♦

PRAYER

Father, work through me . . .

january23

BEHIND CLOSED DOORS

Behind your doors and your doorposts you have put your pagan symbols. Forsaking me, you uncovered your bed, you climbed into it and opened it wide; you made a pact with those whose beds you love.

ISAIAH 57:8

Acceptable, available, concealable, excusable—perhaps no other vice can be better described this way than lust. It has plagued us as a human race ever since Adam and Eve were cast out of the Garden of Eden, and it generally seems to be more of a problem for us Adams!

Who are you when nobody is watching? What do you do behind closed doors? God made it clear to the Israelites that their lustful practices and their sexual sin were really a form of idolatry! Whenever we give in to self, we turn from God.

Lust is so very hard for us guys to fight. It seems that everything is against us—our raging hormones, our loose society, and our sex-saturated media. What a battle! But when you think of it, what an opportunity to daily learn to trust our Father's love for us, to know that he is *not* holding out on us when he tells us to be faithful to one woman, that his way is best and ultimately most satisfying.

The first place to start in dealing with this universal problem of lust is to call it what it is. The saying "you can look at the menu; you just can't order" doesn't cut it in God's eyes. According to him, looking is the same as ordering, and lusting is the same as worshiping idols.

May we have the honesty to call sin what it is. May we dare to trust God's design and remain faithful to him—even behind closed doors. ♦

PRAYER

May my eyes be filled with your Word, Lord...

january24

THROUGH THE FIRE

You let people ride over our heads; we went through fire and water, but you brought us to a place of abundance.

PSALM 66:12

Have you ever felt used, manipulated, betrayed? It's tough when people trample over us in their frantic race to please themselves; it is profoundly more painful when the trampling is done by someone we love.

The psalmist must have known this firsthand when he penned the words above. Yet his perspective was completely opposite from what most of us would think. He believed that God not only allowed the hurt and the trials but also redeemed them as tools of refinement.

Just a couple of verses earlier, the psalmist writes that God had refined his people "like silver." Before refining takes place, the metal has to first be extracted from its ore through a process called smelting. At that point, the silver is silver; it's just not pure. The impurities—in the form of base metals such as lead—are then separated by intense heat. What remains is the metal in its pure and precious form.

Maybe you are already a follower of Christ. By grace, you have already been extracted from the ore of your old sinful nature. But there's still some refining to be done. The process can be a painful one. Yet it is often in the most intense heat that God's greatest work is accomplished in our lives.

Whatever you are going through—whoever may have hurt you—fix your gaze on the work God will accomplish as you trust him. The fire will not burn forever. God *will* lead you eventually to that place of abundance! ♦

PRAYER

I am broken and weak, Father ...

JUST DO YOUR JOB

Suppose one of you has a servant plowing or looking after the sheep ... Will he thank the servant because he did what he was told to do? So you also, when you have done everything you were told to do, should say, "We are unworthy servants; we have only done our duty."

LUKE 17:7, 9–10

When you think of servants you've read about in books or seen in movies, who do you think of? Alfred, the loyal butler of Bruce Wayne in the Batman series? Mary Poppins, the magical babysitter for the Banks family?

Most of us, if we're honest, would say we would rather be the people who *have* the servants than to *be* servants. But according to Jesus, this is the status of every believer. In this passage, Jesus says some very harsh words. He essentially says, "Just do what you're supposed to do."

Why would Jesus be so harsh? What about Jesus' words in John 15:15: "I no longer call you servants, because a servant does not know his master's business. Instead, I have called you friends, for everything that I learned from my Father I have made known to you"? Why is Jesus so harsh here? Probably because he knew we'd need a kick in the pants sometimes. Sometimes we start whining and thinking of ourselves more highly than we ought. Sometimes entitlement creeps in. We think we deserve to be served.

But that's not our role in the story. Our role is to be servants. Doing our jobs. Serving.

Just like Jesus. ♦

PRAYER

Lord, when it comes to servanthood, I feel ...

A MIGHTY WARRIOR

"Pardon me, my lord," Gideon replied, "but how can I save Israel? My clan is the weakest in Manasseh, and I am the least in my family."

JUDGES 6:15

Ever feel like a weakling? That's how Gideon felt. His people—the Israelites—were being cruelly oppressed by the Midianites. The oppression got so bad that the Israelites began praying to God for help. For them prayer was a last resort, a Hail Mary pass.

God heard their prayers. The angel of the Lord appeared to Gideon and said, "The LORD is with you, mighty warrior."

How would you have reacted had the angel of the Lord appeared to you? Gideon's reaction can be seen in the verse above. There he was, threshing grain in a winepress, because he feared that it would be taken away by the Midianites. Not exactly hero material. Yet little did he know that, in God's math, *weakling plus Almighty God equals invincible*. That meant he could go from being a zero to a hero with God's power on his side.

Maybe you feel like Gideon. Small. Weak. Not that impressive. Maybe you need to be reminded that God didn't make a mistake when he called you by name and set before you a challenge you didn't think you could accomplish. Don't forget what Gideon eventually learned: *weakling plus Almighty God equals invincible*.

With God on your side, you can do anything. ♦

PRAYER

Please help me, God . . .

HOW SOON WE FORGET

Aaron's sons Nadab and Abihu took their censers, put fire in them and added incense; and they offered unauthorized fire before the LORD, contrary to his command. So fire came out from the presence of the LORD and consumed them, and they died before the LORD.

LEVITICUS 10:1 – 2

Nadab and Abihu were priests by virtue of their birth—sons of Aaron, Israel's high priest. As such, they had a lot of responsibility in handling the worship and offerings from the people. The fire on the altar of burnt offering was never to go out—it was holy fire. So perhaps Nadab and Abihu did something that made that fire "unholy." In any case, they did something "unauthorized." God's reaction was swift and strong, for his priests—those who represented the people before him and vice versa—had to be without reproach.

Beyond that, however, is a flagrant disrespect for God, a forgetting of who God is. Look back at Exodus 24:9–11: "Moses and Aaron, *Nadab and Abihu*, and the seventy elders of Israel went up and saw the God of Israel. Under his feet was something like a pavement made of lapis lazuli, as bright blue as the sky ... They saw God, and they ate and drank" (emphasis added).

Nadab and Abihu "saw God" and "ate and drank" with him. Imagine such an experience. Yet somewhere later, in the valley, in the hustle and bustle and frustrations of daily life, they didn't bother, or care enough, to check the fire of the offering. Maybe they didn't think it mattered. One little rule broken—who cares?

Apparently God does.

While this can seem odd and ancient, the lesson is clear: When God gives you a place of leadership—in your home, at work, at church—you are responsible to remember who God is and what he expects of you.

Little things? They matter. ♦

PRAYER

Lord, in my position of leadership, help me to remember whom I ultimately serve ...

WHAT'S IN A NAME?

Sing to God, sing in praise of his name, extol him who rides on the clouds; rejoice before him — his name is the LORD.

PSALM 68:4

In Western culture, personal names are little more than labels to distinguish one person from another. In the Scriptures, one's name not only identified them; it referred to the character and the essence of one's nature. Naming carried special significance. It was often a sign of authority and power. This is evident in the fact that God revealed his names to his people rather than allowing them to choose their names for him.

Who is God? Look at his names. He is: The Strong One. The Most High. The Holy One. The Light. The Lord. The Provider. A Prince and a Savior. A Sanctuary. A Shelter. A Sure Foundation. The Alpha and Omega. The Ancient of Days. The Author of Peace. The Creator. Yahweh. King of Kings and Lord of Lords. Master. My Defender. My Fortress. My Rock and My Shield. My Redeemer. My Protector. I AM. The Amen.

God is God.

And as vast, as wonderful, as awesome, as great, as powerful, and as strong as God is, he comes to us — as weak and helpless, blind and deaf, lame and mute as we are — to redeem us. That is reason for celebration and rejoicing.

Call on the name of God. You'll be glad you did. ♦

PRAYER

Heavenly Father, I call on you because ...

january29

THE RIGHT FIT

And this is love: that we walk in obedience to his commands. As you have heard from the beginning, his command is that you walk in love.

2 John 6

Obedience commands a central theme throughout Scripture. From the story of creation to the end of Revelation, few pages fail to deal—directly or indirectly—with God's call to obedience.

Yet in the world today obedience to God is often ignored, dismissed, or glossed over. Why? Could it be because obedience slaps us in the face? It reminds us that we are not in control; we are not in charge. Prideful, we set out on our own course, thinking our way is better.

If we are honest with ourselves, we want to be God. We say to God, "My way is better than your way." We want to exhibit our power, flaunt our egos, seize center stage, and commandeer the throne to control our own little world.

When we proudly step into God's shoes, we discover a bad fit. Just as when a three-year-old tromps around the house in her daddy's shoes, it does not work well. It may be cute, but to let the child live her life in shoes too big would be disastrous.

Obedience demands that we take pride out of the prominent position in our lives. God, instead, is placed on the throne. We get our words from him. We follow them or become lost in our sinful disobedience. The choice is ours. Choose obedience. ♦

PRAYER

Lord, help me to listen and obey when ...

SNOW DAYS

There remains, then, a Sabbath-rest for the people of God; for anyone who enters God's rest also rests from their works, just as God did from his.

HEBREWS 4:9–10

When we ignore our need for rest, we do so at the peril of others and ourselves. Because we do not rest, we lose our way. We miss the compass points that show us where to go. We make faulty judgments. We miss the solitude that gives us wisdom. Consequently, our lives are in danger. Errors in our decisions to forgo rest may cost us our lives as well.

Rest is not optional. Rest was never meant to be a luxury, but a necessity for growth, maturity, and health. God commanded and Jesus demanded believers to withdraw. We do not rest because our work is done; we rest because God created our physical, emotional, and spiritual components with a need for periodic breaks. The old proverb is true: "If you don't come apart, you will come apart."

Do you remember snow days? As a child, when it snowed, you would get up in the morning and immediately turn on the radio to see if school was going to be closed. And when it was canceled, you rejoiced. You had a free day, completely unplanned, in which you could do anything you wanted. It always turned out to be the perfect day.

We need to create our own snow days, or at least some snow time. We need blocks of time on a regular basis to rest our bodies and recharge our souls in order to remain free of burnout and breakdown.

That day—that time of refreshment—is what Jesus had in mind when he instructed his followers—then and now—to come to him for rest. In coming to Jesus, he gives us the snow day we've been listening for. ♦

PRAYER

Jesus, help me to find times when I can rest, especially when...

TAKING GOD SERIOUSLY

Nevertheless, God was not pleased with most of them; their bodies were scattered in the wilderness.

1 CORINTHIANS 10:5

In the exodus, the ancient Hebrews escaped the slavery and punishment of Egyptian rule. On their journey home to Israel, they witnessed the miracle of God's parting the water at the Red Sea that brought doom to their Egyptian pursuers. These people had everything. God guided them with a cloud by day and a pillar of fire by night. They were surrounded by unparalleled privileges. God's presence was constant. His workings were evident. In fact, one would think these people would be the epitome of godliness, if for no other reason than out of gratitude for what God had done for them. But they were not. As they journeyed from Egypt, they played games with their lives and with their God.

That is dangerous business.

What happened to these potential saints? What caused their demise? The supernatural became commonplace. God-talk abounded. But they lacked a reverence and awe for God. They became calloused to the divine and nonchalant in their values, and their heritage was forgotten. Their relationship with God became a farce.

Sound familiar? Never in the history of the world has one country been so blessed. We in America are inundated with churches, Christian radio and television, Christian magazines and books, Christian schools, Christian conferences and seminars. With all this exposure to Christ, our churches should be overflowing with godly men and women. Are they? Instead of making light of what we should honor and playing around with God, we should heed Israel's warning and take him seriously. ♦

PRAYER

God, in a world where you have become entertainment, help me to respect you when ...

february1

THE BOOK OF BOOKS

All Scripture is God-breathed and is useful for teaching, rebuking, correcting and training in righteousness, so that the servant of God may be thoroughly equipped for every good work.

2 TIMOTHY 3:16–17

The Bible is the book of books. In fact, the word *Bible* even means "books." About 170,000 Bibles are distributed each day in the United States. The Bible has been translated into over 1,200 languages. The Bible was the first book ever printed—in 1454 on the Gutenberg press. *Life* magazine called this the single most important event of the second millennium. The Bible has been the world's bestseller ever since. In October 1987, an original Gutenberg Bible was purchased for over five million dollars. It was the largest price ever paid for a printed book.

The Bible was originally made up of books written in three languages— Hebrew, Aramaic, and Greek. The entire Bible was written over a 1,500-year span. It contains 66 books written by over 40 different authors ranging from government officials, peasants, military officers, and fishermen to a prime minister, cupbearer, and religious teachers. It contains 1,189 chapters and over 31,000 verses and is divided into two major divisions—the Old Testament and the New Testament. It presents a consistent picture of the one true God, one cause of mankind's troubles (sin), and one universal remedy (Jesus). It starts with God and shows us the way to God. It will remain until the end of the world.

If you believe these things, read this book and meditate on it; put it in your hearts, inside, where you can never lose it. If you believe these things, take the message of Jesus Christ and go out, proclaiming it wherever you go. Never be ashamed of God's Word. His Word is true, a firm foundation, and it will stand forever. ◆

PRAYER

Lord, help me to set aside time for your Word and apply it when ...

february**2**

CRITICIZE OR FORGIVE?

And forgive us our debts, as we also have forgiven our debtors.

MATTHEW 6:12

Criticism, even when it is valid, reminds us that we have failed in some way. We didn't measure up to someone's expectations, and when they remind us of that, their words are hard to take.

Sometimes critics have ulterior motives. Some will try to make themselves feel better by putting others down. You've probably had the experience of being upended by a nasty remark. When that happens, it is easy to be hurt and forget that others are just as broken and in need of forgiveness as … well … you are.

Jesus understood the brokenness of the human condition. He was criticized by some of the most important people of his day. Still, no one knows the human heart like he does. He forgave prostitutes and cheating tax collectors. He forgave his best friend, Peter, for pretending not to know him. He even forgave the people who crucified him. He knows our weaknesses but gives us the strength to overcome. He doesn't stand in criticism of our every move; he stands waiting to forgive.

Jesus' command in the Lord's Prayer seems hard to obey: "Forgive us our debts, as we also have forgiven our debtors" (Matthew 6:12). But when you think of how much he has forgiven you, you might be more willing to extend the gift of forgiveness instead of criticism. ♦

PRAYER

Lord, help me forgive instead of criticize …

february3

EXTRA GRACE REQUIRED

Dear friends, let us love one another, for love comes from God. Everyone who loves has been born of God and knows God. Whoever does not love does not know God, because God is love.

1 JOHN 4:7–8

We all have people in our lives who absolutely drive us nuts. Sometimes they're called EGRs, because to be around them, Extra Grace is Required. Maybe they're socially awkward, and conversations with them are about as invigorating as reading tax code. Or maybe they're loudmouths who force their opinions on others. Whatever the case, one thing is true about all of these EGRs: they matter intensely to God.

If we're brutally honest with ourselves, we don't want them to matter to God. Because if God loves that kind of riffraff, what does that say about *us*?

And then John comes along with this passage—the kind of passage that hits you in the face like a sledgehammer. There's nothing vague about this verse. If you say you love God and there is someone against whom you have a hidden grudge—then you don't really understand what it means to love God.

To love God means to love whom and what God loves. Think about it: If you're passionate about your wife, friends, kids, or family, and someone comes along and badmouths them, you're going to get angry. Because to love you is to love what you love.

God brings out the big guns whenever he starts to see pride in our lives. And it's good to remember that if the truth were told and all secret thoughts and actions of our lives were brought to light, we would be ashamed. But God loves us anyway. That's just the way God is. And that's the way we should be too. ♦

PRAYER

Make me mindful, Lord, of your attitude of grace . . .

february**4**

OWNING UP

All of us have become like one who is unclean, and all our righteous acts are like filthy rags; we all shrivel up like a leaf, and like the wind our sins sweep us away.

ISAIAH 64:6

Have you ever met someone who has a hard time admitting when he's wrong? If you're a guy, chances are that saying those three words — "I was wrong" — is one of the toughest things you can do. We go to extraordinary lengths to avoid admitting it when it's true.

We have a variety of diversionary tactics. The comparison game: "Hey, it's not like I'm a serial killer." The excuse game: "You don't understand the situation." The blame game: "If so-and-so hadn't done such-and-such, I wouldn't have done thus-and-so." The defense: "What makes *you* so perfect?" The halfhearted apology: "That was not the most right I have ever been."

This is the kind of attitude the Bible calls pride. And the Bible states that "God opposes the proud" (James 4:6). People who refuse to admit when they're in the wrong are some of the most dangerous people in the world. They make their own rules; they can't be told they're wrong. They are fundamentally unteachable.

Contrast this with the attitude shown by Isaiah in this verse. He knows he has done wrong. Even the things that no one else saw, he knows God has seen. He longs to look back at the movie of his life and not see certain scenes. He pleads with God not to remember those things — to forgive him.

So you have a choice. You can be like the proud who refuse to own up to their sins. And in the process, you'll have God oppose you. Or you can be like Isaiah — a man ruthlessly honest before his loving Creator. How will you choose? ♦

PRAYER

Lord God, I admit that I . . .

february5

SPECIALLY CREATED

God said, "Let us make mankind in our image, in our likeness, so that they may rule over the fish in the sea and the birds in the sky, over the livestock and all the wild animals, and over all the creatures that move along the ground."

GENESIS 1:26

In this passage, the first fact that jumps out is that God creates mankind in his "image." While theologians and philosophers have argued for centuries about what this "image" includes, they all agree that in some amazing way human beings are like God.

If you're a father, you undoubtedly remember the birth of your child. What a miracle—a tiny, new person who, through an amazing process, enters the world carrying your image. Every birth is a reminder of God's creative work.

God's creation of the first man was a unique, special act, forming a living being profoundly different from the other animals, and this means *every* human being—male and female, husbands, wives, children, neighbors, bosses, employees, competitors, political opposition leaders, Christians, non-Christians—even those we might consider "enemies."

One strong application involves how we see ourselves. Regardless of our shortcomings, mistakes, and losses, we are good and special—we are like God. You aren't simply an animal in an evolutionary chain. You aren't an object. You aren't a number. No—you are a unique creation of a loving God, made in his image. As leaders in the civil rights movement used to say, "You are somebody!"

Another application is how we see others. Regardless of how irritating or obnoxious people are, we need to remember that they, too, carry God's image. Even those who seek to cheat or harm us are in God's "likeness."

So how are you treating God's special creations? ♦

PRAYER

Lord, knowing that I was created in your image, I feel ...

february**6**

GLOBAL WARNING

The LORD said to Cain, "Why are you angry? Why is your face downcast? If you do what is right, will you not be accepted? But if you do not do what is right, sin is crouching at your door; it desires to have you, but you must rule over it."

GENESIS 4:6–7

Here we find the first two children mentioned in the Bible and the first story of sibling rivalry—and it ends in tragedy.

We don't know why Abel's sacrifice was accepted and Cain's was rejected. It may have had something to do with the contents of the sacrifice, with Cain ignoring God's command. Or perhaps Cain had made his sacrifice with a bad attitude, simply going through the spiritual motions. Whatever the reason, Abel passed the test, and Cain failed—and he was mad.

God gave Cain a clear warning to reverse his course. But Cain persisted, feeding his resentment until he did the unthinkable: he killed his brother.

James presents the progression of sin: "Each person is tempted when they are dragged away by their own evil desire and enticed. Then, after desire has conceived, it gives birth to sin; and sin, when it is full-grown, gives birth to death" (James 1:14–15)—carried out literally by Cain.

God doesn't tempt us, but temptations surround us. And in every tempting situation, "sin is crouching at [our] door." That's when we need to remember God's warning to Cain and the urgency to "rule over it." This begins by asking God for direction and for strength to do what is right. It may mean leaving a physical location or a destructive relationship. It may mean enlisting the help of a Christian brother to hold us accountable.

Sin is crouching. Don't let it pounce. ♦

PRAYER

Dear God, help me flee from temptations . . .

GATES AND COURTS

Enter his gates with thanksgiving and his courts with praise; give thanks to him and praise his name. For the LORD is good and his love endures forever; his faithfulness continues through all generations.

PSALM 100:4–5

The opening words of this passage sound as though someone is going to a professional basketball game, walking through Gate A to courtside seats—ready to cheer on the team to victory. But it's talking about entering God's presence, about worship. Come to think of it, many men seem more dedicated to their sports teams than their church. Some even plan their entire Sunday schedule around an "important" game.

And let's face it. After a late Saturday night, Sunday morning can seem to come too soon, with the prospect of getting up, dressing up, and going to church very unappealing. Yet we often drag ourselves (and our families) there and force ourselves to go through the motions of "worship."

According to this psalm, however, attendance at church services should be occasions of joy in which we fill the air with thankful praise. Even more exciting than the "big game." We should approach worship with joyous anticipation of what the Lord will do.

This positive, joyful attitude comes from realizing that God is good; that his love is deep, strong, and personal; and that he is faithful and true. Understanding that God loves us, remembering what he has done for us, and knowing that we are his people should make us want to shout and sing with joy. What a great God we have!

Next Sunday, approach worship with thanksgiving and praise. "For the LORD is good and his love endures forever." ♦

PRAYER

Forgive me, Lord, for ...

february**8**

HIDE-AND-SEEK

If I go up to the heavens, you are there; if I make my bed in the depths, you are there. If I rise on the wings of the dawn, if I settle on the far side of the sea, even there your hand will guide me, your right hand will hold me fast.

PSALM 139:8–10

Playing hide-and-seek with small children is fun. Often they will simply close their eyes, thinking that if they can't see us, we can't see them. The next stage is for them to go to obvious hiding places—behind a curtain or couch, under a blanket, in a closet—thinking we will never look there. So we go through the motions of "seeking," pretending we have no idea where they are.

We chuckle at these childish ideas and actions; yet many adults do the same with their heavenly Father, thinking they can get away from his presence and knowledge.

Some think they can run from God, moving beyond his sight or reach. Or at least they act that way, hiding sins, disguising true motives, praying in platitudes (if at all), playing at church. It's ridiculous, of course, because God sees and knows everything. But these men and women *hope* they can hide from God because he is a threat to those who are guilty and have something they don't want anyone to discover.

For those who know God and have experienced his love, however, the fact that we cannot be lost to his knowledge is wonderful news. No matter where we are, he is there.

Perhaps you are in uncharted waters and feel as though you have settled on "the far side of the sea." Remember that your loving Father is with you. He is ready to hold you steady in the storm, guide you through, and bring you safely to his harbor. Set your sails to God's wind. ♦

PRAYER

Thank you for seeking me, Lord . . .

february9

POWER-FULL

But you will receive power when the Holy Spirit comes on you; and you will be my witnesses in Jerusalem, and in all Judea and Samaria, and to the ends of the earth.

ACTS 1:8

In this final statement by Jesus to his disciples, he promised that the Holy Spirit would come to them, that they would receive power through the Spirit, and that this power would enable them to be his witnesses throughout the world. A few verses (and days) later, we see the fulfillment of that promise (Acts 2:1–47). Filled with the Holy Spirit, the disciples courageously preached the gospel, and thousands responded. And the church began to spread from Jerusalem into Judea and Samaria and then around the world.

Notice the progression of Christ's promise: power to witness comes *after* receiving the Holy Spirit. Too often we try to reverse the order, witnessing by our own power and authority. When we do that, we are trying to win converts and build our personal kingdom rather than seeking to bring people to the Savior. Witnessing is not showing what we can do for God; it is showing and telling what God has done for us. It is the outpouring of the Holy Spirit's work in our lives.

Submit to Christ, yielding completely to his control. Allow the Holy Spirit to fill you. Then watch God work through you as you witness powerfully to your family, friends, neighbors, and coworkers. God wants to use you to change the world. ♦

PRAYER

Fill me with your Spirit, Lord ...

february10

ONE OF YOUR BEST FRIENDS

Better a patient person than a warrior, one with self-control than one who takes a city.
PROVERBS 16:32

Why can't I lose weight? Why can't I get in shape? Why can't I consistently spend time with God? Why can't I get out of debt? Why can't I break this bad habit? Maybe it is because of a lack of self-control. Could it be that many, if not most, of our personal problems are caused by a lack of self-control?

Self-control is one of the best friends we can have. It will enable us to become the people we want to be and to perform the activities we want to do. We need to cherish this friend always. It is a real lifesaver.

Yet self-control exacts a high price. Following one of the outstanding performances of famed Polish concert pianist Ignacy Paderewski, a fan said to him, "I'd give my life to play like that." The brilliant pianist replied, "I did." On another occasion, Paderewski was asked by a fellow pianist if he could be ready to play a recital on short notice. The famous musician replied, "I am always ready. I have practiced eight hours daily for forty years." The other pianist said, "I wish I had been born with such determination." Paderewski replied, "We are all born with it. I just used mine."

We can't become concert pianists just by exercising enough self-control, but when it comes to living effectively each day, we have the makings of triumph if we will apply our wills and come under God's control and pay the price.

Self-control has your best interest at heart. People exercising self-control are happier and healthier because they are fulfilling their inner potential. It is one of the best friends anyone could have. ♦

PRAYER

God, help me to exercise self-control when ...

LOVING OTHERS LIKE FAMILY

Be devoted to one another in love. Honor one another above yourselves.

ROMANS 12:10

The apostle Paul wrote, "Be devoted to one another in love." To be devoted means we are "full of tenderness" or "affectionate." Paul uses a compound Greek word (*philostorgos*) that denotes "love of the family." The word translated "love" is a familiar Greek word, *philadelphia*. It means literally "love of the brethren." It is quite intriguing that Paul employs two words—love of family and love of brothers—to communicate the need for commitment in loving. The deep affection and abiding commitment made between natural family members should be expressed in the spiritual family as well. We are to love our brothers and sisters of faith as we love our brothers and sisters of blood. Brotherly kindness is an affection that family members have for one another.

Jesus has given authority to the entire world to judge whether or not we are believers on the basis of our love for fellow believers. Love is the badge that identifies us as believers of Jesus Christ. Anytime we do not show love toward fellow believers, we forfeit our right to authentically represent Jesus Christ in the world. People around us who are bored by doctrine and can't fathom theology do understand love. People look at Christians before they look at our creed. They form their opinions about our religion when they see how we behave. If they like the melody, they will listen to our words. If what they hear is discordant, then the lyrics of our faith seldom register in their lives.

As believers in Jesus Christ we need to make a clear, unequivocal commitment to loving each other as a family, for our sake and for the sake of our witness to a fallen world. ♦

PRAYER

Father, help me to love others when . . .

LOVE, LUV

This is how God showed his love among us: He sent his one and only Son into the world that we might live through him. This is love: not that we loved God, but that he loved us and sent his Son as an atoning sacrifice for our sins.

1 JOHN 4:9–10

Remember your first love? You weren't sure about what was happening, just that you felt attracted to her. And your attempts to express those feelings were probably pretty awkward. Through the years, your love experiences have grown, and you've gained a deeper understanding of that powerful four-letter word, *love*—a basic human need.

Love is a popular topic. We talk about it, write about it, and sing about it. *Everyone* wants to love and be loved. But true love becomes obscured in all the verbiage and confused by counterfeits. True love moves beyond talk into action. John states that we can see true love by checking out what God did: he *sent* his Son, and Christ gave his life. God's love sends, gives, serves, feeds, heals, and dies. For God, *love* is an action verb.

True love is also others-centered. In modern society, we sing, "Give *me* some lovin'," and we meet *our* needs by "making love." Again, God provides the contrasting example—Christ came to earth to give himself *for us.*

How can we respond to such sacrificial, selfless love? By loving God and others in the same way (see 1 John 4:11–12).

Thank God for his great love for you, and demonstrate your gratitude by giving yourself to others, just as Christ gave himself for you. ♦

PRAYER

Lord, seeing how you loved and continue to love me ...

february**13**

LAVISHED LOVE

See what great love the Father has lavished on us, that we should be called children of God! And that is what we are! The reason the world does not know us is that it did not know him. Dear friends, now we are children of God, and what we will be has not yet been made known. But we know that when Christ appears, we shall be like him, for we shall see him as he is.

1 JOHN 3:1–2

If you are a father, you know what having a child means to you and to your son or daughter. The relationship is deep and profound. And this is true, regardless of whether the child has been born into your family or adopted.

God uses this image to describe our relationship with him. We are children of God! Through the work of Christ and our faith in him, we have been *born* again and *adopted* into God's family. God is our Father, and Christ is our brother.

Paul wrote that God's plan is for believers to be "conformed to the image of his Son, that he might be the firstborn among many brothers and sisters" (Romans 8:29). This means we are becoming more and more like him as we grow and mature. No wonder the world does not know us—we've changed.

And if God has chosen to make us his children now, just think of what he will do for us in the future! Through John, God says we will be like Christ, bearing fully the family likeness. Truly God has "lavished" his love on us.

What love! What a plan! What a future!

Regardless of what the world thinks, you are special. Regardless of your status in society, you are a member of God's family. Regardless of pessimistic predictions, your future is bright.

You belong to the King! ♦

PRAYER

Abba, thank you for . . .

february14

THE CURE

For I am convinced that neither death nor life, neither angels nor demons, neither the present nor the future, nor any powers, neither height nor depth, nor anything else in all creation, will be able to separate us from the love of God that is in Christ Jesus our Lord.
ROMANS 8:38–39

Whether through separation, withdrawal, loss, isolation, or abandonment, loneliness has become a modern epidemic. Cut off from loving relationships — by divorce, death, conflict, or circumstances — people feel empty and alone. We picture a single individual sitting on a bench at dusk or someone on a dusty road, with downcast eyes and slumped shoulders, trudging one halting step at a time. But even in a crowd, at a party, in church, surrounded by happy, animated faces, individuals can be lonely. And we are adept at masking those feelings with forced smiles, all the while dying on the inside.

Is that how you feel — as though no one really knows you or cares about you and what you're going through? Whatever is causing your loneliness, remember that God is the cure. You may be separated from others, but you're not far from him. He loves you and cares for you, and he's close beside you.

Remember, *nothing* can separate you from God. If you doubt that statement, reread today's passage and highlight all the places, powers, and possibilities that Paul eliminates. Then in case he forgot something, he adds, "nor anything else in all creation."

So no matter what you face, no matter where you are — high above the clouds, in the deepest cave or ocean, at work, in the car, or at the mall — you can never be lost to God's love. ♦

PRAYER

Lord, give me the assurance of ...

february15

WALK RIGHT IN

We do not have a high priest who is unable to empathize with our weaknesses, but we have one who has been tempted in every way, just as we are—yet he did not sin. Let us then approach God's throne of grace with confidence, so that we may receive mercy and find grace to help us in our time of need.

HEBREWS 4:15–16

Jesus knows us, and he knows what we face—the limitations of being human; the stresses, strains, and sorrows of daily life; the temptations; the pain. Leaving the glories of heaven, Jesus stooped to become one of us. Although he was fully God, he became fully man. Then, limited to a physical body in time and space, he struggled, suffered, and was tempted. He knows what it means to be human.

This doesn't mean Jesus overlooks our disobedience, excuses, and mistakes. We still need to turn away from sin and turn toward him. But it does mean he feels our pain and understands what we are experiencing.

Now Jesus sits at the Father's right hand as our Savior, friend, brother, and mediator.

Because of who Jesus is, what he has done for us, and where he is, we can come boldly into the throne room through prayer, confessing our sin, admitting our needs, and asking for help. This is like a small boy walking into his father's office. Dad drops everything to focus on his son.

As a result of Jesus' life and death, you can talk to God at any time, confident that your loving high priest will listen and will give you mercy and grace. Talk to the one who understands you fully.

Jesus knows what you're going through. ♦

PRAYER

You know me perfectly, Lord …

february16

STICKING CLOSE

One who has unreliable friends soon comes to ruin, but there is a friend who sticks closer than a brother.

PROVERBS 18:24

Companions don't cost much and can be easily found. And during the good times, they quickly flutter alongside, like moths to a light. We may think of them as "friends," but the relationship is much more shallow than friendship. As long as we have something they can use or enjoy (prestige, power, money, fun, food, or drink), they will hang around and follow us almost anywhere. But when the light goes off—the first sign of trouble appears, the party ends, or the money runs out—these mere acquaintances can quickly disappear. We can't rely on them for help, support, or even encouragement in a time of need.

Unfortunately, many confuse superficial companions with *true* friends. But the two differ dramatically. A genuine friend stays close, even (especially) during tough times. A real friend accepts and supports, even (especially) when everyone else has left. Deep friendship lasts over the years, even (especially) when miles come between.

Do you need a friend? When everyone else has deserted you, even those you thought were close, you have a friend *who sticks closer than a brother*. His name is Jesus, and he gave his life for you. And he will never leave you or forsake you (Hebrews 13:5). ◆

PRAYER

Lord Jesus, my Savior, my true Friend . . .

JOY — AN INSIDE JOB

Rejoice in the Lord always. I will say it again: Rejoice!

PHILIPPIANS 4:4

Dr. Victor Frankl, author of *Man's Search for Meaning*, was imprisoned by the Nazis in World War II because he was a Jew. His wife, children, and parents were all killed in the holocaust. The gestapo stripped him of his clothes. He stood totally naked before them, but inside he was filled with God's joy. As they cut off his wedding band, Viktor said to himself, "You can take away my wife, you can take away my children, you can strip me of my clothes and my freedom, but there is one thing no person can ever take away from me — and that is my freedom to choose how I will react to what happens to me!" Even under the most difficult of circumstances, joy is a choice that transforms our tragedies into triumph.

Let's face it. Not everything goes our way. Things don't always work out as we planned. Some days are disasters. Other days are worse than that.

Happiness comes easily when everything goes our way. Joy is different. It's deeper. Joy is an attitude we select. Happiness is external. Joy is an inside job where we opt to rejoice, regardless of the circumstances.

Don't confuse happiness with joy. Happiness is a buoyant emotion that results from the momentary plateaus of well-being. Joy is bedrock stuff. Joy is a confidence that operates, irrespective of our moods. Joy is the certainty that all is well, however we feel.

Joy is a divine dimension of living that is not shackled by circumstances simply because we have chosen to respond in a positive manner. Circumstances seldom generate lasting smiles and laughter. Joy comes to those who determine to choose it in spite of their circumstances. ♦

PRAYER

Lord, fill my heart with your joy that I may better serve you when ...

THE GLUE OF GRACE

To each one of us grace has been given as Christ apportioned it.

EPHESIANS 4:7

God often breaks us in order to remake us. For almost anything good to be made, it first must be broken. A tree is broken, and a house is built. Soil is broken, and a crop is grown. Grain is broken, and bread is baked. People are broken, and caring and compassionate believers are reborn. Often it is out of our brokenness that our greatest influence comes. Often before God uses a man or woman greatly, he first breaks them severely.

A church ordered new stained-glass windows for its sanctuary. All the windows arrived except for the largest panel at the front of the church. The congregation anxiously waited for this panel's delivery. When the large piece arrived, they found the glass had been broken in transit. The people were dismayed. But then a skilled artist in the church asked if he could take the pieces and try to make a suitable replacement window. In a short while, the artist unveiled the window he had fashioned. The entire congregation felt that the artist's masterpiece was more beautiful than the original. What was broken was remade into something spectacular.

God's grace sometimes comes in ways we would never expect.

Grace is the glue that takes the pieces of our broken lives and binds them into something new and beautiful. It is the welcome mat that declares to the repentant prodigal, "Welcome home." It is the sponge that cleans the blotched record of our sins so they are remembered no more. Grace is the announcement that there is life after failure and hope for broken, rebellious people. ♦

PRAYER

Thank you for giving your grace to me . . .

WE SHARE GOD'S GLORY

We all, who with unveiled faces contemplate the Lord's glory, are being transformed into his image with ever-increasing glory, which comes from the Lord, who is the Spirit.

2 CORINTHIANS 3:18

As the glory was manifested from God to Jesus, it has now been manifested from Jesus to all believers. We don't possess it, mind you; we radiate it. Recall the account of Moses' going before God to intercede for the people.

"Then Moses said, 'Now show me your glory.' And the LORD said, 'I will cause all my goodness to pass in front of you … But,' he said, 'you cannot see my face, for no one may see me and live'" (Exodus 33:18–20).

When Moses returned from Mount Sinai he "was not aware that his face was radiant because he had spoken with the LORD" (Exodus 34:29).

Like a glow-in-the-dark figure, Moses had no light of his own. But after standing near the most brilliant light in the universe, he glowed. His face was charged with the glory of God.

In like manner, God's glory affects our lives. We have been given the privilege of beholding God face-to-face in Christ. His glory in our hearts transforms us from within.

As we look more and more into Christ's face, we radiate more and more of his nature. ♦

PRAYER

Let your light shine through me this day …

OUR SEARCH FOR JESUS CAN'T WAIT

You will seek me and find me when you seek me with all your heart.

JEREMIAH 29:13

If we don't find God, we have missed the very reason for our existence. Compared to knowing the One who made us, everything else is just crumbs.

Deep down inside, all people have this hunger. God's handprint is on us. His very breath spoke the world into existence. He set eternity in our hearts. We, therefore, are incurably spiritual by nature. That's why every human society—no matter how primitive—has some concept of a higher power, some vision of a reality that goes beyond the natural. On one level, this explains why science has not eradicated religion from the earth. Technological achievement cannot meet the deepest needs of the human heart. That's why millions of people read their horoscopes every morning, and millions more call psychic hotlines.

People are hungry for spiritual truth and if they cannot find it by normal means, they will reach for anyone or anything claiming to give them an answer. Something inside us drives us to seek ultimate meaning outside ourselves. God puts that *something* inside us. Augustine passed on this oft-quoted prayer: "You have made us for yourself, and our hearts are restless until they rest in you." All of us are on a search for the Savior. We desperately want to find him.

The search for God can't wait. The longer you wait, the more clouded the mirror will get. Seeing the whole picture merely requires the clarity that discovering God can bring. Searching for God is good; finding him is much better. ♦

PRAYER

Thank you for letting me find you, dearest Lord ...

WILL WE OPEN THE GIFT?

Those who cling to worthless idols turn away from God's love for them.

JONAH 2:8

One of the many tragedies of life is that God's grace—his free gift of unmerited favor and love—is too often left as an unopened package. And if Jonah had chosen not to receive God's free gift of grace, he would have forfeited his hope of salvation, his chance for reinstatement, and his opportunity to become reusable and reclaimed for God's work.

The conclusion of the movie *The Fugitive* has uncanny parallels with Jonah's life. As Dr. Kimball continues to run from the police and the federal marshal, he learns the identity of his wife's real killer. In the end, Dr. Kimball eludes each of his potential killers, only to be arrested by the federal marshal.

However, after Dr. Kimball slides into the backseat of the federal marshal's car, the marshal takes off Dr. Kimball's handcuffs and hands him an ice pack. Since at the outset of the chase the marshal had said that he didn't care if Kimball were innocent or guilty, Dr. Kimball says to the marshal, "I thought you didn't care."

The marshal replies with a chuckle, "I don't. Don't tell anybody, OK?"

In Jonah's story, it appears that God didn't care. With the storm threatening Jonah and the large fish swallowing him, it even appears that God was trying to kill Jonah. But he was not. God cared (and, unlike the federal marshal in *The Fugitive*, he wanted all to know it). He was trying to save Jonah. He wanted him to live not as a fugitive but as a free man.

When we stop our running and accept the grace that God offers, we also will live in freedom and fulfillment. ♦

PRAYER

I don't want to run anymore. I want to live in the freedom of your grace ...

THE WEIGHT OF HONESTY

Therefore each of you must put off falsehood and speak truthfully to your neighbor, for we are all members of one body.

EPHESIANS 4:25

Run to my arms; glad am I, George, that you killed my tree; for you have paid me for it a thousand fold. Such an act of heroism in my son is more worth than a thousand trees, though blossomed with silver, and their fruits of purest gold.*

So goes the account—according to Parson Weems—of the reaction of George Washington's father on hearing from his son the truth that he did kill the cherry tree with his hatchet. Although the story is well-known, its validity is highly questionable. Yet we would all like to believe that the first president of the United States of America was an honest and truthful man.

Honesty is one of those virtues that is highly esteemed by many but just doesn't seem to work in the day-to-day practices of life. We tend to hold on to it for as long as it is light enough to carry and then drop it as soon as its weight becomes too heavy to bear.

One of the marks of Christ's followers, however, ought to be their honesty, which means both the presence of truth and the absence of deception. It means that others see us for who we really are. It means living our lives in the light, out in the open. How difficult this is for us guys! May God help us to walk today beneath the weight of honesty. ♦

PRAYER

Reveal to me, Spirit, anything false in my life . . .

---

*This quote can be found at http://xroads.virginia.edu/~CAP/gw/chap2.html.

STRIVING TO BE YOUR BEST

Be perfect, therefore, as your heavenly Father is perfect.

MATTHEW 5:48

This quality of excellence and the desire to be and do one's best has been implanted into the believer's soul. Some people immediately give up alcoholic drinks after conversion. One man, after giving his heart to Christ, began immediately improving his handwriting. He remarked, "All things must be done well for Christ, even the little things." Others have changed attitudes. Still others have cleaned up their foul mouths. Employers have treated their employees with greater dignity and respect. Once God enters a life, the believer shares the ambition to do all things extraordinarily. This desire permeates a believer's being and changes his actions, thus transforming his character.

We must remember that excellence is not perfection but the pursuit of perfection. And pursuit is what Jesus had in mind when he stated, "Be perfect, therefore, as your heavenly Father is perfect" (Matthew 5:48). Too, excellence is not being *the* best; it is becoming *your* best. Excellence is a process of becoming the best man you can be in all areas of life. This process involves intense and continual effort, prompting a lifetime challenge that is all-consuming. ◆

PRAYER

Lord, make me perfect—for you ...

february24

IS YOUR PASSION HOT?

Very truly I tell you, whoever believes in me will do the works I have been doing, and they will do even greater things than these, because I am going to the Father.

JOHN 14:12

Passionate people never work for money. This is not to say that they do not earn a great deal of money. But the likes of William Shakespeare, Thomas Edison, Estée Lauder, Walt Disney, Sam Walton, and Bill Gates, who all became wealthy, were inspired not by money but by a drive to fulfill an inner longing to make a difference in this world. Passionate people don't just get a job. A job is something one does for money. Passion is something one does because he is inspired to do it. And passionate people would do it even if they were paid nothing beyond food and the basics. They would do it because it is their life.

Call it what you want—urge, burden, compulsion, force—passion originates with God. Passion is the birthplace of a dream, the trailhead of a new path God calls us to follow.

Significant passion originates with God and takes root in receptive and obedient hearts. Passionate people have their hearts engaged in their work. Their work moves them like a lover ignites their soul. Passion comes from the heart of God to embrace our hearts, and it compels us to act. Passion without action is just a dream, and action without passion is drudgery, but passion with action is sheer delight.

Passion is not a privilege of the fortunate few; it is the birthright of every human being. You can show the world all you are capable of—all that, deep down, you know you can be. Decide now that you are going to let passion into your life. ♦

PRAYER

Lord, enliven my life with passion that I might ...

YOU CAN'T BURY YOUR ANGER

Fools give full vent to their rage, but the wise bring calm in the end.

PROVERBS 29:11

Any archaeologist can tell you that nothing buried remains that way. So why do we assume we can bury something as unstable as anger? We let little things agitate us, but instead of confronting them, we bury them. Over time, our anger becomes increasingly dangerous, like an emotional bomb waiting to go off.

Some of the bombs dropped on England in World War II are still killing people. Sometimes they are discovered and blow up at construction sites, in fishing nets, or on beaches. Undetected bombs become more dangerous with time because corrosion can expose the detonator.

What is true of bombs that are not dealt with is also true of people who have unresolved anger. Buried anger explodes when we least expect it. And when anger explodes, it does all sorts of damage. It severs relationships. It causes ulcers. It leads to murder. When anger is turned inward, it leads to depression; when it is turned outward, it leads to aggression. You have to deal with anger, not bury it.

Dealing with anger is like preventing the bombing raids on England from ever happening. You don't have to worry about buried bombs because there aren't any. Anger only has as much control over you as you give it. Unfortunately, it's not as easy as counting to ten. You have to reason away your anger by asking yourself, "Why does anger have control over me in this situation?" When you've found the answer, you've found your bomb prevention.

The more resolute you are in retaining a peaceful spirit, the less power anger will have over you. Remain calm in Christ, and keep anger above ground. ♦

PRAYER

God, give me your peace that I may resolve my anger for ...

THE SIDES OF FORGIVENESS

"Lord, how many times shall I forgive my brother or sister who sins against me? Up to seven times?" Jesus answered, "I tell you, not seven times, but seventy-seven times."
MATTHEW 18:21−22

Forgiveness is the act of setting someone free from an obligation to you that is a result of a wrong done against you. Several sides are evident in forgiveness.

The practical side of forgiveness means that forgiving someone is simply a deliberate, singular, and volitional decision by which one person chooses to consider another person no longer in debt. It's like saying, "On February 26, I willfully and deliberately choose to forgive you of the wrong you did to me."

The theological side of forgiveness means that you place the person's case in God's court. You are no longer responsible for the behavior of that person, and you are saying to God, "It's your business."

The relational side of forgiveness means that you seek reconciliation with the person who has injured you. This does not mean necessarily that you will be best friends with the offensive person or that you will have a relationship with them, but you relinquish repayment for the wrong.

The transformational side of forgiveness means that since God has forgiven us, we are to forgive others.

Forgiveness is difficult because it is costly. The cost may be the pain of expressing our hurt and disappointment without any satisfactory release and restoration from the one who did the offending.

Some Jewish rabbis taught their followers not to forgive beyond three offenses. Peter, no doubt, thought that forgiving seven times equaled going the second mile. Jesus responded to Peter's inquiry by noting that true forgiveness knows no limits. Go, therefore, and do likewise. ♦

PRAYER

Today I need to forgive ...

february27

A STARRING ROLE

Those who are wise will shine like the brightness of the heavens, and those who lead many to righteousness, like the stars for ever and ever.

DANIEL 12:3

Do you want to be a star? Everyone these days seems to be searching for fame and fortune—sending home videos to TV producers, calling radio talk shows, auditioning for bit parts in movies, making the news, pushing to get on camera during live interviews, winning the contest, game, or lottery, and so forth. Perhaps the drive for significance is what motivates otherwise mature adults to act foolishly for fifteen seconds of personal publicity. In reality, even the most famous of celebrities quickly fade from our memories. For example, can you name the winner of the Super Bowl two years ago? The current Miss America? The NBA's MVP last year? This year's Oscar-winning "Best Actor"? The Olympian currently reigning as "the world's best athlete"? The winner of the People's Choice Award for "Funniest Person in America"? Oh, being recognized, winning awards, and being popular is nice and certainly feels good, but fame is not worth giving one's life for.

If you really want to be a star, forever, in the eyes of the only one who truly counts, check out this prophecy in Daniel. God's stars are wise and *lead many to righteousness.* Think of those with whom you can share the marvelous news of God's love and forgiveness in Christ. Shine on! ♦

PRAYER

I confess, Lord, that I . . .

PLAN A

So he said to me, "This is the word of the LORD to Zerubbabel: 'Not by might nor by power, but by my Spirit,' says the LORD Almighty."

ZECHARIAH 4:6

A dominant aspect of human nature is to depend on our own cleverness, resources, and strength. We want to take charge, to get it done. In fact, one of the first short sentences voiced by children is, "I do it myself!" Submission seems a foreign concept, especially for men (maybe that's why we tend to not ask for directions). So when we find ourselves in trouble or in need, we tend to suck it up, flex our muscles, and work hard, trying plans A to Z. Then, finally, in desperation we may turn to God, asking for his guidance and empowerment.

In contrast, God wants us to depend on him, to turn to him *first* as our "plan A." And this only makes sense—he is all-powerful and all-knowing; he loves us; and, if we have trusted Christ as Savior, we have the Holy Spirit living in us. Depending on God means bringing our ideas, dreams, problems, conflicts, and relationships immediately to him, listening to his Word, and then following his instructions.

Are you worried? In trouble? Struggling? Questioning? Instead of trusting in your own "might" and "power," submit to the Lord Almighty.

Let the Spirit move you. ♦

PRAYER

Holy Spirit, I want to depend on you . . .

march1

LEAD ON!

David shepherded them with integrity of heart; with skillful hands he led them.

PSALM 78:72

Are you a born leader? Who are the first people who pop into your mind when you hear the word *leader*? Got them? OK, now think about the term *Christian leader*. Who comes to mind now? Is this group the same as the one you thought of before, or is it a different one? If different, what is it that sets these people apart from each other? Is it just the word *Christian*, or is it something more?

David was known for his integrity. If your actions inspire others, then count yourself among the leaders. But if those actions inspire others to pray and read the Bible more to grow in Christ, you are a Christian leader. You don't have to be a Joel Osteen, publishing book after book, or a Shannon O'Dell, pioneering the online megachurch with a multicampus ministry. Your actions can be as simple as reading your Bible in the break room at work or praying before you have lunch in your cubicle or on the construction site. People will notice these things! Not only will other Christians look to you for leadership; non-Christians will be drawn to your honesty and integrity. Some may even ask you about your faith. Be ready with an answer, as 1 Peter 3:15 advises.

Don't be afraid to lead. Embrace each opportunity God gives you to show how a man of God can inspire and embolden the hearts of others to obey the call to action. ♦

PRAYER

Help me, Lord, to be willing to lead by my example . . .

march**2**

CHANGED!

Meanwhile, Saul was still breathing out murderous threats against the Lord's disciples ...
As he neared Damascus on his journey, suddenly a light from heaven flashed around him.
ACTS 9:1, 3

Sometimes religion can get in the way of encountering Jesus. Saul was very religious. The problem, however, was that he understood that God was good, which meant that Saul wanted to be like God, which meant trying to be good.

But when you try to be good, you soon realize that you're not. So you start *pretending* to be good. But this image takes a lot of work to maintain, and you know, down deep, that it's phony. So you feel worse because in addition to being rotten, you're also a liar. So you work at external behavior and start looking around for people even worse than you so you can feel better about yourself in comparison.

And that leads to being mean. So in addition to being rotten and a liar, you become a grade-A jerk. It's a downward spiral. Trying to become good enough to gain God's approval simply doesn't work. And as in the case of Saul, this religious cycle can even turn someone into a murderer.

The problem, Jesus says, is on the inside, and only God can change a person there. This change is available, but only if we wake up and realize it. Saul's breakthrough came, not by customs, religion, rules, and church, but through an authentic encounter with the living God, who transformed him into the amazing evangelist, missionary, and Bible writer we know as Paul.

He can change you too, from the inside out. ♦

PRAYER

Lord God, only you are good ...

ALL OPPOSED, SAY ... ?

I will stay on at Ephesus until Pentecost, because a great door for effective work has opened to me, and there are many who oppose me.

1 CORINTHIANS 16:8–9

Open door or *closed door* has become a catchphrase in Christian circles—and for good reason. The idea is found in Scriptures such as the one quoted above. There is a danger, however, that one might assume any kind of obstacle—any encounter with the least bit of resistance—constitutes a closed door.

The apostle Paul writes about his plan to stay for a while in Ephesus, reasoning that God has opened the door for some great work there. Yet with the very next stroke of the pen, he calmly states that there is also incredible opposition in that city. Sounds more like a closed door, doesn't it? Or does it?

Clearly, Paul does not base his idea of an "open door" on the ease or the speed at which the task will be completed. He is not so naive as to think that the gospel will gain any ground without Satan putting up his best fight. The door may be wide-open, but that doesn't mean an enemy army isn't waiting on the other side! The truth is that with great opportunity comes great opposition!

What kind of opposition are you facing today? Don't be discouraged! God isn't necessarily closing the door. It could be that he is asking you to persevere and hang on to him as he leads you to victory.

May you find hope in the words of the 1782 hymn "Awake My Soul to Joyful Lays" by Samuel Medley:

> *Though numerous hosts of mighty foes,*
> *Though earth and hell my way oppose,*
> *He safely leads my soul along—*
> *His lovingkindness, O how strong!*

PRAYER

Help me remain faithful, Lord ...

march**4**

WHEN LIFE HITS HARD

For though the righteous fall seven times, they rise again, but the wicked stumble when calamity strikes.

PROVERBS 24:16

Rocky Balboa—the Italian Stallion—is a fictional character created by Sylvester Stallone who has inspired men for many years. In *Rocky Balboa*, the 2006 film starring Stallone, Rocky shares something with his son that is true both inside and outside the boxing ring: "It ain't about how hard ya hit. It's about how hard you can get it and keep moving forward. How much you can take and keep moving forward. That's how winning is done!"

In James 1:3, we are told that trials and the testing of our faith produce perseverance. The Greek word used for perseverance (*hupomonē*) means to stay under, to endure. It carries with it the idea of standing up under pressure and choosing to not run away.

Rocky is an inspiration to us. The ultimate example of endurance, however, didn't come from a boxer in a ring but from a man in a garden whose sweat was like drops of blood—a man who chose to hold fast and not run from the suffering he knew was coming, a man who said to the Father, "Not my will, but yours be done" (Luke 22:42).

Are you under pressure today? Maybe you've been knocked down again and again. Christ, through his Spirit, can give you the strength to stand up and get back in the fight. Persevere! "That's how winning is done!" ♦

PRAYER

I can't do this in my own strength, Lord ...

THE GREAT WAIT

Sovereign Lord, as you have promised, you may now dismiss your servant in peace. For my eyes have seen your salvation, which you have prepared in the sight of all nations: a light for revelation to the Gentiles, and the glory of your people Israel.

LUKE 2:29–32

In Luke 2, Joseph and Mary take the infant Jesus to the temple to be dedicated to the Lord. There we meet two people—a man named Simeon, who had been waiting his whole life to see the Messiah, and a woman named Anna, who really loved God. In fact, "she never left the temple but worshiped night and day, fasting and praying" (verse 37). And she was old—eighty-four years old. She, too, had been waiting to see the Messiah.

In fact, all of Israel had been waiting. It had been four hundred years since the Lord had last said *anything* to the people of Israel. This is sometimes called the "intertestamental period" by Bible scholars. But really it should be called the "intertestamental silence." No prophets. No Scripture. No word from God for more than four centuries.

But after four hundred years, the Messiah was there in the temple! Of course, Jesus didn't start his ministry for thirty more years.

Sometimes God doesn't do things as quickly as we'd like. And we get angry with God or disappointed with him. But just because nothing *seems* to be happening doesn't mean that God *isn't* doing something or getting ready to do something big. Instead of being frustrated while you wait, you can spend time talking with God and gaining reassurance of his presence. As God shows us in the life of Jesus, waiting to see what God will do is truly worth the wait. ♦

PRAYER

Lord, I am waiting for ...

A HEAVENLY MATH LESSON

As Jesus looked up, he saw the rich putting their gifts into the temple treasury. He also saw a poor widow put in two very small copper coins. "Truly I tell you," he said, "this poor widow has put in more than all the others."

LUKE 21:1–3

In Luke 21, Jesus provides an extraordinary math lesson. While at the temple, Jesus sees a poor widow put in two small copper coins. These two coins, *lepta*, were the smallest coins in the Roman currency. They were worth about 1/100 of a denarius, or five minutes of labor at minimum wage.

Hers is a minimal gift, at least on the surface. But then Jesus looks at these two coins and says, "This poor widow has put in more than all the others."

While we might question Jesus' math, Jesus insists that what he has said is true. Now, he isn't saying that the others' contributions are worthless. Instead, he exalts a contribution that otherwise would have been underappreciated. The widow made a great sacrifice in order to give.

Sometimes little gifts cost a great deal more than big gifts do because their cost is in personal sacrifice. Love in action means sacrificing. The more you love someone, the more you're willing to sacrifice.

Many times we think of an offering we give on Sunday or the time spent with someone as a great sacrifice. Yet we hold back from "giving until it hurts"—the real nature of sacrifice.

The widow gave every cent she had. In heaven's accounting books, she gave more than anyone. God's measure had nothing to do with economics and everything to do with love. The more you love God, the more you are willing to sacrifice to the One who gave everything to you. ♦

PRAYER

Lord, I'm prepared to sacrifice …

IN A BAD PLACE

In my distress I called to the LORD, and he answered me. From deep in the realm of the dead I called for help, and you listened to my cry.

JONAH 2:1 – 2

Pitcairn Island is one of the remotest, hardest-to-reach places on the globe. It is a tiny island in the middle of the Pacific Ocean, just south of the Tropic of Capricorn. It is home to about forty-six people. Getting there would take weeks — even with modern transportation. First you'd fly to Tahiti, which is 4,200 miles away. Then you'd take a boat for about 1,200 miles. But since the island has no natural harbor, only a ring of rugged volcanic cliffs that jut out of the ocean, you'd have to transfer to a rubber dinghy, take your climbing gear, and scale the 900-foot rock cliffs that face the sea.

Yes, Pitcairn Island is about as far as a person can go to get away from it all and still actually be on earth. But this is what the story of Jonah teaches us — that God can be present with Jonah, even in the belly of a whale.

Jonah ran from God, directly disobeying God's specific instructions to go to Nineveh. He was filled with disgust and loathing for the very people to whom God told him to preach. Jonah was not in a good place.

If God were like us, you'd expect him to get royally ticked off. Thankfully, God is not like us. God deals with Jonah with grace, kindness, and mercy.

Jonah's story is our story. We have all run from God. And we've ended up in some pretty bad places. But God sees. God hears. God knows. God helps us and forgives us.

No matter where we are. ♦

> PRAYER

Lord, this is where I am . . .

march8

IN THE MIDST OF THE STORM

The LORD said, "Go out and stand on the mountain in the presence of the LORD, for the LORD is about to pass by."

1 KINGS 19:11

You could make a case that friendship can save your life. It did for one of the most important figures in the entire Old Testament—the prophet Elijah.

You might recall the story. Right after the most triumphant moment of Elijah's life—the Mount Carmel Smackdown (see 1 Kings 18)—the evil queen Jezebel threatens to kill Elijah. This is a brand-new development in the history of Israel. Before that, kings might have hated God's prophets, but they would never dare to touch the Lord's spokesmen. This is a whole new level of evil.

Elijah runs away in stark fear and then enters a phase of what psychologists call depression. He sleeps a lot and wishes he were dead. He is nearly suicidal. And worst of all, he feels utterly alone.

Like a loyal friend, the Lord tends to his needs. An angel brings Elijah food and water. Most of all, the Lord gives Elijah words of encouragement and an assurance of his presence. He also goes one step further: he gives him a ministry companion—Elisha by name. This friendship truly is a match made in heaven.

We all need the kind of friend that God was to Elijah—the kind of friend who encourages us when the darkness of this world threatens to overwhelm us, the kind of friend who reminds us we're not alone. Yes, friends like this are truly a gift from God. Do you have a friend like that? ♦

PRAYER

Lord, I treasure the friends you have provided . . .

march9

A REALLY BAD DAY

David was greatly distressed because the men were talking of stoning him; each one was bitter in spirit because of his sons and daughters. But David found strength in the LORD his God.

1 SAMUEL 30:6

Ever have a bad day—a really, really bad day? David had one. Before he was a famous king, David and his men returned home to their camp one day and found that a band of raiders had taken everything they had, including their families.

The Bible says that "David and his men wept aloud until they had no strength left to weep" (30:4).

Ever have a day like that? The story gets worse. David's men blame him for the loss of their wives and children. So at this point in his life, David has hit rock bottom. His family has been kidnapped and his possessions taken. His men want to kill him. So what does David do? "David found strength in the LORD his God."

At this point, we can see that a change took place. David leads a daring rescue and eventually overtakes the Amalekite raiders, and saves all of the kidnapped people.

The story ends well.

But really, the key to the story is what happened in that moment when a broken and confused David dropped to his knees and "found strength in the LORD his God."

If life ever threatens to overwhelm you, take some advice from the life of David. Stop everything and figure out a way to strengthen yourself by meeting with the Lord your God.

It just might turn a terrible day into an utterly triumphant one. ◆

PRAYER

Meet me today, God ...

march**10**

THE ULTIMATE TEST OF FAITH

On the third day Abraham looked up and saw the place in the distance. He said to his servants, "Stay here with the donkey while I and the boy go over there. We will worship and then we will come back to you."

GENESIS 22:4–5

What do you do when you're quite sure that God is asking you to do something that looks—at least on its face—like happiness suicide? This is the test that Abraham faced when God asked him to sacrifice his son, Isaac. Abraham was flying blind here. There was no Bible, no "Christian Living" section at the local Christian bookstore, and no centuries-long lineage of saints.

So what did he do? One of the keys to this passage is what you might consider a "throwaway" line. Check out the passage above. Abraham says, "Stay here with the donkey while I and the boy go over there. We will worship and then we will come back to you." Do you see what's going on here? Abraham is convinced that, even though the command to sacrifice Isaac makes no sense, he can trust that God will be merciful.

In essence, Abraham focuses on God's promises and his character, not on trying to get explanations for his circumstances. Abraham figures that if he just relies on what he already knows about God, somehow everything will all work out in the end.

Do you have that kind of faith—the faith that considers what is true of God and acts, regardless of appearances? When God asks us to do something that seems hard, we must trust that God is good and always has our best interests in mind. ♦

Heavenly Father, I believe that you . . .

SACRIFICIAL LOVE

A Samaritan, as he traveled, came where the man was; and when he saw him, he took pity on him.

LUKE 10:33

After the devastating tsunami that hit Japan on March 11, 2011, a video surfaced on CNN. A camera had captured a startling image of the tsunami waves rising through a valley as people climbed to higher ground up on the hills. As the wave of debris and destroyed houses thundered closer, the camera zoomed in to show a group of people down below moving slowly—way too slowly. They also were way too close to the rising, deadly surge of water. It soon became apparent why these people couldn't move fast—they were carrying people who were unable to move themselves. Yet the people refused to move to safety if it meant leaving the others behind.

In Jesus' parable of the good Samaritan, the priest and the Levite each asked himself what would happen if he were to stop to help the man lying in the road. But the good Samaritan reversed the question: "If I do not stop to help this man, what will happen to *him*?" This is the essence of love.

Is that the kind of love you have for others—the kind that would risk death to save lives, the kind of love that is willing to give instead of to grasp? ♦

PRAYER

Fill my heart with your love, Lord ...

march12

TAKE IT SLOW

My dear brothers and sisters, take note of this: Everyone should be quick to listen, slow to speak and slow to become angry.

JAMES 1:19

The airline just "misdirected" your luggage.

The sports car you bought is a lemon.

Your meal at the restaurant has a hair in it, but the manager won't give you a discount.

What do you do? You speak out, right? You complain, write a letter, post a blog, and maybe even make a YouTube video decrying the injustice. The unfairness of it all just makes you mad!

How we respond is evidence of who lives in our heart. You can see the level of hostility and frustration in people's lives by watching almost any news show. One pundit debates another, and it seems as if no one is listening. There is no restraint, no lack of verbal assaults. There is also no evidence of the fruit of the Spirit.

We Christians are called to demonstrate patience, not to speak too hastily or harshly but to always be willing to listen. We're also told not to become angry too quickly or allow frustration to dictate our opinion of things. We are called to be slow to speak and slow to become angry.

Ephesians 4:26 tells us that anger is not sinful—but we must respond appropriately when we are angry. Is it possible to swim against the current, to be countercultural by showing kindness to that restaurant manager, self-control to the salesman who sold you a lemon, and patience to those who sent your suitcase to Guam? Absolutely.

When God opens the door of opportunity to show evidence of his power in our lives, we can do so, knowing that the Holy Spirit can use us to be an example of God's love. ♦

PRAYER

Lord, help me think before I react . . .

HONEST TO GOD

Then the man and his wife heard the sound of the LORD God as he was walking in the garden in the cool of the day, and they hid from the LORD God among the trees of the garden.

GENESIS 3:8

You know the story: Eve listened to the serpent and bit the fruit. Then she gave it to Adam, and he followed suit. Suddenly they saw themselves and the world differently, and they tried to hide from God. In responding to God's call, Adam said, "I was afraid because I was naked; so I hid" (3:10). Then God asks Adam how he knew he was naked and if he had disobeyed and eaten from the tree. Listen to the ensuing conversation (3:12–13):

The man said, "The woman you put here with me—she gave me some fruit from the tree, and I ate it."

Then the LORD God said to the woman, "What is this you have done?"

The woman said, "The serpent deceived me, and I ate."

Talk about not taking responsibility for his actions. Adam made excuses, passed the buck, and even blamed God ("the woman you put here with me"). Eve was no better, of course—quick to blame the deceiving serpent.

And we've been making excuses for our actions ever since. We see it in our kids. With more than one child, Mom and Dad are never quite sure who is to blame because the kids blame each other. And if we're honest, we have to admit that we do the same thing. Confronted with a temptation, we give in—and then the excuses begin.

Instead, we need to man up and take responsibility for our actions. In fact, the first word of the gospel is "repentance," confessing our sins and acknowledging our need for Christ. When do you tend to hide from God or to make excuses? ♦

PRAYER

God, help me be your man ...

march14

COME CLEAN

Confess your sins to each other and pray for each other so that you may be healed. The prayer of a righteous person is powerful and effective.

JAMES 5:16

Confession is good for the soul. When we hide sin, we hide ourselves from others. But when we come clean, we can, as James writes, live together whole and healed.

James is not suggesting confessing sin to a preacher or priest. We confess our sin first to God, but we must confess our sin to those who have been affected by our sin. Private sin requires private confession; public sin requires public confession.

When New York's Citicorp Center was completed in 1977, it was the seventh tallest building in the world. The structural engineer was William J. LeMessurier. One year after the building opened, LeMessurier came to a frightening realization. Without his approval, joints that should have been welded were bolted. Under severe winds the building would buckle.

LeMessurier weighed his options. If he blew the whistle on himself, he faced lawsuits, probable bankruptcy, and professional disgrace. He could keep silent and hope for the best. But lives were at stake.

He did what he had to do. He confessed the mistake, and three months later, the problem was corrected.

One engineer commended LeMessurier for being a man who had the courage to say, "I got a problem; I made the problem; let's fix the problem."

You may be at that point where you realize your life is like that flawed building. You know you have points of weakness that make you vulnerable to collapse. Sin is corroding the very foundation of your life. What do you do?

You come clean, get help, and get fixed. ♦

PRAYER

God, I offer up all my sins to you . . .

march**15**

NO FAIRY TALE

*He told them, "This is what is written: The Messiah will suffer and rise from the dead
on the third day, and repentance for the forgiveness of sins will be preached in his name to
all nations, beginning at Jerusalem. You are witnesses of these things."*

LUKE 24:46−48

If you know anything about basketball, you know that Lebron James is one of the
top twenty players to ever play the game. He's a must-see—a man who is faster
than nearly everyone on the court, who can jump higher than men eight inches
taller than he is.

When James played in Cleveland for the Cavaliers, a billboard covering most of
a building read, *We are all witnesses.* Translation: What James did—and continues
to do—amazes us. And we will tell people about him and marvel in our hearts at
what we're seeing.

Although this parallel might seem strange, this is *exactly* what was going
on with the early church. They were witnesses. Jesus appeared to them. That
experience defined their lives.

You see, *something* happened on Easter Sunday that changed the course of
history. There were witnesses who told this story. Many of them were killed
because they wouldn't stop insisting that Jesus was God and had beaten death.

This is history, not fairy tales. Fairy tales don't have witnesses. And it's much,
much bigger than basketball. ♦

PRAYER

Lord, I believe . . .

march**16**

PLAY MISTY FOR ME

When Methuselah had lived 187 years, he became the father of Lamech. After he became the father of Lamech, Methuselah lived 782 years and had other sons and daughters.

GENESIS 5:25–26

This passage gives the answer to the Bible riddle, "Who was the oldest man who ever lived and yet died before his father?" The answer — Methuselah. He lived 969 years, but his father, Enoch, never died; instead "God took him away" (Genesis 5:24).

When reading this chapter, most people wonder how people could live so long. Imagine fathering a child at your 187th birthday! The answer is unclear. Some think it's because the effects of sin were just beginning to be realized. Others posit that diets were better at that time than they are today. Whatever the reason, people lived way longer then than in the twenty-first century.

Time is relative. Ten minutes at the end of a boring meeting can seem like an eternity. But ten minutes in a close basketball game when your team is behind can seem like a few seconds. In the same way, when we're young, living to 70, 80, or 100 seems like a very long time. But every octogenarian will tell you that those years passed quickly.

In reality, life is short, no matter how long we live. James says our lives are like "a mist that appears for a little while and then vanishes" (James 4:14). Whether we live to be 30 or 300, the end comes very quickly.

Instead of wondering, "How long will I live?" we should ask, "How can I live well?"

The missionary C. T. Studd wrote these well-loved words: "Only one life, 'twill soon be past; only what's done for Christ will last." Amen. ♦

PRAYER

Heavenly Father, help me to live each day as though it may be my last — for you . . .

ST. PATRICK'S MISSION

After the earthquake came a fire, but the LORD was not in the fire. And after the fire came a gentle whisper.

1 KINGS 19:12

Kidnapped by pirates as a teenager, Patrick was taken from his well-to-do home in Roman-Britain in AD 405, transported to Ireland, sold to a farmer, and given responsibility for the man's sheep.

Patrick had grown up in a Christian home. His father was a deacon in the church, his grandfather an elder. But the faith had not been real to him until one day, while tending sheep in the barren hills of Ireland, he encountered the great Shepherd and purposed to follow him.

Eventually, Patrick escaped from slavery and returned to Britain, where he became a priest. Then, in a dream, he heard an Irish voice pleading with him, "Holy boy, we are asking you to come home and walk among us again."

Return to the land of his servitude? An unlikely mission. But Patrick was a slave to Christ now, and the Lord gave him a sense of compassion for the Irish. "I was struck to the heart," he later wrote.

Patrick returned to primarily pagan Ireland, determined to bring the gospel to people enslaved by superstition and Druid worship. By the time he died, about AD 461, he had started a movement in the church that transformed ancient Ireland.

Patrick did not turn a deaf ear to the voice of the Spirit, and the gospel spread throughout Ireland. Patrick heard a voice—the still small voice of God prompting him to action. And he went to the people of Ireland. To whom is the still quiet voice of God prompting you to go? ♦

PRAYER

Lord, I'm listening . . .

march18

UNDER A WING AND A PRAYER

Show me the wonders of your great love, you who save by your right hand those who take refuge in you from their foes. Keep me as the apple of your eye; hide me in the shadow of your wings from the wicked who are out to destroy me, from my mortal enemies who surround me.

PSALM 17:7–9

David wrote this psalm while he was being persecuted by King Saul. This was no minor persecution from fellow citizens. David was running for his life, pursued by the king and his soldiers. Quite literally, David's enemies were "out to destroy" him. But as he was being falsely accused and pursued by Saul, David knew his mighty God, his Savior, loved him dearly. He knew he could call out to God, who would hear his prayers and save him from his enemies.

You may not be chased by a king, but you probably have people who are against you for some reason or another. Persecution can come from a variety of sources—strangers, coworkers, neighbors, even family members. They may be spreading rumors about you and trying to harm you in many ways. You may feel surrounded. When this happens, remember that God loves you and wants the very best for you. Regardless of the danger and problems you are encountering, God will protect you from them or guide you through them. He will "save" you and give you refuge "in the shadow of [his] wings." Thank God for his love and ask him for help. You are the apple of God's eye. ♦

PRAYER

Lord, please save me . . .

march**19**

YOUR MISSION IN THE MARKETPLACE

[Jesus prayed:] "As you sent me into the world, I have sent them into the world."

JOHN 17:18

On Sunday the church gathers, but on Monday through Saturday the church scatters. In the marketplace, followers of Jesus Christ live as God's ambassadors. We are his representatives, his messengers. We are on a mission.

Jesus' strategy always involved believers' going into the world to penetrate the marketplace. The marketplace is the largest mission field in the world. We rub shoulders every day with people who need the power and grace of the gospel of Jesus Christ.

What can you do in your work setting to minister and witness to those around you? Make an impact list. List the people you work with for whom you will pray. And begin praying for them each day.

Begin each day by consecrating your workplace. Dedicate it as a sanctuary to God. Make it a holy place where God is present and God can work. And then each day look for opportunities to minister, to serve, to help, to offer assistance.

Here's the point: As we perform our jobs in the marketplace, we may not be able to do everything, but we can do something. So do something for God, his kingdom, and his work. ♦

PRAYER

As I head into my workplace today, Lord, I want to serve you . . .

march20

IT MAKES ME WANT TO SHOUT!

Shout for joy to the LORD, all the earth. Worship the LORD with gladness; come before him with joyful songs. Know that the LORD is God. It is he who made us, and we are his; we are his people, the sheep of his pasture.

PSALM 100:1–3

The psalm writer declares that "the LORD is God." What does this mean? It sounds as though he is saying, "God is God."

Knowing that people have many competitors for the position of "god" in their lives—back then, idols of wood and stone, and these days, idols of money, relationships, position, power, and more—he may have been asserting that only one true God exists, namely, the Lord.

Or the writer may have been highlighting the meaning of the word *God*. The Lord is not a creature or an impersonal force. He is all-knowing, all-powerful, and ever-present—perfect in love and justice. Our God is infinite, eternal, not limited by time or space. He knows us completely, inside and out, past, present, and future. This God loves us and cares for us, and he deserves our total devotion, as sheep with their shepherd.

With the knowledge that he was created and now belongs to God, no wonder the writer of this psalm feels moved to shout for joy (verse 1), sing joyful songs (verse 2), and praise God's name (verse 4).

God created you too. He loves you, cares for you, and wants only the best for you. How does that make you feel? Shout for joy! ♦

PRAYER

You, alone, are God Almighty ...

THE "RUST" OF THE STORY

Let us acknowledge the LORD; let us press on to acknowledge him. As surely as the sun rises, he will appear; he will come to us like the winter rains, like the spring rains that water the earth.

HOSEA 6:3

Remember your first car? Whether new or used, it was a prized possession, and you were so proud of it. Where is it now? Probably in a junkyard, mined for parts, discarded, and rusting.

Nothing on earth lasts forever. Possessions break and decay. People disappoint and desert. Homes crumble, burn, collapse, or are blown away by time, firestorms, earthquakes, or tornadoes. Investments lose value. Physical prowess diminishes with age or disease. Salespeople, advertisers, and politicians promise and forget ... or simply lie.

Looking solely at the world around us, we can feel insecure, adrift, lost. More than anything, we need a sure relationship, a solid foundation, and a secure future.

God's message through his prophet Hosea is that he is near and that he will be there when we need him. Using examples from nature, Hosea highlights the truth that we can count on God.

When you feel tossed about by winds of change and the shifting sands of time, stand on God's solid ground—find your security in him. When you feel abandoned, isolated, or abused, call out to him—he will come. And this relationship will always be true—no rust, decay, collapse, or unfulfilled promises. Come close to God—he is close to you.

God *will* appear. God *will* come. ♦

PRAYER

Thank you, Lord, for ...

march22

GETTING OUR ATTENTION

He reached down from on high and took hold of me; he drew me out of deep waters.

PSALM 18:16

God can use the crises of our lives — whether sickness, accidents, job loss, divorce, or anything else — to get our attention. At few other times can God get through to us with such crystal clarity. In those moments we can change our focus as well as our direction.

What would you do if a dedicated Christian businessman in your church lost his job and after several weeks of job searching came to you to talk? Interestingly, he wanted to know what you thought about his leaving the business sector and enrolling in seminary to pursue a ministerial vocation. He prefaced his remarks by saying, "You know, I've been doing a lot of serious thinking lately."

He was a fine Christian layman. Eventually he found other jobs and never enrolled in seminary. But by his own admission, his eyes and ears had previously been closed to God's voice. It took the loss of a job to jar him out of his complacency.

Here's the point: God uses the crises of life, those near-tragic events in our lives, to jar us, to wake us up, to get our attention. In our uncomfortable experiences he desires to get through to us.

We must never forget that God not only comforts our affliction but also arouses us from a state of complacency. These encounters with God, while they may be uncomfortable, are teachable moments — provided, that is, that we allow God to speak and have his way with us.

Whatever the crisis, God can use it to rivet our attention on him. He wants to speak to us. His words may be uncomfortable, but they will be useful. ♦

PRAYER

God, please speak and have your way in my life that I might follow you . . .

march23

THE TEST OF TIME

Search me, God, and know my heart; test me and know my anxious thoughts. See if there is any offensive way in me, and lead me in the way everlasting.

PSALM 139:23–24

It is easy to get caught up in things that rob us of our time and add nothing to our lives. As kids, we sat on the couch on Saturday mornings and wasted hours watching cartoons. Today, with game apps for iPods and phones, we don't even have to stay at home on the couch—we can take the mindless distractions with us. Instead of taking notice of those around us, we pop in the earbuds and lose ourselves in music and gaming. Our minds can become consumed with distractions, and we lose our grip on the people and responsibilities that really matter.

David, the shepherd-turned-king, was well aware of the intimate knowledge God had about his life. God knew him thoroughly—warts and all. David readily welcomed God's input, treasuring God's guidance.

Look at where you are spending your time, money, and energy. Are there things in your life that you know are stealing time away from your responsibilities or family, or from doing things that will make a difference? Like David, ask God to search you and know your heart. If he reveals something, take steps to make a positive change. Strive to be a faithful steward of all you have been given, including your time, for none of us know how much time we have left. ♦

PRAYER

Lord, help me get my priorities straight...

THE POWER OF INFLUENCE

I looked for someone among them who would build up the wall and stand before me in the gap on behalf of the land so I would not have to destroy it, but I found no one.

EZEKIEL 22:30

During the eighteenth century, many Quakers were wealthy slave owners. John Woolman, a Quaker, dedicated his adult life to eliminating the practice of slavery among his brethren. He spent more than twenty years visiting Quakers along the East Coast. He did not criticize, nor did he make them angry. He merely asked questions: "What does it mean to be a moral person? What does it mean to own a slave? What does it mean to will a slave over to one's children?"

By 1770, a century before the Civil War, not one Quaker owned a slave.

Certain individuals, like John Woolman, have that kind of irresistible and flaming influence that brings out the best in others. Their influence is like a fire on a cold, lifeless piece of iron. The small, soft flame curls around the iron, embracing it and never leaving the iron until it melts under the flame's irresistible influence.

Influential individuals have a clear sense of direction. They refuse to quit because they know that life cannot deny itself to the person who gives it his all.

Influential individuals will not allow their principles to be compromised. They know that when one door is shut, another door that is bigger and wider will soon be opened. They demonstrate a care and compassion for the people around them. Love keeps the flame of influence burning brightly. Because of John Woolman's efforts the Quakers were the first religious group in America to denounce and renounce slavery.

John Woolman was determined to change the minds of his fellow Quakers. His influence transformed his church and his state. He stood in the gap. ♦

PRAYER

Lord, help me to influence . . .

ALIVE AGAIN

When he had said this, Jesus called in a loud voice, "Lazarus, come out!" The dead man came out, his hands and feet wrapped with strips of linen, and a cloth around his face.

JOHN 11:43–44

When a body is entombed, it has no contact with others. It has been sealed up, because it is lifeless and unable to be productive, unable to interact. Jesus has the power to release the entombed and give new life. He can roll the stone away from a tomb!

In the case of Jesus' friend Lazarus, when the stone in front of his tomb was rolled away, Lazarus did not automatically get up and walk out, full of life. For Lazarus to leave his tomb, Jesus had to call him by name and instruct him to come out. Instantly, Lazarus returned to life. Though still in the bondage of his death clothes, he got up and walked out.

Perhaps you feel that missed opportunities or failures have rendered you "lifeless" today. Yet the means for freedom from guilt or pain has been accomplished. The stone has been rolled away. It is time to listen to God's voice, then rise up from your tomb—the state of lifeless inactivity—and be an effective witness for God. Leave behind that which binds you, and live in the glory God has for your future. ♦

PRAYER

Lord, be active and alive in me that I might also be active and alive . . .

march26

KNOWN AND LOVED

You have searched me, LORD, and you know me. You know when I sit and when I rise; you perceive my thoughts from afar. You discern my going out and my lying down; you are familiar with all my ways.

PSALM 139:1–3

Popular TV shows and movies often picture a sinister government agency spying on citizens—reading correspondence, recording calls, checking financial transactions, watching movements. We abhor the possibility of that happening because we highly value privacy and resist control. And we carefully hide our secrets. This goes much further than e-mails, phone calls, and bank accounts; we also hide our sins of commission and omission. We may be afraid of being found out, discovered. Often, however, we simply fear rejection. What if the *real* person, hidden behind the facade, were uncovered? So consider ...

What if someone knew ...

> ... your deepest thoughts and emotions?
> ... your true motives?
> ... your complete personal history?
> ... your talents, abilities, and gifts?
> ... your dreams and desires?

Would you feel threatened? Afraid? Embarrassed? Relieved?

God knows. He has "searched" you. He understands who you are, what you have done, and why you do what you do. He even knows your secrets. And he stands ready to forgive, heal, correct, guide, affirm, protect, and conform you to the image of his Son (Romans 8:29).

Follow God's ways. He knows and wants what's best for you.

No need to hide. You are known; you are loved. ♦

PRAYER

I know that you know me, Lord ...

march**27**

RADIATE CHRIST'S LIGHT

You are the light of the world.

MATTHEW 5:14

Jesus made it absolutely clear that he wants his followers to radiate his love to those around them. That's why he talked about light. A tiny tungsten filament charged with electrical energy naturally radiates light and dispels darkness. It has no choice. The very nature of light is such that it must shatter the darkness around it. In the same way, true Christians should, by their very nature, radiate something of the work of God in their lives to the people around them. We are the light of the world; we must, therefore, radiate that light and dispel darkness.

Jesus anticipated that some believers might choose to limit their candlepower, to refuse to shine their lights—and he forbade it. "Let your light shine!" he commanded. He did not, and he does not now, leave believers the option of letting their worlds remain in undisturbed blackness.

Jesus made it obvious that he wants us to spread his influence to every corner of this dark, fallen world. It's not enough that we simply take our lights out of hiding. He wants us to put them on a lampstand where everyone can see them! God wants the light of his love to be held high so it can permeate every bit of darkness.

How long will it take for us to realize that we are his agents of light? It is through the channels of our daily lives that God shines the light of his message of love into a dark world. You *are* light. Shine. ♦

PRAYER

Help me to shine brighter when . . .

march28

FIND US FAITHFUL

Be faithful, even to the point of death, and I will give you life as your victor's crown.

REVELATION 2:10

Faithfulness is not a word we hear often these days. Sometimes we hear it at retirement parties, or we use it to describe our dog, or we think of it when we refer to "Old Faithful" at Yellowstone National Park. "Old Faithful" is famous for its faithfulness—it's like clockwork!

It's not easy to find someone who can be counted on—one who is dependable through thick and thin. The fact is that not everyone who volunteers actually comes through. Faithfulness is not just a religious duty we employ on Sundays or when we are supposed to be Christian. When we tire of our roles and responsibilities, it helps to remember that God has planted us in a certain place and told us to be dependable and reliable. Christ expects us to be faithful in the very place he puts us.

In the eleventh century, King Henry III of Bavaria grew tired of court life and the pressures of being a monarch. He made application to Prior Richard at a local monastery, asking to be accepted as a contemplative and spend the rest of his life in the monastery.

"Your Majesty," said Prior Richard, "do you understand that the pledge here is one of obedience? That will be hard because you have been a king."

"I understand," said Henry. "The rest of my life I will be obedient to you, as Christ leads you."

"Then I will tell you what to do," said Prior Richard. "Go back to your throne and serve faithfully in the place where God has put you."

Not bad counsel. Go forth and do likewise, faithfully. ♦

PRAYER

God, you have always been faithful to me. Help me to be faithful to others when . . .

HE'S ALWAYS THERE

Then Satan entered Judas, called Iscariot, one of the Twelve. And Judas went to the chief priests and the officers of the temple guard and discussed with them how he might betray Jesus.

LUKE 22:3−4

In Luke 22, Judas—a beloved and chosen disciple of Jesus—somehow gets to the place where he betrays Jesus and plots with his enemies to have him killed for thirty pieces of silver.

Jesus is gathered for his final meal with his closest friends. Even as Jesus is about to deliver up his life for the sake of his friends, one of them is about to betray him.

You see, Judas got lied to by Satan. Judas forgot that God is always there. He may have met the leadership team in private, but God was not fooled. As with all secretly plotted sin, God was there.

God is always there. Nothing is hidden from God. We can't fool God.

You know the rest of the story. Judas ended up killing himself, probably out of shame or hopelessness. He could not undo what he had done. He gave in to the lie once more.

We don't have to give in to the lie. No matter what we've done, God is always there, waiting to forgive. If you've got something to talk over with him, he is waiting to listen. ♦

PRAYER

Lord, I messed up ...

march30

DOWN TO THE DREGS

This is what your Sovereign LORD says, your God, who defends his people: "See, I have taken out of your hand the cup that made you stagger; from that cup, the goblet of my wrath, you will never drink again.

ISAIAH 51:22

It was a dark night, and there was a chill in the air. A man had his face to the ground. One could tell from his trembling body that he was in anguish. In spite of the cold, sweat could be seen dripping off his brow as he began to cry out, "Father, if you are willing, take this cup from me; yet not my will, but yours be done" (Luke 22:42).

As Jesus prayed on the Mount of Olives, he knew what lay ahead. He knew that in a few moments he would begin drinking from the cup of God's fury against sin. The thought was almost unbearable. That cup was not meant to be his. Up until that point, he had known only sweet communion with the Father. Now the Father had taken the cup of wrath out of the hands of sinners and placed it before him; and he was about to drain it to its dregs.

Jesus knew all this even before he wept on the Mount of Olives. He knew it in the upper room as he shared the Passover meal with the Twelve. There can be no exchange in history more amazing or more profound than what took place that night: God took the cup of his fury out of the hands of guilty sinners and gave it to his Son to drink. In exchange he offers to all of us the cup of peace—the cup of the new covenant in Christ's blood! Have you received that peace? ♦

PRAYER

Thank you, Father, for the cup of peace . . .

march31

THE FORCE OF FAITH

Though it is the smallest of all seeds, yet when it grows, it is the largest of garden plants and becomes a tree, so that the birds come and perch in its branches.

MATTHEW 13:32

Strength exists in smallness. A spark can start a fire, an acorn grows into a tree, and a single idea can spur an individual to change the world. Faith, regardless of its size, can change desperate circumstances into a hope-filled situation.

Jesus' parable about a mustard seed is a parable about smallness affecting greatness. The mustard seed was known for its smallness. In Jesus' day, a particular variety of mustard plant in Palestine grew rapidly from a minuscule seed into a bush and then into a tree. Mustard seeds were so small that the naked eye could barely see them. Yet the result was a strong-branched tree.

Look closely at the central character of the parable. The Lord himself sows the mustard seed that grows to gigantic proportions. The seed is his gift of faith to us. The issue is not the size of our faith but the object of our faith. Faith needs to be directed toward God. Even the smallest amount of faith can be the difference in whether or not you finish strong.

In 1972, NASA launched the exploratory space probe Pioneer 10. By 1997, twenty-five years after its launch, the satellite was more than six billion miles from the sun, beaming back radio signals to scientists on Earth from an eight-watt transmitter, which radiates about as much power as a bedroom night light.

In like manner, the seed of faith planted within us is like that tiny eight-watt transmitter. We can keep going and going and going. God has implanted us all with the faith we need. As long as we keep our hearts focused on him, God can work. ♦

PRAYER

Strengthen my faith, Lord, for the task at hand . . .

FAITH HAS ITS REASONS

He was chosen before the creation of the world, but was revealed in these last times for your sake. Through him you believe in God, who raised him from the dead and glorified him, and so your faith and hope are in God.

1 PETER 1:20–21

Doubts come for a variety of reasons—persecution, sickness, loss. We can feel distant from God and question what we have professed to believe, wondering if it is really true.

Certainly first-century believers could have felt that way. That's why Peter wrote and highlighted the truth that Jesus was *revealed*; that is, he had come in space and time as a living, breathing human being. That's an historical fact. Jesus of Nazareth lived and then was executed by the Romans—dead and buried. But, proving beyond doubt that his claims were true, Jesus came back to life, rising bodily from the grave. The resurrection happened; the tomb is empty.

Faith in God is not a blind leap in the dark, against all reason. Jesus is the indisputable proof that God exists and that he loves us. God sent Jesus to live on earth as a man and to die on the cross as the perfect sacrifice for our sins. His resurrection and ascension show us that he was and is God's eternal Son. Thus we can be confident that God is real and true and that we will have eternal life, just as he promised.

When doubts creep in like evening shadows, remember the facts about Jesus. When problems hit like a surging tide, hold on to the reality of Christ. When despair threatens to engulf you in darkness, take hope in God's promise of deliverance and eternal life. Jesus was chosen, revealed, raised, and glorified! ♦

It's true!

PRAYER

Thank you, Jesus, for . . .

PROMISE KEEPER

God said, "This is the sign of the covenant I am making between me and you and every living creature with you, a covenant for all generations to come: I have set my rainbow in the clouds, and it will be the sign of the covenant between me and the earth."

GENESIS 9:12–13

After saving Noah and his family through the flood, God established his "covenant" with them, all living creatures, and all who would follow (that includes us). He promised never again to destroy the earth by means of a flood. And he gave the rainbow as a sign of his covenant.

We tend to equate the word *covenant* with *contract*, and we know how little contracts seem to mean these days. Every week, we hear of another high-profile athlete who wants to renegotiate his contract, often simply because someone else at the same position is making more money. But in the Bible, covenants were much more serious and binding—these were solemn agreements, often involving a special ceremony and, as in the case here, a special sign.

Here are the important points to remember. First, God initiated this covenant, and it was totally on him. Noah and his family (and everyone else mentioned) didn't have to make any promises or do anything—it was all God, all grace. Second, God always keeps his word—he will do what he says.

The Bible is loaded with God's promises. He promises forgiveness of sins and new life to all who put their faith in Christ as Savior. He promises his presence and strength for life's journey. He promises to bring us home to live with him eternally in heaven.

So when rainy days and Mondays get you down, look for the rainbow. Let God's covenant with his people and his promises to you lift your spirits and give you hope. ♦

PRAYER

Thank you, Lord, for these promises …

april3

A CHANGED LIFE

To him who loves us and has freed us from our sins by his blood, and has made us to be a kingdom and priests to serve his God and Father—to him be glory and power for ever and ever! Amen.

REVELATION 1:5–6

By saying "to him be glory and power for ever and ever," John praises Christ by acknowledging his eternal glory and power. Overwhelmed by what Christ has done for him, John responds with enthusiastic adoration for his Lord and Savior.

What has Christ done for you? How has he changed your life? When hearing dramatic conversion testimonies, we may downplay our relationship with God and what we can do for him because our stories are not nearly as dramatic. Even worse, we diminish his work for us.

Many hesitate to tell others about Christ because they don't feel that the changes in their lives have been spectacular enough. But we should witness for Christ because of what he has done for us, not because of what we have done for him.

Think about it. Christ demonstrated his great love by freeing you from your sins through his death on the cross, guaranteeing you a place in his kingdom, and making you a priest to administer his love to others. The fact that the all-powerful God gives you eternal life is nothing short of spectacular.

Praise God through your words and works. You are a priest of the kingdom! ♦

PRAYER

Jesus, thank you for ...

april4

OURS FOR THE TAKING

If you keep my commands, you will remain in my love, just as I have kept my Father's commands and remain in his love. I have told you this so that my joy may be in you and that your joy may be complete.

JOHN 15:10–11

Here we are at what is known as the Last Supper. The disciples are not yet getting it. The betrayer has gone out into the night. Jesus has a few final hours in which to give to his disciples words that will carry them through the coming hours, days, weeks. "I am the true vine," he says. "Remain in me, as I also remain in you" (John 15:1, 5).

And then the amazing statement: "As the Father has loved me, so have I loved you" (verse 9). This statement should give us pause. How odd that he then has to add, "Now remain in my love." Are we *that* prone to stray from true love? Apparently so. And the way to remain in his love? Obedience. "If you keep my commands, you will remain in my love" (verse 10). And when we obey? "Your joy may be complete" (verse 11).

Joy and obedience. One sounds like freedom; the other sounds like rules. But in reality, both are freedom. Obedience protects us from false joy—from following after something that makes us feel good but might be wrong or sinful. A commitment to finding joy *along with* obedience helps us to find true joy because we are following God's will for our lives. We are remaining in his love.

Joy is found in obeying, and obeying is discovered in God's Word and in seeking God's guidance daily. There is no greater joy than staying within the boundaries of obedience to our Savior. You save yourself a lot of pain and regret; you don't hurt other people by sinning against them; and you live the life God called you to live.

Obedience is the way to true joy. In these final sayings before his death, Jesus showed us the way to find the joy he himself had. Such a gift to us! ♦

PRAYER

Jesus, I want to partake in your kind of joy . . .

NO ONE WILL TAKE YOUR JOY

Now is your time of grief, but I will see you again and you will rejoice, and no one will take away your joy.

JOHN 16:22

The disciples do not know the horrifying events that will soon crash into their lives. They will run from their Master and grieve over his death, and then doubts will surely overwhelm them, causing them to wonder if they have spent three years wasting time with a master manipulator. Satan will seek to deceive them in any way possible.

Jesus knows what he is soon to face, but even as he knows of his impending death, he cares for these followers to whom the future of Christianity will be entrusted. They need extra reassurance to make it through the events of the coming days unscathed. He speaks these words of assurance, of hope. If they will just listen and believe, their sorrow will turn to joy. They will see him again—for real. Then they will be able to ask anything in his name, and their joy will "be complete."

Grief turned to joy; joy complete—all centered around the resurrection. Because of the resurrection on Easter morning and the coming of the Holy Spirit, Jesus' presence will be so real, so vital, that he will hear every request, every need, every concern, every desire, and he will answer.

Imagine such a promise! Imagine that it is true for us! Hey wait—it is! "Ask and you will receive, and your joy will be complete" (16:24). This is joy so complete that no one and nothing can ever take it away. ♦

PRAYER

Jesus, I am asking for complete joy—joy that nothing can ever take away . . .

HE SAW THE JOY AHEAD

Since we are surrounded by such a great cloud of witnesses, let us throw off everything that hinders and the sin that so easily entangles. And let us run with perseverance the race marked out for us, fixing our eyes on Jesus, the pioneer and perfecter of faith. For the joy set before him he endured the cross, scorning its shame, and sat down at the right hand of the throne of God.

HEBREWS 12:1–2

The writer of Hebrews reminds us that since a great crowd—faithful people who in some cases died for their faith (many are listed in Hebrews 11)—surrounds us, we should look to their examples and get rid of anything that would slow us down. Like any good runner focusing on the finish line, we focus on Jesus, our ultimate example, the goal of our faith. He saw "the joy set before him" and endured the cross. When we think about him, we should be encouraged not to get tired and give up.

Like cross-country runners, we all will wind through pleasant smooth pathways and up and down difficult hills (or mountains!). In order to keep going, we must strip away sin that entangles us and seeks to trip us up.

Why should we keep running? Because there is an end to the race. Jesus endured because of the joy he saw ahead. You can endure for the same reason. There is joy ahead.

Are you weary of enduring hurt? Of feeling that you can't take another step? Can joy be enough to look forward to? Yes, joy is the best enticement of all. If it was enough for Jesus, how could it not be enough for you? You can endure because of the joy set before you. Deep, abiding joy that no one can take away. Constant joy unmarred by sin and evil. Eternal joy in the presence of God and all the witnesses who have gone before.

After all, that whole crowd is cheering you on. ♦

PRAYER

I am running, Jesus, because of the joy set before me …

EYES OF JUDGMENT

As she stood behind him at his feet weeping, she began to wet his feet with her tears. Then she wiped them with her hair, kissed them and poured perfume on them.

LUKE 7:38

The text tells the story beautifully. Jesus is invited for dinner at a prominent religious leader's house and is approached by a woman in that town who is living a sinful life. We're not told exactly what she has been doing; perhaps she is a prostitute.

She knows where Jesus is and goes there with an alabaster jar of perfume. She stands behind him, at his feet, weeping and wetting his feet with her tears. Then she wipes the feet with her hair, kisses them, and pours perfume on them. All the religious people have rejected this woman. But Jesus seems different, so here she is, taking a chance.

Imagine if Jesus had sat up and said indignantly, "Why are you touching me? Don't you know I'm God?" Think about the emotional trauma this woman would have felt. And if you recoil inside at even the idea of Jesus' saying that, then you're on the right track.

Not only does Jesus *not* say that; he rebukes his host for criticizing the woman. Jesus then informs his host that the woman is forgiven by God.

People judge by external appearances, but God sees the heart (see 1 Samuel 16:7). The challenge is for us to see people the way God does. ♦

PRAYER

Lord, take away my eyes of judgment . . .

LISTEN

The Sovereign LORD *has given me a well-instructed tongue, to know the word that sustains the weary. He wakens me morning by morning, wakens my ear to listen like one being instructed.*

ISAIAH 50:4

When you wake up in the morning, what first brings your mind out of its state of peaceful slumber? Is it an alarm clock, a noisy bird, a passing train, the voices of your kids? We are usually awakened by what comes through our ears—by what we hear.

Isaiah wrote prophetically that the Messiah would be awakened each morning with a whisper from God, teaching him words he wanted the people to hear.

Jesus was completely in tune with the Father. He continually reminded his followers that he did not speak on his own but said—and did—only those things he learned from the Father.

Christ modeled for us the kind of stance we are to take with God—that of a listener. Peter observed that Jesus held the words of eternal life (John 6:68). The crowds claimed that his teaching had authority unlike any they had ever heard (Mark 1:22). Jesus' words were perceptive and powerful. They brought healing as well as conviction. Yet Christ was a teacher second and a listener first.

Each morning, as you are beckoned from your beauty sleep, be attentive first to that whisper in your ear, that voice which says, "I have loved you with an everlasting love; I have drawn you with unfailing kindness" (Jeremiah 31:3). ♦

PRAYER

Quiet my thoughts, Lord . . .

april9

BATTLE IN THE BARLEY FIELD

Eleazar stood his ground and struck down the Philistines till his hand grew tired and froze to the sword. The LORD brought about a great victory that day. The troops returned to Eleazar, but only to strip the dead.

2 SAMUEL 23:10

More than strength or skill, a great warrior must possess courage and determination as well as a willingness to sacrifice, to lay it all on the line. Perhaps no one else in the Old Testament met these qualifications better than Eleazar, son of Dodai. One of King David's three mighty men, Eleazar is remembered for what took place in a field of barley one fateful day (1 Chronicles 11:12–14).

Picture this: David's army is assembled in the field, taunting the Philistines. The enemy begins to rush wildly toward them. Overcome with fear, the Israelite soldiers drop their weapons and run for their lives—but not Eleazar. He digs his feet deep into the dark soil of that barley field, draws his sword, and stares the enemy straight in the eye.

Eleazar fought so hard that day alongside his king that, after the dust had settled and the Philistines lay dead at his feet, his hand had literally become frozen to his sword!

What about you, man of God? Are you ready to stand your ground, though the forces of darkness advance in all their fury and everyone around you flees in terror? Will you fight alongside your King until, in exhaustion, your hand freezes to the hilt of your sword—the Word of God? And as the dust settles, will you be found with your feet still firmly planted in the soil of the fields that are ripe for harvest (John 4:35)? ◆

PRAYER

God, give me courage to ...

THE GOD WHO WANTS TO COME OVER

After David was settled in his palace, he said to Nathan the prophet, "Here I am, living in a house of cedar, while the ark of the covenant of the LORD is under a tent."

1 CHRONICLES 17:1

One of the indicators that you've got a good friendship is when you can totally let down your guard and relax with someone. You know, the kind of friend who comes over and puts his head in your fridge, and the two of you can just hang out. At some level, it doesn't even matter what you do—even menial tasks get done a lot faster and are more enjoyable when you do them with a friend.

We value friends like that because of their loyalty. If your friend sees that you need help with something, he's the first person to volunteer. In fact, it would disappoint him if you didn't ask him to help. Who cares if it's sledgehammering concrete for six hours straight—that's what friends do!

Here's the amazing thing. God is the kind of person who doesn't mind coming over and sledgehammering.

In this passage, David feels pangs of guilt because he's in a palace made of the finest building materials while God's place is out in a tent. You'd think God, because he's God, after all, would demand better service. But God doesn't require an ornate palace, because that's not the kind of thing God cares about. God wants more than anything to just hang out with his people, to experience life with them.

Do you view God that way? Whether it's relaxing and watching sports on TV or building a fence or dealing with traffic during your morning commute, God wants to "come over." And he doesn't care that the place isn't picked up. ♦

PRAYER

Lord, come on over . . .

SUPPORTED BY THE ROOT

Do not consider yourself to be superior to those other branches. If you do, consider this: You do not support the root, but the root supports you.

ROMANS 11:18

Very often, we men look to ourselves for not just *some* of the answers but *all* of the answers. Others will often look to us for the solution to some broken situation or for a comforting word of advice. This sometimes leads us to see ourselves as able to be everything to everyone in all circumstances.

We see through the writing of the apostle Paul that those who came to have more faith in themselves and whose faith in God became diminished were reminded of whose they really were. In order to grow, they were pruned back so that others who acknowledged their faith in God could be grafted into the root that provides the strength and support (see also John 15:2).

Others will look to us for answers, but if we are to provide true wisdom, we must be grafted in. We must be connected to the root that provides nourishment so we can have the counsel to provide what is needed when others lean on us.

The only way to accomplish this is if we know on whom to lean. We can't be arrogant and think we have all the answers. We should be in awe of the One from whom real wisdom and knowledge come—the only one who can provide all the answers.

When we are grafted into the root, not only are we gaining nutrition and support; we are also accepted and taken in by the root as one of its own. ♦

PRAYER

Lord, may my branch go down deep in you . . .

GOD WANTS YOU MISERABLE

*Then the L*ORD *God provided a leafy plant and made it grow up over Jonah to give shade for his head to ease his discomfort, and Jonah was very happy about the plant. But at dawn the next day God provided a worm, which chewed the plant so that it withered.*
JONAH 4:6–7

Jonah sat under the lean-to he had built, waiting on the expected destruction of Nineveh that did not come. He became angry when God did not do what Jonah wanted him to do. Jonah was using God for his own purposes rather than understanding that God uses us for *his* purposes. So, like a curiosity seeker at a hanging in the wild wild West, he had sat down to take in what he thought would come. Here was a man who sought ease and comfort.

We are not much different. We live in a comfort-seeking society. So we are surprised to learn that God sometimes wants us to be miserable. Yes, God is a God of comfort. He comes into our lives to bring comfort, joy, peace, and happiness. But sometimes God comes to bring discomfort—to issue a wake-up call, to move us out of complacency, to stretch us spiritually, to challenge our comfort zones, to help us see beyond the walls of our measly existence, to break down the barriers we erect because of our prejudices and hatred.

It takes rain to make a rainbow, a strong wind to propel a kite toward the heavens, the weight of resistance to build muscles, stress on piano strings to make music, pain to appreciate paradise, and discomfort to develop character. Don't miss those times. The misery and discomfort are never intended for a lifetime (unless you never see God through them). They are never intended to break you but to *make* you, never intended to destroy you but to develop you. God is molding and making you into a godly man. ♦

PRAYER

I'm miserable, Lord. Help me ...

WHEN HOPE DIES

When the centurion, who stood there in front of Jesus, saw how he died, he said, "Surely this man was the Son of God!"

MARK 15:39

The year: AD 30. The place: outside the city of Jerusalem, at the foot of a hill called Golgotha—place of the skull. The time: twelve noon, the sixth hour. The sun should have been high; it was midday. Instead, the atmosphere seemed strangely cold and dark.

Jesus had been nailed to the cross with square spikes about a third of an inch thick at the head. Then he began his slow, agonizing death. The lungs would fill with fluids, causing him to drown.

The year: AD 30. The place: still outside the city of Jerusalem. The time: three o'clock in the afternoon, the ninth hour. The pitiful sight of the men dying has left an eerie silence over the crowd of onlookers at the foot of Golgotha. Out of the silence, Jesus, on the cross in the middle, shouts, "It is finished!" It sounds more like a cheer than a cry, as though he is heralding triumph.

A centurion stands erect, his eyes intent on this Jesus. *How can a crucified criminal act so convincingly like the victor?* His heart was pounding. *Who is this man? Could he be the Son of God?*

Why would the biblical writers speak of a Roman centurion? The writers wanted us to understand that the ones who put Jesus on the cross were not just the teachers of the law and the Pharisees, not just the crowd or Pilate or the Romans or Judas. The Roman centurion stands for all of us. We are as responsible as anyone else. We took part in nailing Jesus to the cross.

The year: present day. The place: your hometown. The time: now. What will be *your* response to Jesus? ♦

PRAYER

Thank you for dying in my place, Jesus . . .

april14

DO-OVERS

While he was still a long way off, his father saw him and was filled with compassion for him; he ran to his son, threw his arms around him and kissed him.

LUKE 15:20

The movie *City Slickers* is about three New York City men, who were approaching midlife crises, participating in a cattle drive out West. Phil's life was a wreck. He was in a hopeless job and was facing a divorce. He broke down and began crying. "I'm at a dead end!" he sobbed. "I'm almost forty years old; I've wasted my life!"

One of his friends tried to console him. "But now you've got a chance to start over," he said. "Remember when we were kids? We'd be playing ball, and the ball would get stuck up in a tree or something. We'd yell, 'Do-over!' Look, Phil, your life is a do-over. You've got a clean slate!"

How is a guy like Phil ever really going to be helped? The answer is only through the kind of do-over one can get from God. After all, God is the world's biggest dispenser of do-overs. He loves granting them to contrite and humble recipients.

Jesus tells a story about a young son who squanders his inheritance. His only hope is to return home. He is not sure his father will welcome him back. But his dad does. He gives him a do-over.

The son in Jesus' story represents you. The father represents God. God relishes in granting do-overs. God loves to give us a new beginning.

God is a waiting father, longing for his children to return home. Go home. Experience the divine method of resolution and the untold blessings that come from it. ♦

PRAYER

Thank you for giving me the chance to start over...

april15

MONEY MATTERS

No one can serve two masters. Either you will hate the one and love the other, or you will be devoted to the one and despise the other. You cannot serve both God and money.

LUKE 16:13

Luke 16 is almost entirely about money. There are at least a few reasons why having money can be ruinous to the soul, and they all have deeply spiritual implications. For example, if we have money, we begin to think we can solve all our problems. Having money can, indeed, solve many problems. It can get your leaky roof fixed, your grumbling stomach fed, your children educated in the best schools, your achy back massaged. So the temptation is to begin to believe that *all* problems can be solved with money. This isn't true. Neither cancer nor death can be erased with money.

We can become addicted to comfort and security. Once we have peace, safety, and comfort, we tend to not want to let go of them. We begin to see discomfort as something to be avoided. And you know what's uncomfortable? Giving away money to help other people. We begin to believe it would be better to hoard our money, to make sure we always have enough. We begin to worship comfort and safety. Jesus' life was anything but comfortable, and it certainly wasn't safe. So we become less like Jesus.

Jesus had an antidote for money worship, and we find it in Luke 16:13. We can't avoid the choice — God or money. What we do with our money and how generous we are with it depend largely on whether we think of ourselves as *owners* of the money or as *stewards*. The Bible is clear that we are stewards. All money is on loan from God, and we are obligated to invest it wisely. ♦

PRAYER

Lord, this is how I feel about money . . .

YOUR PLACE IN LIFE

Do not let your hearts be troubled. You believe in God; believe also in me. My Father's house has many rooms; if that were not so, would I have told you that I am going there to prepare a place for you? And if I go and prepare a place for you, I will come back and take you to be with me that you also may be where I am.

JOHN 14:1–3

Soon Jesus will die on the cross, rise from the dead, and ascend into heaven, leaving his disciples on earth. To help prepare them for life without him, Jesus explains that he will be going to his Father in heaven and will be preparing a place for them there. He also promises to return.

The disciples are confused, not really believing that Jesus has to die, not realizing that he will come back to life, and thus not understanding at all what he means by going to the Father and "preparing a place" for them.

But we have the perspective of history. We *know* that Jesus died on the cross. And we *know* that he rose from the grave and later ascended into heaven. Thus we can be confident that he is there *now*, preparing for us to join him.

What a great promise! If you have trusted in Christ as your Savior, your future is secure. He has a place for you in the "Father's house." No one can stop you; nothing can deter you; no one can steal your hope … because Jesus has promised.

And he is coming back to take you there.

As a member of God's forever family, you have a place in his house. ♦

PRAYER

What an amazing promise, dear Savior, that you …

april**17**

OVERCOMERS UNANIMOUS

I have told you these things, so that in me you may have peace. In this world you will have trouble. But take heart! I have overcome the world.

JOHN 16:33

Jesus is about to be captured, arrested, tried, convicted, and crucified. Soon his disciples will be left to carry his message throughout the world. Jesus knows they will be tested, tempted, and persecuted. So in these final instructions, he warns them and gives them a promise.

Note that Jesus doesn't tell the disciples they "might" or "could" have trouble. He says they "will"—it is a certainty. Yet in their troubles they can have peace and be encouraged.

Until Christ returns, we Christians—"Christ-ones"—will always conflict with the world. We stand out with a different allegiance, different values, and a different lifestyle. We threaten the status quo by refusing to compromise our faith, by living for Jesus, and by calling people to turn from their sins and give their lives to the Savior.

That doesn't make us popular. We *will* have trouble.

With all this trouble, however, we can have peace. Knowing that our Lord has defeated sin, death, and all of the temptations and attacks of Satan should give us courage to face adversity with calmness of spirit during any trial.

Whatever "trouble" you face, take heart! You can be an overcomer because Jesus has "overcome the world."

Be an overcomer. ♦

PRAYER

At times I feel assaulted on every side, Lord . . .

TAKE A STAND

We had previously suffered and been treated outrageously ... but with the help of our God we dared to tell you his gospel in the face of strong opposition.

1 THESSALONIANS 2:2

Courage can be defined as "the ability to do what is right even when we don't have to." Embedded in courage is conviction—the issues of the heart that one will live by and die for. Convictions are the mainsprings of action, the driving powers of being, the embodiment of one's life. Martin Luther King Jr. often told his children, "If a man hasn't discovered something that he will die for, he isn't fit to live." When we show our courage, we live out our convictions, as we say no to those things that are wrong and yes to those things that are right.

The opposite of courage is not cowardice but conformity. It is often stated as, "Be one of the boys"; "Go along with the crowd"; "Come on, everyone is doing it." In some situations we can't always walk away. We are, therefore, at times forced to take a stand. At those pivotal moments, surrounded by enemies, we show the crowd who we are and whom we serve.

Martin Luther, the Reformer, stood at the door of the Wittenberg Chapel, nailing up his ninety-five theses exposing the heresy and hypocrisy of people having to pay the church for their sins to be forgiven. At the Diet of Worms on April 18, 1521, he stated, "Here I stand; I can do no other. God help me. Amen."

Sometimes in different ways we are forced to say the same thing. *Here I stand. I can do no other.* ♦

PRAYER

Here I stand, Lord, firmly with you ...

april19

SOARING

Even youths grow tired and weary, and young men stumble and fall; but those who hope in the Lord will renew their strength. They will soar on wings like eagles; they will run and not grow weary; they will walk and not be faint.

ISAIAH 40:30–31

Long-distance runners know about "hitting the wall." That's the time in a race when the runner feels totally depleted—legs dead, skin rubbed raw, feet hurting with each step, joints aching, vision blurred, lungs unable to get enough breath. And the mental fatigue is even worse, with the mind filled with thoughts of doubt and quitting. At that point, runners long for renewed strength—a second wind.

Life is like a marathon, and at times we can feel totally depleted, especially in times of facing problems and conflicts. We can feel like slowing down or even quitting, with our eyes fixed on our circumstances and struggles. That's when we need to change our focus and find hope in the Lord.

When you feel overwhelmed by life—exhausted, frustrated, weak, discouraged—remember that even young and strong people tire. But God's power and strength never diminish. He is never too tired or too busy to help and listen to you. And God's strength is your source of strength.

When you feel all of life crushing you and are convinced you cannot go another step, remember that you can call on God to renew your strength.

Trust God to lift you on wings like eagles' wings. Soar in faith! ♦

PRAYER

Dear Lord, I'm so tired . . .

THE MUSTARD SEED

Jesus asked, "What is the kingdom of God like? What shall I compare it to? It is like a mustard seed, which a man took and planted in his garden. It grew and became a tree, and the birds perched in its branches."

LUKE 13:18–19

Because we're not living in first-century Israel, the truths inherent in Jesus' parable of the mustard seed may seem a little opaque. Here are a couple of truths about the mustard plant to aid our understanding:

- *It has the smallest seed in agriculture.* Ever seen a mustard seed? It's smaller than the head of a pin—about as large as a big grain of pollen. Yet some varieties can grow to ten feet in height.
- *Mustard grows like ivy.* It has a voracious growth pattern that overpowers all other plant life. It spreads like wildfire! You can't just chop it down, like a tree; you have to pull it out and uproot every shoot. If you miss even a bit, it will grow right back.

Jesus is saying that something as small as your commitment to devote your life to him can have magnificent impact. There's something a bit dangerous about being a follower of Jesus. Little things make a big impact. And little plants can take over and change everything.

How does knowing what you now know about the mustard plant change how you view the parable and the lesson Jesus was communicating? And what does it say about your potential to change the world? ♦

PRAYER

Heavenly Father, grow in me the seed of faith . . .

YOU'RE IT!

[You] have been chosen according to the foreknowledge of God the Father, through the sanctifying work of the Spirit, to be obedient to Jesus Christ and sprinkled with his blood.

1 PETER 1:2

God took the initiative and chose you to be a part of his family. Your salvation is no accident. He chose you long before you chose him. He knew all about you and chose you anyway. He took the initiative. Your salvation is no fluke; it was God's idea from the very start.

On what basis did he choose you? The answer is *mercy*—the divine disposition to extend compassion when justice demands punishment. God's choosing you is based on his mercy, not on your performance. You deserve punishment for your sin, for the wages of sin is death. But God in his mercy says, "I want you in my family. I choose to forgive because of what my Son did for you." God did not choose you because you deserve it, earned it, or were good enough.

Revel in being chosen! The next time you find yourself in a battle, don't look at the trials; focus on the God who loves you. Don't look at the world that assaults you; gaze at the Christ who accepts you. Don't look at the pressures that consume you; see the Savior who chose you. ♦

PRAYER

Thank you for choosing me to be yours . . .

SUCH A DEAL

"Look, I am about to die," Esau said. "What good is the birthright to me?"

GENESIS 25:32

Although Jacob and Esau were twins, they were quite different. Jacob was a homebody and a cook, while Esau was an outdoor guy, a hunter. As the older brother (just barely), Esau was first in line for the inheritance—that was his "birthright."

At this point in their story, we see Jacob's taking advantage of his brother's hunger. After a long day in the wild with no success, Esau is so hungry that he thinks he is going to die. Actually, it takes sixty-five days to starve to death, but Esau isn't thinking straight. So when Jacob offers him food for his birthright, Esau takes the deal.

Looking back, we might say, "What an idiot! He sold his future for a bowl of stew!" and we'd be right. But before we condemn Esau too hastily, we should consider that this sort of deal happens every day. Men often trade the future (wife, kids, reputation, career) for a present satisfying of what feels like an urgent physical need. The flirtation, the suggestive comment, the porn, the opportunity—and like Esau, they give in to those urges and let sexual desire drive the decision. They make a terrible choice, a stupid trade.

When tempted to make such a deal, remember Esau and his fateful decision. Then ask God to give you the strength to choose his way. Don't be an idiot and trade your future for a bowl of stew! ♦

PRAYER

I know I'm weak, Father. Keep me strong and focused on you ...

LIVING BETWEEN THE STEPS

The grace of our Lord was poured out on me abundantly, along with the faith and love that are in Christ Jesus.

1 TIMOTHY 1:14

Scripture is clear that life lived in the presence of God is rich both with longing and fulfillment, times of darkness and times of light, times of sweet days and times of dark nights.

The Spirit led Jesus into the desert. Jesus experienced darkness in Gethsemane and on the cross. Lament in the Psalms is as familiar as an old pair of slippers. Even Paul, the model of Christian optimism, said he had times when he was perplexed and felt weak. Yet, in spite of the unpredictable days, the one constant is grace—God's grace infused in our being to make our days and nights bearable.

The story is told of a young man who was constantly helping others. When asked why, he described his tour of duty in Vietnam. It was his job to clear minefields, and he watched many friends get blown up before his eyes. "I learned to live between steps," he said. "I never knew whether the next one would be my last, so I learned to get everything I could out of the moment between when I picked up my foot and when I put it down again. Every step I took was a whole new world, and I guess I've just been that way ever since."

A grace-filled life is living between the steps. It understands the remarkable gift of today. Today is a gift, you know; that is why it's called "the present." In our unpredictable todays, we must find all the life we can, and live it to the fullest. Abundant life is determined not by how long we live but by how well we live. ♦

> **PRAYER**

I want to live today to the fullest ...

NO ALIBIS, NO REGRETS

Remember your Creator in the days of your youth, before the days of trouble come and the years approach when you will say, "I find no pleasure in them."

ECCLESIASTES 12:1

On the walls of many locker rooms hangs the framed statement "no alibis, no regrets." The message reminds the athletes to leave it all on the field, to give their all and their best. But this could also be an apt summary of Solomon's last words here in Ecclesiastes.

Bible scholars believe that Solomon wrote this book near the end of his life. A brilliant man, Solomon had not been very wise in his choices over the years. Reflecting on his life, he could clearly see his foolish mistakes and how most of his pursuits and accomplishments were "meaningless." Here, at the end, he summarizes and concludes with this challenge to young people: "Remember your Creator in the days of your youth."

In essence, Solomon is stating, "Honor God, *now*, while you are young and have your whole life ahead of you. Then you'll be able to look back with no regrets."

Unfortunately, the opposite often occurs. Young people, filled with energy, optimism, and self-confidence, don't see or *feel* the need for God. So they race along, living for self and reaping the consequences of a meaningless life. Face it — nothing is more tragic than a bitter old person, broken physically, emotionally, and spiritually, feeling abandoned, voicing complaints and regrets.

Regardless of our age, we would do well to heed Solomon's advice, to learn from *his* mistakes. It will mean that we put and keep God at the center of life, with our values and actions focused on him and his will. Then, at the end of life's game, we will be able to have "no alibis, no regrets." ♦

PRAYER

Creator God, I want to remember you each and every day of my life ...

THE CHOICE

As for me and my household, we will serve the LORD.

JOSHUA 24:15

Joshua was a strong leader and a man of God. He led, not just with words, but by example. And he expected no less of himself than he demanded of the people. Time and again, we see Joshua making tough choices, leading the troops into battle, and interceding with God for the people.

At this point in his distinguished career, Joshua has just led the Israelites into and through the Promised Land. They have defeated the Canaanites and are beginning to settle in. So once again, he reminds the people of their most important decision and action: serving God. Joshua knows that the land is filled with divine alternatives, false gods vying for devotion. So he puts the choice before them: the idols in the land or the Lord God Almighty. Then he states unequivocally: "As for me and my household, we will serve the LORD." Clearly Joshua was the spiritual leader in his family as well.

We haven't trekked through the wilderness to Canaan, but we still encounter false gods in the land. These gods are more subtle than Asherah poles and statues of Baal, and if we're not careful, we can shift attention and allegiance to them. A career, the pursuit of wealth, a love relationship, and other things can easily become idols when given a high spot in our ranking of values and life priorities. Real men, godly men, know the right choice to make. They take the lead and declare their loyalty to the Lord.

Where are you in this story? Choose to be like Joshua, declaring his allegiance and leading his family to the Savior. ♦

PRAYER

I want to be your leader, Father, to lead people, including my family, to you ...

HE LIVES!

In their fright the women bowed down with their faces to the ground, but the men said to them, "Why do you look for the living among the dead? He is not here; he has risen! Remember how he told you, while he was with you in Galilee: 'The Son of Man must be delivered over to the hands of sinners, be crucified and on the third day be raised again.'" Then they remembered his words.

LUKE 24:5–8

The women had planned to put spices on Jesus' body. They had seen him die on the cross and carried to a tomb. They knew the spot. But Jesus was gone! In his place stood two angels, who reminded them of Jesus' prediction that he would be crucified but then, on the third day, be raised from the dead. Then the women remembered.

If they had listened, understood, and believed in the first place, they would not have expected to find his body in the tomb. None of Jesus' followers had heard his prediction, however; thus they all were surprised by his resurrection. Breathless with excitement, the women rushed back with the wonderful news, but the eleven disciples and the others didn't believe their report.

Do you believe? Because Christ rose from the dead, we know that our world is heading for redemption, not disaster; that death has been conquered, and we too will be raised from the dead to live forever with Christ; that Christ is alive and ruling his kingdom; and that God's power that brought Jesus back from the dead is available to us so that we can live for him in an evil world.

Do you believe? Then live with joy and hope and power.

Jesus is alive! ♦

PRAYER

I serve a risen Savior . . .

YOU'RE CRUCIAL

Christ himself gave the apostles, the prophets, the evangelists, the pastors and teachers, to equip his people for works of service, so that the body of Christ may be built up.
EPHESIANS 4:11–12

Being picked last is the worst. Ever experience that? It's like a college running back entered in the NFL draft. He wants to get picked in the early rounds. If he is, it means he is a contributor—someone important, someone who is thought of as providing a critical ingredient necessary for winning.

But if he is the last one standing, it means he is nearly worthless. Deadweight. A nonfactor.

In this passage, Paul makes it clear that God doesn't view people the way the world does. He doesn't see some people as important and others as unimportant. Paul uses the metaphor of the body. He repeats the word *one* several times in this passage to drive the point home: we all either work together or this thing won't work.

In a body, there are no unimportant parts. What is more critical—your thumb or your right kidney? Your cornea or your hamstring? *Every* part is critical—even the seemingly insignificant parts (like that little flap that covers your esophagus so that when you swallow, food doesn't enter your lungs).

It doesn't do any good to beat yourself up because you don't have flashy gifts. Paul says that God "equip[s] his people for works of service, so that the body of Christ may be built up" (4:12). God made you who you are. And God believes your role is critical in this world and in his church. Do you? ♦

> **PRAYER**

Lord, I believe that ...

TREASURE IN HEAVEN

Where your treasure is, there your heart will be also.

MATTHEW 6:21

What do you treasure? We men tend to treasure the tangible—a nice putter, a vintage tool, a trophy in a cabinet. But the Bible says those things are like dust in the wind. Only the Word of the Lord will pass with our soul from this life into eternity.

Our treasures should be first and foremost with God, for then our actions and responses will be rightly directed. So how can you build up treasures in heaven? Through the process of getting the Word of God into your heart.

It is now the time of year for people to start planting seeds for their gardens or farms. In preparation for this annual event, we turn over the soil and treat it with compost and fertilizer so that it is prepared—nutrient rich. In this environment, seeds can grow and produce a bountiful crop—the very thing they were designed to produce.

Are you nutrient rich in the Word of God? Are you storing up for yourself treasures that no one can steal and that will never turn to dust? Are you providing others with what they need so they can flourish and produce rich fruit? ♦

PRAYER

Lord, help me to focus on treasures that matter...

HE HAS COME!

The Spirit of the Lord is on me, because he has anointed me to proclaim good news to the poor. He has sent me to proclaim freedom for the prisoners and recovery of sight for the blind, to set the oppressed free, to proclaim the year of the Lord's favor.

LUKE 4:18–19

Returning to his hometown of Nazareth, Jesus went to the synagogue on the Sabbath. There he stood and read this familiar passage from Isaiah 61:1–2. After reading, he sat down and explained that the passage was referring to him, that he was the promised Messiah who would deliver God's people from their bondage.

Most of the people who heard Jesus that day did not understand what he meant, because they expected the Messiah to free Israel from Roman rule. But Jesus meant that he would free poor, imprisoned, blind, and oppressed people from their sins. Jesus came, not to establish a worldly kingdom by restoring Israel to its former glory, but to rule in people's hearts.

That's the good news. Jesus is here, and he offers new life to all who will trust in him. To the spiritually impoverished, he offers the riches of his glory. To those enslaved by their sins, he offers forgiveness and freedom. To those blinded by grief, who see no escape from their troubles, he offers a future and a hope. To those oppressed by anxieties and enemies, he offers justice and vindication. Rejoice and live in this time of "the Lord's favor."

Jesus, your Messiah, has come! ♦

PRAYER

Thank you, Jesus, for ...

SAVING ACCOUNT

When the kindness and love of God our Savior appeared, he saved us, not because of righteous things we had done, but because of his mercy. He saved us through the washing of rebirth and renewal by the Holy Spirit, whom he poured out on us generously through Jesus Christ our Savior, so that, having been justified by his grace, we might become heirs having the hope of eternal life.

Titus 3:4–7

Christians will often use the word *saved* when referring to their relationship with God. They may say, "Jesus saves"; "when I was saved"; "I got saved"; or something similar. That expression comes from passages such as this one that refers to Jesus' work for us on the cross. When we turn away from our sins and give our lives to Christ, trusting in him alone for salvation, God forgives and thus saves us from the penalty we deserve.

Paul points out that this is all about God and his mercy and grace—we can do nothing to merit forgiveness and eternal life.

God also *saves* us from the evil and corruption in the world, keeping us close to him, marking us as his very own children, and making us more and more like his Son. That's the work of the indwelling Holy Spirit, who is changing our focus, values, and desires.

And God will save us in the future, giving us eternal life when we die.

Is Christ your *Savior*? If so, you are a justified heir, with power for the present and hope for the future. Thank God for his love and work for you. Praise him for his generous goodness.

When God reigns, he pours. ♦

PRAYER

Father, I bow in humble gratitude . . .

may1

DO YOU WANT TO GET WELL?

When Jesus saw him lying there and learned that he had been in this condition for a long time, he asked him, "Do you want to get well?"

JOHN 5:6

Thirty-eight long years he had lived with a crippling condition. Thirty-eight years he had lain by the pool alone with no one to help him. Thirty-eight years of hopelessness and depression. Then a man approaches him and asks him one simple question: "Do you want to get well?"

In reading the account of the lame man by the pool of Bethesda, you might wonder why on earth Jesus asked him that question. *Of course he wants to get well! Did you not hear just how long this man has been lying there crippled?* But think about it for a minute. Do you know anyone (yourself included) who has struggled for years with some kind of debilitating sin or destructive habit? How about a broken relationship filled with bitterness? Does that person really want to get well? Do you?

God's healing is available, but it might hurt a little. You might have to swallow your pride. Christ wants to lift you up; he wants to restore you. But you have to be willing. Jesus asks the same question today: "Do you want to get well?" ♦

PRAYER

Give me the desire to be made whole . . .

A DEADLY DELICACY

Knowledge puffs up while love builds up.

1 CORINTHIANS 8:1

Our society holds knowledge in high regard. It is seen as a key capable of unlocking endless opportunities. People base their status on what university they attended or how many letters they have after their names. We like to believe that "knowledge is power."

In Scripture, however, we find a different view. While knowledge in and of itself is not evil, we are warned about mishandling it. Paul reminded the Corinthian believers that knowledge has the tendency to puff us up with pride.

An intriguing illustration can be found in nature in the form of the puffer fish. We all know about this creature's ability to blow itself up into a spiny ball, but did you know that this little fish can be lethal? Toxins can be found in its skin and internal organs; yet despite the dangers, some people insist on eating its meat! Extreme care must be taken in preparing the dish, and some diners have been poisoned or even killed by this deadly delicacy!

Knowledge can be sweet, but if used in the wrong way, it can be very destructive. If we become conceited by how much we know (or think we know), we become puffed up and our misused enlightenment can actually poison those around us!

God is more concerned about how you love than about what you know. Don't be a puffer fish! ♦

PRAYER

Lord, help me to build up others . . .

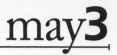

REFUSING THE PARDON

God was reconciling the world to himself in Christ, not counting people's sins against them. And he has committed to us the message of reconciliation.

2 CORINTHIANS 5:19

In 1830, a man by the name of George Wilson was convicted of stealing from the U.S. Mail in Pennsylvania and endangering the life of the mail carrier. Later, he received a presidential pardon from Andrew Jackson. He refused it, however.

The judges didn't know what to do. The case was taken to the Supreme Court. In 1833, in *United States v. Wilson*, the court made this statement (recorded at Justia.com) regarding the refusal of a pardon:

> A pardon is a deed to the validity of which delivery is essential, and delivery is not complete without acceptance. It may then be rejected by the person to whom it is tendered, and if it be rejected, we have discovered no power in a court to force it on him.

The apostle Paul states that, through Christ, God reconciled the world to himself—he granted us an unimaginable pardon. But Paul goes on to state that we must be reconciled to God—it is our responsibility to accept his pardon.

Why would anyone refuse? Pride is a probable culprit. By accepting a pardon, a man is admitting he is guilty and in need of mercy. Shame is another. Some of us just find it too hard to accept forgiveness after the wrong we've done. Hatred is a third possibility. Some may not be able to accept the fact that there is a God and that he has the power to pardon.

Let us not refuse the pardon God offers us in Christ! ♦

PRAYER

Pardon me, Lord, for . . .

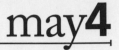

HEART TRANSPLANT

I will give you a new heart and put a new spirit in you; I will remove from you your heart of stone and give you a heart of flesh.

Ezekiel 36:26

Something happened in the Garden of Eden when Adam took the fruit from his wife and bit into its forbidden flesh. Something happened, something so profound it was almost unnoticeable: Adam's heart turned to stone. He had spiritual heart failure and died that day to the warm friendship with God he had previously known.

Since that time, we have all been born with hearts that are cold toward God and hardened toward his work in our lives. We are like stillborn babies. We enter into the world already spiritually dead.

But two thousand years ago, a baby was born fully alive with a heart that beat for God. That baby grew into a man, and that man changed the world. God knew our state. He knew that the only cure for our disease was a complete heart transplant. So he sent his Son to the cross to die for us, and now the risen Christ is able to rip out our hearts of stone and replace them with his own heart of flesh, restoring the relationship lost since the Garden of Eden.

What kind of heart do you have? Have you paid a visit to God's operating room? Have you entered into life that is truly life? ♦

PRAYER

God, you know that my heart is like ...

may5

OUT OF HIS MIND

When they came to Jesus, they saw the man who had been possessed by the legion of demons, sitting there, dressed and in his right mind; and they were afraid.

MARK 5:15

This is one of the weirder stories from the Gospels, and one of the most moving. In the region of the Gerasenes, Jesus encounters a demon-possessed man. The townspeople tried to lock up the man in chains, but he was so strong he kept breaking the chains. The Bible explains that "night and day among the tombs and in the hills he would cry out and cut himself with stones" (Mark 5:5).

Think about that for a second. Can you imagine his torment? How long had this been going on? Living in a graveyard, howling in pain, cutting himself.

Jesus comes and drives a legion of demons out of the man and into a herd of pigs that will eventually drown in the sea. The townspeople then see a sight they never thought they'd see: the formerly demon-possessed man, sitting calmly next to Jesus, all cleaned up and dressed. Mark's gospel tells us he was "in his right mind."

What a beautiful phrase—"in his right mind." We don't need to be demon-possessed to experience what it's like to be "out of our minds." Sin prevents us from being in our right mind. It always makes us pay more than we want and drift farther away from God than we ever planned. The forgiveness and healing Jesus offers can bring us back into a right frame of mind. ♦

PRAYER

Bring me back, Lord . . .

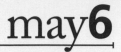

may**6**

FAITH TRANSFER

*The L*ORD *had said to Abram, "Go from your country, your people and your father's household to the land I will show you . . ."*
*So Abram went, as the L*ORD *had told him; and Lot went with him.*

GENESIS 12:1, 4

You're sitting at your desk and you get word that your boss wants to see you. Not exactly sure what's up, you try to think positively as you walk down the hall. He invites you to take a seat, and he proceeds to compliment you about your work and point out your great potential. Then you hear, "I want you to move to . . . [the other side of the country]." If you've been there, you know the mixture of excitement and apprehension this brings. You like the prospects of a pay raise and the upward move in the company. But the move would mean leaving church, friends, neighborhood, and familiar places, not to mention buying a new house and establishing new relationships and routines.

Now imagine being transferred across the world with nothing guaranteed.

That's what Abram faced. God told him to leave everything behind—all his family and connections—and to head out to a yet-to-be-named destination. And the Bible reports, "So Abram went, as the LORD had told him."

Because of Abram's move, his act of absolute faith in God, Paul reminds us, "Abraham believed God, and it was credited to him as righteousness" (Romans 4:3). Abram (Abraham) moved because he believed.

God wants men of action—those who will move out in faith. What's holding you back? ◆

PRAYER

I'll go where you want me to go, dear Lord . . .

ALWAYS FAITHFUL

Know therefore that the LORD your God is God; he is the faithful God, keeping his covenant of love to a thousand generations of those who love him and keep his commandments.
DEUTERONOMY 7:9

The Old Testament contains dozens of names for God, each one emphasizing an important aspect of his character. In this passage, Moses describes him as "the faithful God."

Faithfulness is important in any relationship. Without that assurance, we feel insecure and fearful about the future. A faithful person is someone we can count on during tough times, someone who is loyal and true, and someone who keeps promises and commitments.

In contrast, *unfaithfulness* has become a byword of modern culture. Husbands and wives break marriage vows; parents abandon children; workers and employers break commitments; skilled lawyers look for loopholes in contracts; family members abuse each other; friendships dissolve over trivialities. We long for the security and hope that faithfulness brings. Faithfulness breeds trust and leads to security, confidence, and peace.

In Moses' statement that "he is the faithful God," we find that promise. While others break their commitments, God keeps his. Though everyone else deserts us, God will be there. And notice that God is "keeping his covenant of *love*." No matter what happens and regardless of what we've done or how far we've strayed from him, he never leaves us. That's a promise we can live with!

Your faithful God keeps his promise of love. ♦

PRAYER

Thank you, loving Father, for . . .

BESIDE QUIET WATERS

The LORD is my shepherd, I lack nothing. He makes me lie down in green pastures, he leads me beside quiet waters, he refreshes my soul. He guides me along the right paths for his name's sake.

PSALM 23:1–3

Picture a shepherd in the Middle East, guiding, protecting, and leading his flock to an oasis to feed and be refreshed.

David describes such a scene and the picture of complete contentment. Ah, quiet waters, green pastures, sunny skies, light wind rustling leaves along the bank—lambs lying down, relaxed, at peace. With every need met, they lie in still solitude, secure and safe. Although the breezes are gentle, the grass comfortable, and the water plentiful, the secret to each lamb's contentment is not the weather or pasture or stream—it is the loving shepherd, the one who leads, guides, and restores.

Today, people desire to be like the lamb described in this psalm. They want to live comfortably. Even more, they long for fulfillment, peace, and soul restoration. And many spend their lifetimes searching for the right formula or setting or program, restlessly looking for soul comfort in a person, place, or lifestyle. That's a dead-end search, as evidenced by all the fearful, insecure, and unhappy people who seem to have everything.

Instead, the secret to contentment is the loving shepherd.

Do you want real peace and restoration? Remember the secret. Stay close to your Shepherd. ♦

PRAYER

Guide me, dear Shepherd ...

DISTRESS SIGNAL

I call to God, and the LORD saves me. Evening, morning and noon I cry out in distress and he hears my voice.

PSALM 55:16–17

Nothing hurts more than betrayal and abandonment by a loved one—an unfaithful wife, an unscrupulous and dishonest business partner, a backstabbing friend, or a deceitful teenager. And the hurt can be much more than emotional, involving loss of money, career, reputation, and health. How do you respond? Where do you turn?

Consider King David, whose beloved son Absalom was working against him, undermining his rule and plotting a violent overthrow of the kingdom. Understandably David was in great "distress," and we can hear his pain in these words. As David wrote this psalm, probably during the time of Absalom's rebellion and his adviser Ahithophel's treachery, he must have felt devastated and alone, abandoned by his son and close friend. So he poured out his grief, anger, and confusion to God. And he didn't just pray once—he called on his Lord continually, all day—"evening, morning and noon." David was confident that God would hear his prayer, give him courage and strength, and save him from his enemies.

Are you feeling overwhelmed—surrounded by enemies and abandoned by friends? God has not left you, and he stands ready to save. Call on the Lord to give you his presence, peace, and power. God hears. God knows. God understands. ♦

PRAYER

I feel like David, Lord. I desperately need you . . .

AID STATION

I will refresh the weary and satisfy the faint.

JEREMIAH 31:25

Jeremiah had just predicted that Judah, God's chosen people, would be conquered by Babylon and taken captive. But God's next message through his faithful prophet was that eventually the nation would be brought back from captivity and restored completely.

Soon after this prophecy was given, the first part was fulfilled: the army of Nebuchadnezzar besieged Jerusalem, conquered it, and took many of its citizens back to Babylon. Imagine what those captives must have been thinking and what they must have felt. Did they learn their lesson? Did they continue to trust in God? Did they remember God's promise of release and restoration?

Although you have not been conquered by a foreign army, you can feel defeated and even like a captive living in another land. A load of bills, obligations, and responsibilities weighs heavily, draining strength and exhausting reserves. You may feel like an exhausted and depleted runner—weary and faint, wondering how you can continue. But as one of God's people, a member of his holy nation, remember this promise in Jeremiah. God's aid station is just around the next turn. Keep running the race; keep obeying his word; keep trusting in his love. God keeps his promises, and he will "refresh" and "satisfy." ♦

PRAYER

I'm exhausted, Savior. I need . . .

may11

CHOSEN AND CHERISHED

But you are a chosen people, a royal priesthood, a holy nation, God's special possession, that you may declare the praises of him who called you out of darkness into his wonderful light.
1 PETER 2:9

It begins on the playground when we stand among the leftovers when choosing teams. But the process continues at every stage of life as awards and honors are bestowed, and we're left out. Our society seems obsessed with recognition for achieving greatness of some sort—or at least notoriety. With a steady stream of awards shows and people being crowned or titled "champion," "all-American," "world's greatest," and so forth, all of us runners-up or also-rans can feel like losers.

This passage is an antidote for identity crisis or an affliction of low self-esteem. Peter affirms that all those who belong to Christ are "chosen," "royal," "holy," "God's special possession," and "people of God." Take a moment and focus on each of these positive and profound descriptions. In short, God—the only one whose opinion really counts—thinks highly of us, his people.

All of this is true, not because we are such wonderful people. Quite the opposite. We were far from God and, in fact, his enemies, completely and totally lost and in darkness. But because of the Lord's grace and mercy, we have been declared forgiven, new, and good, and now we can walk in "his wonderful light."

How do you feel about yourself? What defines your worth as an individual? Instead of comparing yourself to others or trying to match the world's standards for beauty, significance, happiness, strength, and success, find your true identity in Christ. Rejoice in who he has made you, and "declare the praises" of your loving and merciful Lord.

You are chosen by God—walk in the light. ◆

PRAYER

Lord, knowing what you think about me …

may12

FRUITFUL LIVES

The fruit of the Spirit is love, joy, peace, forbearance, kindness, goodness, faithfulness, gentleness and self-control. Against such things there is no law.

GALATIANS 5:22–23

When the timing is right, we come to realize the love of the Father through his Son and through the Holy Spirit actively working in the heart. As men, we don't like to talk about our feelings—our heart—but they determine who we are. Our whole being, from the very depths of the heart, yearns for our Father in heaven. From this we pursue a relationship with the Savior, who can fill the vacuum within.

The Old Testament provided God's people with laws that would help them live holy lives. The New Testament recounts how Jesus came to fulfill the law given through Moses. When we recognize our need for a Savior, we fill that void in the heart with Jesus.

So now we are not bound to the law, but our lives, being filled with the Holy Spirit, have the ability to act according to the Spirit. We have the ability to delight in what is godly, because our nature is now so infused with the Spirit that we desire to live according to the ways of the Spirit! We begin to show evidence of the fruit of the Spirit. We desire to act righteously and rejoice to act in a holy manner. Because our being—who we really are—is now complete through the Holy Spirit, we can be in continual communion with God. ♦

PRAYER

Lord, reign in me ...

NOW AND FOREVER

Praise be to the God and Father of our Lord Jesus Christ! In his great mercy he has given us new birth into a living hope through the resurrection of Jesus Christ from the dead, and into an inheritance that can never perish, spoil or fade. This inheritance is kept in heaven for you.

1 PETER 1:3 – 4

Peter's words offer joy and hope in times of trouble and pain. Remember, he was writing to followers of Christ who were suffering for their faith, severely ostracized, beaten, imprisoned, and thrown to lions in Roman arenas. These first-century believers certainly had cause to despair. But Peter told them to move their focus from their conditions to their Savior and his plans for them. He wrote about "hope"—encouraging words for them and for us.

Peter bases his confidence on what God has done for us in Christ Jesus. The proof that our new birth and hope are certain is the resurrection. Jesus is alive, and his promises are true.

We are called to a *living* hope. This means we have hope today, not just at some point in the future. Eternal life isn't just for after death; it begins when we trust Christ and join God's family. And regardless of the pains and trials, we know that this life is not the end, and those sorrows and struggles are not our final experience. Eventually we will live with Christ for eternity.

God gives you new life, *now* and *forever*. You have his power and presence as you live for him each day. And you have an incorruptible inheritance reserved in heaven in your name. Praise God! ♦

PRAYER

Life can get discouraging, Father, but I find my hope in . . .

ROOTS

And I pray that you, being rooted and established in love, may have power, together with all the Lord's holy people, to grasp how wide and long and high and deep is the love of Christ, and to know this love that surpasses knowledge—that you may be filled to the measure of all the fullness of God.

EPHESIANS 3:17–19

When we know Christ, we become "rooted and established in love." Paul uses the word picture of a tree with long roots descending deep into nourishing soil. The tree stands strong and healthy because of how and where it is rooted.

With that as a given, Paul urges his first-century readers and us to fully understand that Christ's love reaches every aspect of our existence. It is wide, covering the breadth of our experience and reaching the whole world—wherever we go, his love is there. It is long, continuing the whole length of our lives. It is high, rising to the mountaintop experiences, the thrilling heights of honor, celebration, and elation. But it is also deep, reaching us in the valleys, in the depths of discouragement and despair, and in death. No matter where we are or what we are going through, God is there, loving us and keeping us close.

When you are far away from family and friends, God is there. When you feel old and alone, God is there. When you exult in a great victory, God is there. When you face death, God is there.

He loves you and wants you to be "filled to the measure of all the fullness of God." ♦

PRAYER

I love you, Lord, and I know you ...

UNDER CONSTRUCTION

Being confident of this, that he who began a good work in you will carry it on to completion until the day of Christ Jesus.

PHILIPPIANS 1:6

What was the last construction job you worked on? It could be as small as fixing a child's toy or as ambitious as building a deck. Whatever the case, you didn't want to be judged on the quality of your work until you were finished. Until then, the project was under construction. You had a vision for the outcome and a plan for getting there, and step by step you proceeded.

Now think of your life as God's construction project, and remember that what God begins, he finishes. God has begun his work—his good work—in you. And you can be confident that he will finish what he has started. His Holy Spirit is shifting and shaping right now.

This means you are not complete—you are in process, under construction. No matter what your temperament, personality, giftedness, successes, and failures, God is working "in you," making you more like his Son Jesus (see Romans 8:29). God's work in you began when you trusted Christ as your Savior, and it will continue until you see Christ face-to-face.

When you feel incomplete or distressed by your shortcomings, remember God's promise and provision. Don't let your present condition rob you of the joy of knowing Christ or keep you from growing closer to him. Be patient—God is not finished with you yet. ♦

PRAYER

I know, Lord, that you are working in me . . .

may**16**

WHY?

And we know that in all things God works for the good of those who love him, who have been called according to his purpose.

ROMANS 8:28

"Why?" we wonder as we struggle to reassemble the pieces of a broken relationship.

"Why?" we think as we read of a devastating earthquake or tsunami halfway around the world or dig out in the aftermath of a tornado close to home.

"Why?" we question as we hear of a child struck down by a random bullet in a drive-by shooting.

"Why?" we cry as we stand at the grave of a loved one.

Life is short and often tragic, and each day we are reminded of our finiteness. We don't know the future. We don't know the relationship between events. And we certainly don't know the reasons.

But we do know that God is good and all-knowing. Nothing catches him by surprise—not the car out of control, the malignant tumor, the hurricane, or the disease. So even as we wonder and question the reason and cause for each event, we can be confident that God knows why and that in everything, even in the seemingly senseless tragedy, he is working.

In all things (not "all things," but "*in* all things") *God works* (he's always present) *for the good* (the ultimate good and God's purpose) *of those who love him.*

Take hope and trust in his plan. And remember, this life is not the end; it is only the beginning! ♦

PRAYER

Lord, help me trust you about . . .

WANTED: DEAD AND ALIVE

I have been crucified with Christ and I no longer live, but Christ lives in me. The life I now live in the body, I live by faith in the Son of God, who loved me and gave himself for me.

GALATIANS 2:20

When Paul wrote these words, his readers would have understood *crucified*, since crucifixion was a common Roman method of execution that caused excruciating pain and public humiliation. And believers would have understood the reference to Jesus' death on a cross. But they must have wondered about the meaning, about how a person could be crucified and still live.

Yet that's what Jesus did. He was nailed on that cross for us, taking the punishment we deserved, and he died. But then he rose from the grave and is alive today, now, interceding for us in heaven.

Being "crucified with Christ" means being identified with him on the cross. It means admitting that *we* deserved death, not him, and then accepting his sacrifice for us. When Jesus died, he died in our place, paying the penalty for our sins. He actually became sin for us. Because Jesus died, we can have our sins forgiven by trusting in him as Savior. Because Jesus died, we can live—forgiven, free, and headed for heaven.

Jesus loved you so much that he died for you. Now, by faith, you can live for him. You are alive and free. Thank God!

And Christ lives in you, giving you the strength to live for him. ♦

PRAYER

Thank you, dear Savior, for ...

SEEKING STATUS

We do not dare to classify or compare ourselves with some who commend themselves. When they measure themselves by themselves and compare themselves with themselves, they are not wise.

2 CORINTHIANS 10:12

Did you know that the average American owns 2.8 vehicles? Did you know that if you make $24,000 per year, you are in the top 6 percent of income earned in the *entire world*? Did you also know that out of 194 countries around the globe, Christianity is forbidden in 38 and greatly persecuted in another 14?

If you've ever been to one of the restricted or hostile nations, you know that Christians there live in abject poverty. Because of their faith, they may not even be allowed to attend school or hold a job. Still, these Christians are completely aware of what is important in this life—it's not money or cars. It's sharing the gospel with their friends. They know that their treasure is in heaven.

To the average American man, what is important is having those 2.8 cars, a good paycheck, status in the workplace or community, and kids who get good grades and scholarships. But we often forget that these are only temporary pursuits. We forget that God has already built a mansion for us in heaven, set aside a crown, and has a name of honor unique to each of us whose name is in the Book of Life. We forget that there are those around us every day who need to hear about the opportunity for eternal life offered by Christ.

This doesn't mean we can't strive for greatness. But it does mean we should stop comparing ourselves to the folks down the street. Maybe it means we need to have those folks over for a barbeque, get to know them, and invite them to church. We know God's best is in store for us—let's give others the opportunity to know God's best as well. ♦

PRAYER

Lord, help me to remember what's really important ...

may19

FEAR OF FAILURE

To this end I strenuously contend with all the energy Christ so powerfully works in me.
COLOSSIANS 1:29

A lie believed for long enough will become perceived truth.

We all want to live the dream. What man on earth doesn't strive for success? But sometimes our thinking becomes clouded with lies, and the dream of success slowly becomes the daily reality of just getting by. But God says he has plans for you, plans that will bring success, not harm.

What are the lies holding you back? "It's never been done that way before. I might upset someone if I do this. No one believes I can do this. It'll cost too much money. I can't. This idea is doomed to fail." Fear of failure is the wrong definition of success.

Men need to step up and begin to operate in freedom rather than in fear. Success comes when we not only dream big but also make plans to achieve that dream and then act on those plans. When the outcome is not what we hoped for, we learn from it and keep moving forward. Failure only comes when we stop trying, stop striving toward our goal.

As Christians we know the truth that in all things God works for the good of those who love him. We can't allow ourselves to get bogged down when things don't go our way. We can't hang our heads and take on the "poor me" attitude. Just because something hasn't been done that way before doesn't mean it is doomed to failure.

Try something new. See what works. Make adjustments to what doesn't work. Find people who believe in you. Seek out investors. Start saying, "I can." ♦

> **PRAYER**

Lord, I can! . . .

MINORITY REPORT

Caleb silenced the people before Moses and said, "We should go up and take possession of the land, for we can certainly do it."

NUMBERS 13:30

Twelve men went up to scout out the land. Twelve men returned. Ten were intimidated and frightened by what they had discovered in Canaan, and in dramatic terms they described their findings and recommended against moving forward. But two men, Joshua and Caleb, took the opposite position, urging Moses and the people to "take possession of the land." But the people were not swayed; they were practically overcome by despair after hearing about fortified cities and the "giants" who inhabited them.

Joshua and Caleb tried again, declaring this message:

> "The land we passed through and explored is exceedingly good. If the LORD is pleased with us, he will lead us into that land, a land flowing with milk and honey, and will give it to us. Only do not rebel against the LORD. And do not be afraid of the people of the land, because we will devour them. Their protection is gone, but the LORD is with us. Do not be afraid of them."
> —NUMBERS 14:7–9

Notice the faith flowing through their words, as they focused on doing God's will, trusting in God's strength and protection, and moving forward without fear.

Standing up for our convictions takes great courage, especially when everyone else seems to be against us. Yet that's what God expects us to do. These days, those who follow Christ are in a distinct minority, and we can be easily intimidated by the giants in our way—public opinion, politicians, employers, even relatives. But God wants us to take a stand for him and to move ahead against all odds.

What does God want you to do? Man up and "take possession of the land." ♦

PRAYER

Give me strength and courage to take these steps of faith . . .

GET IN THE GAME

Go to the ant, you sluggard; consider its ways and be wise!

PROVERBS 6:6

No one has to tell an ant what to do. It just does it. They are creatures on the move.

Getting in the game is doing what needs to be done. "A sluggard's appetite is never filled, but the desires of the diligent are fully satisfied" (Proverbs 13:4). God put us on this earth to act. Courageously and diligently we must act.

When it comes to relationships, the courageous take the time to develop the relationships. They invest the necessary energy.

When it comes to purpose, the courageous find a reason for living. They discover how God has gifted them. They seek ways to help others.

When it comes to responsibility, the courageous refuse to look the other way. They do their part and their fair share.

When it comes to spiritual direction, the courageous engage in the necessary disciplines to keep their bearings. These spiritual disciplines keep the wells of refreshment and renewal full of fresh water, leaving their souls with no possibility of drying and parching.

The courageous live by three life-changing words: *Do it now!* They refuse to delay and to procrastinate. They don't evacuate. They see what needs to be done and do it. They choose not to stand on the sidelines and merely watch. They get in the game. ♦

PRAYER

I'm in the game, God. What next?...

GOD'S CLEANSING FIRE

I will hear from heaven, and I will forgive their sin and will heal their land.

2 CHRONICLES 7:14

God's hearing and forgiveness and healing result in our cleansing.

Standing beneath the giant sequoias in King's Canyon National Park, the forest ranger guide told the tour group that fire is necessary for the growth and reproduction of those magnificent trees, the largest and oldest living things on planet Earth. It seems that at one time the U.S. Forest Service had carefully guarded them from naturally occurring, lightning-caused forest fires—only to discover that the trees were not thriving and that no new trees were developing. They came to the conclusion that without periodic fires to burn away the underbrush, the trees would fail to reproduce. It takes the intense heat of a roaring fire to open the seed cones, and the ashes contain just the right mineral mixture on which the trees thrive!

So it is with Christ's followers. Without the intense heat of God's fire we will not thrive and grow and reproduce. Like innocent children, we think the fire will hurt. And at times it just might. We attempt to avoid the crisis of God's cleansing fire. But as in the forest of sequoias, the fire is needed. It is through this outpouring of cleansing that we feel God's love, grace, and comfort. To live without these manifold provisions is to limp through life with deformed characters unable to reach the heights for which we were destined and designed.

Like the forest rangers in the forest, we need to allow God's cleansing fire to periodically occur in our lives. For it is through that fire of forgiveness that our sin debt is canceled. It is through the fiery touch of God, much like a physician cauterizing aberrant tissue, that spiritual healing occurs. ♦

PRAYER

I trust you, Lord, to burn me with cleansing fire ...

MAN OF INTEGRITY

How then could I do such a wicked thing and sin against God?

GENESIS 39:9

You know the story of Joseph and his "technicolor dreamcoat"—how as his father's favorite son, he copped a prideful attitude and irked his older brothers. Totally annoyed, they sold Joseph to slave traders and told their father that he had been killed by wild animals.

Here we see Joseph as a slave to an Egyptian official named Potiphar. Evidently Joseph had grown in his relationship with God because he took the moral high road and made a tough choice in a pressure situation. When Potiphar's wife tried to seduce him, Joseph rejected her advances because it would violate his relationship with his master and, more importantly, with God. We can imagine the lines Mrs. Potiphar used: "It's just the two of us." "What's a little sex between consenting adults?" "No one will ever know!"

Joseph refused and paid the price when the woman falsely accused him of attempted rape, landing Joseph in prison. Joseph could have complained to God, but he didn't. Instead, he kept the faith and became a model of consistent trust and confidence in God. Even when reunited with his treacherous brothers, he held no grudges and forgave, reassuring them with this famous phrase: "Don't be afraid. Am I in the place of God? You intended to harm me, but God intended it for good to accomplish what is now being done, the saving of many lives" (Genesis 50:19–20).

Joseph didn't know God's plan, but he knew God and trusted him, even in the difficult times. And he lived the way he knew God wanted him to live.

Whatever your situation, remember that God knows you, is with you, and has a perfect plan for you. Trust him. ♦

PRAYER

Father, help me make the tough choices that honor you . . .

THE VIRTUE OF COURAGE

Be on your guard; stand firm in the faith; be courageous; be strong.

1 CORINTHIANS 16:13

We admire courage in others, don't we? We write about it, acknowledge it, and applaud it. But courage is a virtue, not by choice, but of necessity, found in people who defeat the sin of indifference.

It was courage that enabled a young sheep-herding teenager named David to go toe-to-toe with the giant Goliath. It was courage that empowered the prophet Elijah to stand against the prophets of Baal on Mount Carmel. It was courage that infused the three Hebrew boys, Shadrach, Meshach, and Abednego, to refuse to bow to the golden statue of Nebuchadnezzar. It was courage that emboldened Daniel to stand for his religious convictions, even if it meant being eaten alive by lions. It was courage that prompted a handful of uneducated disciples to boldly proclaim the message of Jesus Christ, even in the face of persecution and possible death. It was courage that allowed Stephen to face the stones and rocks of hatred.

We need to be courageous men. Granted there are varying degrees and forms of opposition. Sometimes it is violent and brutal—fires and swords have taken down many professing believers; at other times it is subtle and scornful—satire and comedy have also been weapons of choice in some societies. Let's face it, the spirit of this world is hostile to the Spirit of Christ. And the courage needed to stand up against the enemy may sometimes be greater when the opposition is soft-spoken than when it is boisterous.

The apostle Paul's message to the first-century church is the message to the church of the twenty-first century. How do we stand firm, being men of courage? ♦

PRAYER

I am a man of courage. I will stand for you today, Lord ...

THE CREATOR GOD

Through him all things were made; without him nothing was made that has been made.
JOHN 1:3

Flash of Genius is a film about the life of Robert Kearns, a college professor and part-time inventor who took on the Ford Motor Company for allegedly stealing his idea for the intermittent windshield wiper. The movie's title comes from a legal term in patent law, which was in use from 1941 to 1952, called "the Flash of Genius Test" for patentability. It argued that an invention could come to someone out of nowhere and without years of working on it beforehand.

John's opening words to his gospel, "In the beginning," suggest not only the start of the gospel story but the creation of the world as well. "Through him all things were made; without him nothing was made that has been made" (John 1:3). The Bible does not defend divine creation; it simply declares it.

Christianity has always believed in creation out of nothing — *ex nihilo*. We do not believe that the world began with God and something else. It is our belief that behind everything there is God, and *God alone*. Only God creates. We may have a flash of genius that leads to an invention, but we don't create anything. We take existing material, as Robert Kearns did with windshield wipers, and fashion it into something new. We make things. Only God creates something from nothing. The next time you look at the world, don't look for a flash of genius; look at the genius who in a flash brought it all into existence. That is a God worth knowing and worth worshiping. ♦

PRAYER

Thank you, God, for your magnificent creation . . .

RELUCTANT LEADER

Moses said to God, "Who am I, that I should go to Pharaoh and bring the Israelites out of Egypt?"

EXODUS 3:11

Moses was tending his father-in-law's flocks in the middle of nowhere when God got his attention with the burning bush. Then God gave Moses a message; in short, he wanted Moses to lead his people, the nation of Israel, from Egypt to the Promised Land. Moses' quick response was: Who am I to do such a thing? At first, we may conclude that Moses was just being humble, but he continued to answer God with excuses. Check these out:

- I won't know what to say (Exodus 3:13).
- But what if they don't believe me (4:1)?
- "I have never been eloquent, neither in the past nor since you have spoken to your servant. I am slow of speech and tongue" (4:10).

God had answers for each excuse and question. Then, finally, out of desperation Moses pleads, "Please send someone else" (4:13).

But God prevailed. Moses obeyed, and he became Israel's greatest leader.

This story has many lessons. Here are a few:

- God can use anyone.
- If God wants us to do something, he will equip us to do it.
- God will be with us every step of the way as we carry out his will.

To what task has God assigned you? Does he want you to heal a relationship, stand up for truth and morality, teach a Sunday school class, or talk to a friend about Christ? Don't be Moses the excuse maker; be Moses the leader—God's man for the moment. ♦

PRAYER

No excuses, Lord. I want to be your man for your work ...

may27

HE CAME FOR YOU

All of them were filled with the Holy Spirit and began to speak in other tongues as the Spirit enabled them.

ACTS 2:4

History is unchangeable. We read about times and places; we understand things that have happened and even look into the reasons behind the historical events, but they're often impersonal. You may have ancestors who were in America in 1776, when the Declaration of Independence was signed. But even those times are now just stories of generations past. To some of us, World War II is somewhat personal—we know men who were there. Those from the greatest generation are still among us, and we can hear from them the accounts of a time more than six decades ago. Or we have relatives or friends who were in the Korean War, Vietnam, or Iraq. Maybe you're a veteran yourself.

The coming of the Holy Spirit is not just a piece of history. The One who came in the form of a dove at Jesus' baptism, who filled the believers at Pentecost, is alive and active now because God sent the Spirit of his Son into our hearts! This is the evidence that the believer is indeed heir with Christ and a child of God. The Spirit within us enables us, or more so compels us, to call out *"Abba,* Father!" He provides us with the strength to fight against the principalities and powers of this world—the spiritual battles.

Knowing the events of history by reading accounts in Scripture is important. But making the coming of the Holy Spirit a personal experience is more important still. If you're a believer, he came to live within you. ◆

PRAYER

Spirit of the Living God, fill me today ...

151

may28

FREE INDEED!

Therefore, there is now no condemnation for those who are in Christ Jesus, because through Christ Jesus the law of the Spirit who gives life has set you free from the law of sin and death.

ROMANS 8:1–2

All living creatures do what comes naturally to them—they build shelters (nests, dens, houses), find food, and protect their young. In addition, human creatures, created in the image of God, also have great capacity for good as we reflect our Maker and follow him. But because of sin, we humans also have great capacity for evil—and this also comes naturally to us.

Ever since sin entered the world with the first parents, every child enters a sinful world with a sinful nature. Born as sinners, we soon discover that sinning is a way of life. We ignore God, disobey his commands, and work hard at living independent of him, our own way—a way that leads to guilt, condemnation, and death. That is the "law of sin." Sin enslaves and destroys.

God didn't leave us without hope, dead in our sins, however; he sent Jesus to live and die for us. In sharp contrast, Jesus brings forgiveness, freedom, and life. That is the "law of the Spirit."

Because you trusted Christ as your Savior, you have been released. The shackles of sin have been broken by your Lord, and you stand before God forgiven and clean. Now, with a quickened spiritual nature, you have the freedom to choose to do what is right, to obey God, and to love others in his name. And the Spirit will give you the power you need.

The choice is yours. Live for him! ♦

PRAYER

I am free to serve you, Lord …

WHAT'S IN A NAME?

Then the man said, "Your name will no longer be Jacob, but Israel, because you have struggled with God and with humans and have overcome."

GENESIS 32:28

The word *Jacob* means "one who grabs" or "the deceiver," and Jacob certainly lived up to his name. He tricked Esau into trading his birthright for some stew. He deceived his father, Isaac, into giving him the blessing. And he lied to his father-in-law, Laban. But here we see an interesting twist in the story, as God changes Jacob's name and his destiny.

Jacob was about to meet up with his brother Esau, and he wasn't thrilled with the prospects. He assumed that Esau would be out for revenge, to get even for Jacob's deceptions. Jacob didn't know what to do and designed an elaborate plan (another scheme) to appease his brother. He was desperate.

Then the Bible simply says, "So Jacob was left alone, and a man wrestled with him till daybreak" (Genesis 32:24). Where or how Jacob had this encounter with the mystery man, the Bible doesn't say. Jacob couldn't win this wrestling match, but in his desperation, he held on. And God blessed him and changed his life and name. Instead of the "deceiver," he would be "Israel"—"one who has struggled with God."

Names meant a lot to people in Bible times. Today we might do something similar with nicknames. "Tricky Dicky," for example, evokes the image of a certain disgraced U.S. president, and "Sweetness" recalls the great football moves of Walter Payton.

So what comes to mind when people say your name? And if you're known as a Christian ("Christ-one"), do you live up to this description? If not, go to the mat with God and ask him to change you. He will. ♦

PRAYER

Lord, I want to be known as your man. Change my name—change me ...

may30

BUILD IT RIGHT

Don't let anyone look down on you because you are young, but set an example for the believers in speech, in conduct, in love, in faith and in purity.

1 TIMOTHY 4:12

Paul exhorted Timothy to live an exemplary life. The word *exemplary* originates from the word *example* (*typos* in the Greek), from which we get our word *type*. Timothy is to lead by being a "type," a pattern or model of Christ's likeness that others can follow. In his book *Principle-Centered Leadership*, Stephen Covey distinguishes between what he calls primary and secondary greatness. Secondary greatness is leadership that relies on human influence, strategies, and tactics to get what it wants. Primary greatness, on the other hand, is related to the strength of a person's character.

Too often, we set our sights on secondary greatness—wealth, position, public recognition—without paying the price in terms of character development. Character development is always a prerequisite to godly living.

A TV news camera crew filming the widespread destruction of a hurricane in south Florida approached the owner of the only house left standing in the neighborhood. "Sir, why is your house the only one in the entire neighborhood that is standing?" asked the reporter. "How did you manage to escape the severe damage of the hurricane?"

"I built this house myself," the man replied. "I also built it according to the Florida state building code. When the code called for 2x6 roof trusses, I used 2x6 roof trusses. I was told that a house built according to code could withstand a hurricane. I did, and it did."

When our lives are the "type" that is built to the moral and character code of Scripture, it can withstand any hurricane. So build your life right—follow God's plans. Live a life worthy of serving as an example for people to follow. ♦

PRAYER

Lord, give me a firm foundation that I may be a better leader for ...

may31

YOUR JOB—A MINISTRY

Whatever you do, whether in word or deed, do it all in the name of the Lord Jesus, giving thanks to God the Father through him.

COLOSSIANS 3:17

Many jobs are boring, and the threats of layoffs, mergers, and downsizing can bring high levels of stress. But in the midst of undesirable circumstances, attitude can transform a boring, thankless job into a Christian ministry.

When Gordon MacDonald was pastor of Trinity Baptist Church in New York City, he would ride the same bus daily from his home to the church. One day when the bus driver was complaining about the monotony of his job, MacDonald responded, "Every day, when you first get on this bus, before anyone else gets on, dedicate that bus to God for that day. Declare it to be a sanctuary for God for that day. Consecrate it to God's glory, and then act like it is a place where God dwells."

Several weeks later, MacDonald returned from a trip and saw the bus driver. "You've transformed my life," the man exclaimed. "I've been doing what you said every day, and it has made me see my job with an entirely new perspective."

The same transformation could happen to you. At your work, whatever it may be, have an attitude that reflects the positive nature of God's grace on your life.

What can you do in your work setting to minister and witness to those around you? List your coworkers for whom you will pray—and begin praying for them. Begin each day by consecrating your workplace. Dedicate it, like the bus driver, as a sanctuary to God. And then each day look for opportunities to minister, to serve, to help, to offer assistance. We may not be able to do everything, but we can do something.

It might just transform your life! ♦

PRAYER

I dedicate my workplace to you today, Lord . . .

BRIDE-TO-BE

Then I heard what sounded like a great multitude, like the roar of rushing waters and like loud peals of thunder, shouting: "Hallelujah! For our Lord God Almighty reigns. Let us rejoice and be glad and give him glory! For the wedding of the Lamb has come, and his bride has made herself ready. Fine linen, bright and clean, was given her to wear." (Fine linen stands for the righteous acts of God's holy people.)

REVELATION 19:6–8

This is the culmination of human history—the wedding of the Lamb and his bride, all faithful believers from all time. The bride's clothing is the righteousness of the saints, the work of Christ to save us.

In every wedding, the groom waits expectantly for his bride. Then as everyone stands and turns, she walks gracefully toward the altar where the two will be joined as one. The bride is prepared for this moment, dressed exquisitely and focused on the love of her life.

When imagining yourself in a wedding, as a man you see yourself as the "groom." In this case, however, the groom is Christ, "the Lamb." So if you are in the scene—and you are—that makes you the "bride." This is the biblical picture of Christ and his bride, the church. But don't get put out by the feminine noun. Instead focus on two powerful, life-changing truths: the Groom is waiting for us, and we must be ready.

Until that glorious wedding day, we must prepare to meet our Groom, the Son of God. We prepare by staying faithful to him, living for him, telling others about him, and looking for his return.

Are you ready for your wedding day? Put on your wedding clothes. ♦

PRAYER

Lord, dress me in your righteousness ...

june2

GET READY!

He will go on before the Lord, in the spirit and power of Elijah, to turn the hearts of the parents to their children and the disobedient to the wisdom of the righteous — to make ready a people prepared for the Lord.

LUKE 1:17

Looking at your calendar, is there anything for which you're preparing? A holiday? Vacation? A huge, new responsibility? What will it take to get you prepared to meet the new challenge?

When the angel Gabriel appeared to Zechariah the priest to announce the upcoming birth of John the Baptist, the angel told Zechariah that John would "make ready a people prepared for the Lord." As the forerunner of the Messiah, John's task would be to get the hearts of the people ready to welcome the Savior. Repentance and baptism were signs of this readiness.

John's ministry hearkened back to that of the Old Testament prophet Elijah, whose fiery words made enemies of King Ahab and Queen Jezebel, who were textbook examples of disobedience. John also did not shy away from warning the powerful about their need to return to the Lord in humility.

As believers, we have more than a holiday or a job to which we can look forward. Jesus' imminent return is an occasion that demands heart readiness. How are you getting your heart prepared for his coming? Repentance is still a sign of readiness. ♦

PRAYER

Lord, make me ready . . .

A LITTLE REST AND RELAXATION

Come to me, all you who are weary and burdened, and I will give you rest ... For my yoke is easy and my burden is light.

MATTHEW 11:28–30

Every man needs a little rest and relaxation. Between earning a paycheck, church commitments, yard work, keeping the vehicles running, going here and there with the kids, we can get a little run-down.

God knew all about our need to rest. In fact, God saw rest as such an important part of life that even he rested after working six straight days creating everything. Whew!

Rest should come not just to the body but also to the mind and spirit. When all three are at peace, you can completely relax. Jesus offers the kind of soul rest we need. He knows the type of "yoke" the world puts on us — worries, stress, and so on. Putting aside your worries, trusting in the Lord to help when you call, and knowing that the One who is in control will work all things together for good — this brings peace.

Rest and relaxation is not optional. It is a *necessity*. Don't just hope to fit it into your schedule — make it a priority today. Your body, mind, and spirit will thank you for it. ♦

PRAYER

Lord, bless me today with a chance to rest and relax ...

HOLD ON TO UNITY

Be completely humble and gentle; be patient, bearing with one another in love. Make every effort to keep the unity of the Spirit through the bond of peace.

EPHESIANS 4:2 – 3

How often have you seen a minor misunderstanding lead to friction among God's people? Maybe you've been a part of misunderstandings in your own family — between yourself and your parents, your wife, or your kids. Misunderstandings not only cause the disruption of fellowship between individual believers, but unchecked misunderstandings can cause church splits as well. Left unresolved, misunderstandings do not shrink and go away — they snowball and cause more damage than an avalanche!

How can we avoid misunderstandings, or at least, keep them from growing to the point of destruction?

The best advice comes from the apostle Paul. It seems that the members of the church in Ephesus and Colossae were faced with misunderstandings that threatened to tear apart their fellowship. He told both congregations to be completely humble, gentle, patient, and forgiving, and to bear with one another in love (see also Colossians 3:12 – 13).

Humility, gentleness, and patience don't always come easily to men. However, when misunderstandings arise, whether in the family or among friends, if we strive to retain unity, the Spirit will add to us whatever is necessary. Don't let pride block the path of peaceful unity. ♦

PRAYER

Make me an instrument of peace, Lord . . .

EXPOSED

Godly sorrow brings repentance that leads to salvation and leaves no regret, but worldly sorrow brings death.

2 CORINTHIANS 7:10

Caught red-handed. The saying comes from the idea of a murderer with bloodstained hands who has no way of covering up his guilt. None of us like to be caught in sin—to have the curtains thrown back with our guilt and shame laid bare for all to see.

In those moments we suddenly feel sorry and ashamed. But what kind of sorrow is it? Is it sorrow over being caught? If that's the case, we're worse off than before our deeds were exposed. Feeling sorry for ourselves just leads to deeper entanglement with our sin. Scripture tells us this kind of sorrow will eventually destroy us!

So how ought we to feel when our dark deeds suddenly come to light? Paul tells the Corinthian church that one fitting emotion is alarm. Have you ever been shocked by how low you were willing to stoop? Sin is deceptive, and we can get so mired in it that we can't see its ugliness until it is exposed. It's like lying down for a nap in the soft mud of a cave only to turn on a headlamp afterward and find out you are actually caked in bat guano!

God doesn't call us to feel sorry for ourselves; he calls us to repentance—to a complete turnaround in our attitudes and behavior. The right kind of sorrow leads to freedom; it leads to life. ♦

PRAYER

Holy Spirit, turn the light on in my soul . . .

WHO'S NUMBER ONE?

What we preach is not ourselves, but Jesus Christ as Lord, and ourselves as your servants for Jesus' sake.

2 CORINTHIANS 4:5

Let's face it, most of us guys like to be noticed, to be respected by others. If that means blowing our own horn every once in a while, so be it. Besides, how else will we be picked for that promotion or catch the eye of that blonde we hope to date?

Sadly, this tendency to gain recognition from others finds its way into every area of our lives—even into our witness for Christ. Have you ever led worship, taught Sunday school, helped with the youth group, or gone on a mission trip, hoping that others will think better of you instead of seeking to bring glory to Christ?

In every part of our lives—whether at church, on the playing field, at school, or in the workplace—healthy questions to ask ourselves are: *Who am I preaching here: myself or Christ? Through my words—but even more so, through my actions—am I making much of Christ or much of myself?*

Let's take it a step further. We can ask ourselves: *Do I approach my day with the attitude of a servant? Instead of trying to get my way every time, do I keep my eyes open to those around me who often get overlooked?* Imagine the shock to a cynical world of seeing an army of men shamelessly seeking to bring notice to Christ instead of to themselves!

This world doesn't need great men; it needs a great Savior. May we hide ourselves in him! ♦

PRAYER

Jesus, evaluate me ...

STAND FIRM, BE STILL

Moses answered the people, "Do not be afraid. Stand firm and you will see the deliverance the LORD will bring you today. The Egyptians you see today you will never see again. The LORD will fight for you; you need only to be still."

EXODUS 14:13–14

After serving as slaves in Egypt for many years, the Israelites were finally allowed to leave and to journey to their Promised Land. But soon after giving permission for their departure, Pharaoh changed his mind and sent his army to bring them back. Seeing the approaching army in the distance, many of the Israelites became filled with fear and began to panic. So Moses answered them with this strong prediction of God's rescuing them from their enemies. His answer was simple: "Stand firm and you will see ... The LORD will fight for you; you need only to be still."

"Standing" means staying put, not running away. "Standing firm" means staying put without fear and with determination. "Being still" means carefully watching and listening for God's work.

We may not be pursued by armies, but we will have occasions when we feel chased, trapped, and under attack simply for being God's people. That's when we need to remember Moses' advice to stand firm and watch for God to act on our behalf.

Are you being ridiculed for your faith? *Stand firm.*

Are you being pressured to act immorally or unethically? *Stand firm.*

Are you being forced out because of your commitment to Christ? *Stand firm.*

Do you feel trapped, with no way out of your dilemma? Stand firm ... and look for God's deliverance.

Remember: God works miracles to deliver his people. ♦

PRAYER

Lord, help me to stand firm ...

MADE KNOWN HIS WAYS

He made known his ways to Moses, his deeds to the people of Israel: The LORD is compassionate and gracious, slow to anger, abounding in love.

PSALM 103:7–8

Sports experts love statistics, measurements of how individual athletes and teams have performed in specific situations. The assumption is that knowing a person's tendencies in the past can predict his or her present and future performance. Analysts will say, "He's aggressive at the plate, a first-pitch hitter," "He gets alligator arms when he goes over the middle," "The secret is to get him to dribble to the left," "This goalie is susceptible to the high shot." We can learn much about a person by looking at his or her track record, checking out how he or she has performed and related to others in the past.

We can learn much about God by taking a close look at his past actions and relationships, especially with his people, the children of Israel. What we find is that God is profoundly loving. In fact, time after time when Israel would disobey his commands and even begin to worship idols, God would be slow to punish them, and then he would take them back as soon as they turned from their sin.

The fact that God is "slow to anger" should not encourage us to take him for granted. Instead, we should remember his unending love and resolve to live for him and stay close to him.

Thank God for what he has done in the past—for Israel and for you. And live in the light of his gracious and compassionate love. ♦

PRAYER

Thank you, Lord, for ...

HOMECOMING

The LORD is gracious and compassionate, slow to anger and rich in love. The LORD is good to all; he has compassion on all he has made.

PSALM 145:8–9

Remember falling off your tricycle and skinning your knee? Your mother didn't accuse you of being clumsy; she gently held you close, wiped away your tears, and bandaged your abrasions.

Remember trying to hide the report card with the less-than-acceptable grade? Your parents insisted that you do better, holding you to a higher standard—for your own good.

And remember as a teenager when you came home hours after curfew and found your parents waiting? Although you didn't like the punishment Dad enforced, you knew he cared about you.

Good parents love their children and are "gracious and compassionate" with them.

Some people are afraid of God because they see him as a vindictive law officer trying to catch them in a mistake—like a highway speed trap—so he can punish them. Others picture God as a killjoy, taking all the fun out of life.

But God is a *perfect Parent*; he is what all of us imperfect fathers should be like. "Slow to anger and rich in love," God wants only what is best for us. When we fall, he picks us up, dries our tears, and puts us back on our feet again. When we sin, he hears our repentance and forgives.

When you've fallen or fallen away, go home. Your Dad awaits with open arms. Run to the Father. ♦

PRAYER

Heavenly Father, I admit . . .

SOW SOW

Sow righteousness for yourselves, reap the fruit of unfailing love, and break up your un-plowed ground; for it is time to seek the LORD, until he comes and showers his righteous-ness on you.

HOSEA 10:12

Trying to nurture a beautiful lawn can be a frustrating experience. Certain patches of the yard seem to resist all growth — except weeds, of course. And too often we discover clover, crabgrass, dandelions, and other weeds encroaching at an alarming rate.

In any agricultural endeavor — working on a farm, planting a garden, or just caring for a lawn — we know the importance of fertile, receptive earth. The plants we hope to sprout and grow are directly affected by the seeds we choose and quality of the soil. Grass won't come from dandelion or crabgrass seeds. Tulips in the spring come from tulip bulbs planted in the fall. We expect tomatoes from tomato seeds, not cucumbers. And no seeds, even those of highest quality, will germinate, take root, and flourish in rock-hard, weed-infested soil.

In this passage, the prophet Hosea reminds Israel of this great truth and uses it as a spiritual metaphor. Those who plant seeds of righteousness will reap a crop of God's love, if their hearts are open and ready.

Do you want to experience God's love? Plow the hard ground of your heart by confessing your sins and accepting God's forgiveness. Then sow seeds of righteousness by seeking God and resolving to live for him, and then reap God's bountiful harvest. ♦

PRAYER

I want your harvest, Lord …

ROCKED BY HIS LOVE

The LORD your God is with you, the Mighty Warrior who saves. He will take great delight in you; in his love he will no longer rebuke you, but will rejoice over you with singing.

ZEPHANIAH 3:17

The prophet Zephaniah proclaimed God's message and predicted tough times for Judah. As punishment from God, the nation would be conquered, her cities destroyed, and her people taken captive. Yet with this bad news, Zephaniah included God's message of hope. Because of God's great love for his people, he would rescue and restore them when they returned to him.

If you are a father, you know the joy of rocking and singing your child to sleep. Regardless of what happened earlier, the loving discipline is done for the day. You feel nothing but love for your child as you experience the great joy of being a father, and you know you would do anything to keep your baby safe.

That's the picture here—it's how God feels about you. If you have trusted in Christ, you are God's child—you belong to him. He loves you, takes delight in you, and rejoices over you.

No matter what you have done or where you are, in any circumstance, remember that "God is with you" and is your "Mighty Warrior who saves." Turn back to him, and let him hold you in his arms and rock you to sleep.

Hear his love song again. ♦

PRAYER

Father—Daddy—let me hear you . . .

IF I'D JUST ... JUSTIFIED

Therefore, since we have been justified through faith, we have peace with God through our Lord Jesus Christ, through whom we have gained access by faith into this grace in which we now stand. And we boast in the hope of the glory of God.

ROMANS 5:1–2

Remember when Dad caught you disobeying one of his orders? You were guilty, caught red-handed, and you knew it. And you had to accept your punishment.

Over the years, situations have changed drastically, but the results are the same—disobedience and guilt. Our adult sins take many forms: hatred, gossip, lying, lust, pride, self-centeredness, and on and on. And this time we know that our guilt is much more serious and that we have offended more than Dad or Mom. In fact, we stand guilty before God, for every sin is a defiance of his laws and an affront to his holiness. The reality is that the deserved punishment for our sins is death—eternal death, separation from God forever. But this passage says we have been justified.

Justified means being declared "not guilty." No matter what we have done, we have been acquitted and forgiven because of Jesus ("He was delivered over to death for our sins and was raised to life for our justification"—Romans 4:25). Thus we have "peace with God" and stand in a place of highest privilege. Not only has God declared us "not guilty"; he has drawn us close to himself. Instead of being his enemies, we have become his friends—in fact, his very own children.

Being freed from the shackles of sin and the burden of guilt, we have hope and are free to serve our loving Lord. Thank you, Jesus. ♦

PRAYER

Because of Jesus, I am ...

TAKE A GOOD LOOK

Since, then, you have been raised with Christ, set your hearts on things above, where Christ is, seated at the right hand of God. Set your minds on things above, not on earthly things. For you died, and your life is now hidden with Christ in God.

COLOSSIANS 3:1–3

The world is appealing, with attractive offers of easy wealth, relational happiness, and personal fulfillment. Advertisements for the latest adult toys entice us to materialism; sexy come-ons tempt us to lust and to pursue gratification of our desires; idealized descriptions of "the good life" prompt us to greed and self-indulgence. In addition, we are assured by financial counselors that the right investments can make the future secure.

It's an illusion—a lie. Yet we can believe it and easily "set [our] hearts on things" *below.*

Although we live in this world, it is not God's reality and certainly is not our ultimate destination. Despite conventional wisdom, all the money, sex, power, and pleasure in the world will not bring happiness and meaning to life. Thus we must "set [our] hearts" on what is *above and beyond* this life—God's priorities and eternal life with him. Those are realities, and they last forever.

Don't be taken in by the world and become attached to what is only temporary. Look at your few short years on earth from God's point of view and seek what he desires. You are secure in his love.

Look up and live! ♦

PRAYER

Help me, Lord, to stay focused on you ...

CONTENTMENT DEFINED

Keep your lives free from the love of money and be content with what you have, because God has said, "Never will I leave you; never will I forsake you."

HEBREWS 13:5

Contentment lies not in what is ours but in whose we are. When we come into a relationship with God through his Son, Jesus Christ, we understand whose we are and what we have. Envy causes one to look horizontally—at what others have—so we are never satisfied. Contentment invites us to look vertically—at God. When we look in his direction, we know he is enough.

We live in a consumer world. Our status, intelligence, and even our character are gauged by how much we consume. We are constantly being programmed by society to wipe the word *enough* from our vocabulary. Thankfully, God doesn't share this sentiment. When he sent his Son to earth, he was content with Jesus' death as the price for our sin. And when Jesus was on the cross, his final words were "It is finished" or "It is enough." Jesus died contented.

Being content with less stuff and not envying those with a lot are steps in a process that will take more than a quick prayer or reading a book or hearing a sermon to accomplish.

Are you content today? What will it take to get you there? ♦

> **PRAYER**

Lord, help me to be content with what I have when . . .

THE BEFORE PRINCIPLE

So he went down and dipped himself in the Jordan seven times, as the man of God had told him, and his flesh was restored and became clean like that of a young boy.

2 KINGS 5:14

A letter in a can tied to an old water pump on a trail across the Amargosa Desert read as follows: *This pump is all right as of June 1932. Under the white rock I buried a bottle of water, out of the sun and cork end up. There's enough water in it to prime the pump, but not if you drink some first. The well has never run dry. Have faith. When you git watered up, fill the bottle and put it back like you found it for the next feller.*—Desert Pete

P.S. Don't go drinking up the water first. Prime the pump with it, and you'll get all you can hold.

If you were a lonely traveler shuffling down that parched desert trail with your canteen bone-dry, would you trust this guy Desert Pete? There are no guarantees that what he claims is true. It's a risk. What do you do?

This story illustrates an important principle—the principle of before. The lonely traveler had to prime the pump *before* all the water flowed.

In Scripture the "before principle" is repeated: The Israelites had to march to the Red Sea *before* God parted it. Naaman had to wash seven times in the water *before* God cured him of leprosy. Peter had to obey Jesus' instruction to row out to deep water *before* he caught a boatload of fish.

The weary traveler reading Desert Pete's letter was put to the test in a way similar to how the Hebrew people at the Red Sea, Naaman, and Peter were put to the test.

God honors radical, risk-taking faith. God relishes favoring people who apply the "before principle." Will you take the first step of faith? ♦

> PRAYER

Lord, give me faith that I may trust in you when . . .

WHAT GOD IS LIKE

While he was still a long way off, his father saw him and was filled with compassion for him; he ran to his son, threw his arms around him and kissed him.

LUKE 15:20

What is God really like? There are as many opinions about what God is like as there have been people in the world.

Some of Jesus' parables shed light on God's character. Jesus' portrait of the character of God is so deep and compelling that it challenges every other possible assumption about who God really is. In Luke 15, Jesus tells a series of parables in which he captures the essence of what God feels toward people—toward us. He begins with a comparison, saying God is like a shepherd who searches for a lost sheep and then rejoices when he finally finds it. Yet that parable does not completely do the Father justice.

So he switches to another comparison about a woman who lost some money she really, really needed. And she finds it and hollers at all her neighbors, waking them up, because she's so excited. But even this story does not fully convey the Father's love for people.

And then Jesus settles on his final comparison. God is like a Father whose wayward son left, got tangled up in the wrong crowd, and then realized that he had to go back home to try to beg his way back into the household. When the Father saw him, he ran down the road to embrace this son who had finally come home.

This is what God is like, Jesus says—a devoted, loving Father. And if you really understood that, Jesus seems to be saying, it would change *everything*. Do you know God as your Father? Why not talk to him about the identity he provides through his Son Jesus. If you're in need of forgiveness, just like the son in the story, remember that God is just a prayer away. ♦

PRAYER

God, I believe you are . . .

june17

THE GOD WE CALL DADDY

He said to them, "When you pray, say: 'Father, hallowed be your name, your kingdom come.'"

LUKE 11:2

Oftentimes, you will hear people say things like, "Well, in the Old Testament, God was mean, but in the New Testament, he turns nice." There is at least one person who profoundly disagrees with that statement—Jesus.

One of the more shocking aspects of Jesus' words and life is the way he describes God the Father. Jesus believes that God is the best example of a father the world has ever seen, and he even says to us that when we pray, we should refer to God as *Abba*—a Hebrew intimate name used by children for their fathers. It's like the British word "Papa" or perhaps something like "Daddy." It's not a title; it's a name called out by little kids when their dads come through the door after work.

The apostle Paul also invited believers to use this wording: "The Spirit you received brought about your adoption to sonship. And by him we cry, '*Abba*, Father'" (Romans 8:15).

This was a rather revolutionary idea in the history of the world. The gods of the Romans and Greeks and Mesopotamians were not known for their fondness of humanity. And that's the problem, isn't it? We think of God in this way or equate his behavior with that of our all-too-human fathers.

If you want to learn how to pray, perhaps you shouldn't look at religious people who are experts at praying specific prayers. Maybe the best way is to observe a child's interactions with a father who adores her. Knowing she is loved, the child responds with trust. Maybe then it will be easier for us to pray. ♦

PRAYER

Abba, I offer you my trust ...

june**18**

THE COST OF LEADERSHIP

From everyone who has been given much, much will be demanded; and from the one who has been entrusted with much, much more will be asked.

LUKE 12:48

To be a leader means that at times you will be lied about, misrepresented, mistreated; you will be forced to make decisions that others don't like; you will have to say no at times, even when you would like to say yes; and you may have people say all kinds of false and evil things about you. But in the words of the old Peace Corps ad, "It will be the hardest job you ever loved."

When the lion asked the other animals if they knew he was king of the jungle, he was so confident that he bypassed the smaller animals and went straight to the bear. "Who is the king of the jungle?" the lion asked. The bear replied, "Why, you are, of course." The lion gave a mighty roar of approval.

Next he asked the tiger, "Who is the king of the jungle?" The tiger quickly responded, "Everyone knows that you are, O mighty lion."

Next on the list was the elephant, to whom he addressed his question: "Who is the king of the jungle?" The elephant immediately grabbed the lion with his trunk, pounded him onto the ground several times, dunked him under the water in a nearby lake, and finally threw him up on the shore.

The lion looked at the elephant through sad and bloody eyes and said, "Look, just because you don't know the answer is no reason for you to get mean about it!"

Likewise, the cost of leadership is to be beaten, bruised, and battered. People will be mean to you. They will hurt you and disappoint you. Lead anyway. ♦

PRAYER

God, give me the strength to lead even when . . .

CELEBRATE TOGETHER

Rejoice in the Lord always. I will say it again: Rejoice!

PHILIPPIANS 4:4

We were born to celebrate. God's kingdom, according to Jesus, is like a wedding reception where he wants his friends to celebrate with him as though he were the bridegroom. God's church is the ultimate party place—a place of rejoicing, celebration, and laughter.

God's intent was that his creation—us—would mirror his celebration. We are the recipients of grace. We're convinced that Jesus is the Messiah. We're expectant of his return. We're changed men and women.

When we celebrate, joy is expressed. Joy is the outward expression of the inward knowledge that God has everything under control. Joy is infectious and convinces a watching world that Christianity is real and that Christ can transform a life—no matter what the circumstances.

One of the most memorable events during Special Olympics had to do with a foot race among a group of people with Down syndrome. One of them stumbled and fell. When that happened, the rest of the runners went back as a group, helped the fallen runner get back up, and then all ran together across the finish line. Once across, they hugged and congratulated each other for finishing the race.

I can think of no better picture of authentic community than this. A place where people who are disabled by sin help each other stand up, link arms, and celebrate the finished race together.

A church is a community of believers who have come together to worship the living God. We are a celebrating community. When we do celebrate, those who are outside the walls cannot help but want to be inside the walls. ♦

PRAYER

Lord, give me a joyful spirit so that I may celebrate when . . .

THE WHOLE TRUTH

Therefore each of you must put off falsehood and speak truthfully to your neighbor, for we are all members of one body.

EPHESIANS 4:25

We are not very good at telling the truth. One survey revealed that 30 percent of those consulted admitted they would cheat on their taxes—to a point. The assumption is that a huge lie is more likely to be audited than a small one. That same survey reported that 64 percent agreed with the statement, "I will lie when it suits me, as long as it doesn't cause any real damage." Another survey indicated that about one out of three people admits to deceiving a best friend about something within the last year. What can we do about the truth today?

Pursue the truth. We must comprehend through diligent study and earnest prayer what God has graciously revealed in Scripture. Too many people give false testimony against God himself through ignorance of the Bible. We must fill our minds with the truth of Scripture. We live in a culture that adheres to relativism, subjectivism, and pragmatism. As we study and meditate on the riches of God's revealed truth, instinctively we will know truth from error.

Speak the truth. I encourage you to make the following commitment: "From this day forward, with God's help, I will speak only the truth, always and in every situation, for the rest of my life." Such a commitment will inevitably improve our relationships both with God and with everyone else.

Practice the truth. If we are to proclaim truth, we must live truthfully; otherwise we are merely pretending. You should ask yourself, "Do people trust me to tell the truth?" No matter how truthful we believe ourselves to be, we should continue to check up on ourselves. Make sure your walk matches your talk. ♦

PRAYER

Lord, help me to speak the truth when . . .

june21

BLURRED VISION

Weeping may stay for the night, but rejoicing comes in the morning.

Psalm 30:5

When loved ones die, we feel a sharp pain within. Death is life's bitterest inevitability. It is the end of something we never wanted to end, and in those moments we are forced to look at the world through crying eyes. Tears have a way of distorting things, like a straw appearing bent in a glass of water. When it comes to death, we just can't make sense of some things. We become confused.

That's what happened to Mary. She, too, had come face-to-face with death, and her tears blurred her vision. Outside the tomb in the garden she encountered Jesus, but she didn't recognize him. She looked in the wrong direction. "Thinking he was the gardener, she said, 'Sir, if you have carried him away, tell me where you have put him, and I will get him.' Jesus said to her, 'Mary.' She turned toward him and cried out in Aramaic, 'Rabboni!'" (John 20:15–16).

The voice. She recognized Jesus' voice. It jolted her out of despair. Joy filled her soul. Her tears were transformed into rivers of laughter. Her confusion was reborn into fountains of understanding. She had wanted to see Jesus, and she did. Her prayer to "show me Jesus" had been answered. He was standing in front of her, breathing and talking. He was alive.

In her crisis of confusion Jesus brought understanding. It was her defining moment. Jesus erased the tears with comfort. He removed her confusion and replaced it with clarity. In one climactic moment she saw her Savior, and he was alive! ♦

PRAYER

God, help me to see your joy despite my pain when ...

june**22**

THE HEART OF JUSTICE

Learn to do right; seek justice. Defend the oppressed. Take up the cause of the fatherless; plead the case of the widow.

ISAIAH 1:17

While justice includes an element of judgment and a component of fairness and a pinch of mercy, demonstrating justice moves beyond these ingredients. The virtue of justice involves being in right relationship within the community, with our fellow human beings.

Justice, in biblical times, involved a whole web of relationships that stemmed from Israel's covenant with God. While the punishment of lawbreakers was itself a fulfillment of the covenant, and everyone was given their fair due, and as always mercy was called for, the prophets and the psalmists contended that justice was executed by caring and compassionate action toward everyone in the community.

The Israelites were to father the fatherless and feed the stranger, not because the orphan and the outsider deserved it, but because this was the way God had acted toward Israel. For Israel, the practice of justice was an expression of love — God's love for them and their own love for others.

When we show justice, we act toward others as God has acted toward us. The evidence of justice, then, is when a community embraces those who are the most helpless. When we are compassionate toward others, we view life from their perspective. John, the apostle of love, writes, "If anyone has material possessions and sees a brother or sister in need but has no pity on them, how can the love of God be in that person? Dear children, let us not love with words or speech but with actions and in truth" (1 John 3:17 – 18). Justice is not an abstract word about laws or rights. If a believer fails to help the hurting and care for the wounded, he is lacking the one essential ingredient of Christianity and justice — love. ◆

PRAYER

Lord, help me to pursue justice and love others when . . .

june23

KNOWING THE DESTINATION

Like clay in the hand of the potter, so are you in my hand.

JEREMIAH 18:6

God determined that those who are redeemed shall experience salvation and be "like Jesus." This predestination of God is a decision that sharing in his being will be the ultimate end of salvation. In other words, God has determined the final result. He knows where we are headed before we get there.

A weaver sits at her loom to fashion a beautiful tapestry. She knows beforehand what her final product will be. But the creative process may take some unexpected turns. When she encounters a mistake, she does not undo her days of labor. Instead, she utilizes the mistake to enhance her design. The result is a more beautiful weaving than expected.

Similarly, God knows our final product—a distinctive character. In the pursuit he employs our mistakes and the altered courses of our lives to make a more beautiful character. But for this tapestry to be woven, we need to allow him control of the final product. This submission is not difficult when we understand the love of God. God is the divine potter, and we are like malleable clay in his tender, artistic hands. God says, "Like clay in the hand of the potter, so are you in my hand." He knows beforehand what we are to look and be like.

What do we do while God performs his artistry on our lives? We stand face-to-face, looking into the image of Jesus Christ as revealed in Scripture. The path leading to a distinctive character is made clear by getting personal with Jesus. ♦

PRAYER

Lord, help me to follow your plan for my life and guide me when ...

INTENSE

All the angels were standing around the throne and around the elders and the four living creatures. They fell down on their faces before the throne and worshiped God, saying: "Amen! Praise and glory and wisdom and thanks and honor and power and strength be to our God for ever and ever. Amen!"

REVELATION 7:11–12

How's this for a worship service? In John's vision of the future, he sees the angels and all the believers bowing before God's throne, worshiping and honoring him. By just reading the text, we can't hear the voices—intensity, volume, and inflection—or the emotion. But we can sense it in the angels' posture ("fell down on their faces") and words. Imagine what John must have felt as he witnessed these glorious heavenly creatures wholeheartedly worshiping the Lord. As they remember all that God had done, especially his redemption through the blood of Christ, they give him their full and sincere praise.

Now compare this vision with your typical worship experience, either private or public. Does your praise for the Savior overflow as you pray, sing, and read the Word? Unfortunately, our "worship" activities often become routine and even boring.

What has God done in your life? For starters, he sent his only Son to die for you; he has forgiven you and rescued you from sin; he filled you with his Spirit; he is working in and through you; and he has promised you an unending life after death. Respond in awe and in humble adoration, and give him honor as your King, Lord, and Savior.

Praise the Lord! ♦

PRAYER

Lord, when I think of what you've done, I ...

MANAGEMENT ISSUES

Wealth and honor come from you; you are the ruler of all things.

1 CHRONICLES 29:12

Taking children out to a fast-food restaurant usually means ordering a cheeseburger, French fries, and a soft drink for them. You reach over to take one of her fries, and she says, "Dad, you can't have one. Those aren't your fries; they're mine!"

Several thoughts immediately leap into our minds: *I'm the one who brought you to McDonald's; I ordered you the meal; I paid for the fries with my money. You don't realize that without me you would have no fries. I am the source of your fries.*

I wonder if God has similar thoughts toward his children when we become possessive of our possessions. A theological thread running throughout the Bible is this truth: God owns everything. David's prayer on the topic of the gifts the people of Israel had given for the building of a permanent temple in Jerusalem reflects this truth. He understood that everything he owned and possessed came from God. In like manner, everything you and I have comes from God. Everything.

We are managers, not owners, of what God has placed in our trust. The days we live, the positions we fill, the children we nurture, the people we influence, the homes we inhabit, the things we use, the money in our accounts—all must be recognized as belonging to Someone else. Of these, the stewardship of money can be the most challenging. Martin Luther astutely observed, "There are three conversions necessary: the conversion of the heart, the mind, and the purse. Of these three, it may well be that we find the conversion of the purse most difficult."

Let's get one thing straight: God doesn't need your money. What he wants is what money represents—and that is your heart. A heart that is generous toward God and the things of God is a heart that is close to God. ♦

PRAYER

God, I offer up to you ...

june26

GOING AGAINST THE FLOW

Do not conform to the pattern of this world, but be transformed by the renewing of your mind. Then you will be able to test and approve what God's will is — his good, pleasing and perfect will.

ROMANS 12:2

A man who commits to Jesus Christ lives a countercultural lifestyle. Yet if you make a radical allegiance to Christ, people will think you have gone mad.

The biblical word for going against the flow is *holy*. Paul uses it here. Holy means "distinct, separate, not the same, out of the ordinary, unusual." God is a holy God, and he expects his followers to be holy. A man who is holy is not odd, but *different*. He takes Jesus Christ and his word seriously. He is committed. He goes against the flow.

Consider tennis prodigy Andrea Jaeger. At the age of fifteen, she became the youngest player ever seeded at Wimbledon (a record later broken by Jennifer Capriati). She won eleven professional singles titles, along with thirteen U.S. national junior titles. Once ranked number two in the world, she won matches against tennis greats Chris Evert, Billie Jean King, and Martina Navratilova. But her career was brief, thanks to a serious shoulder injury at the age of nineteen.

The tennis world wondered how she would respond. Most observers assumed that Jaeger, like a child star who never makes it as an adult, would always see her most meaningful days as behind her. But Andrea Jaeger did something that surprised the world. She became a living sacrifice. After becoming an Anglican Dominican nun, she gave her life to serving God and others.

Maybe God is not calling you to be a priest or a preacher. He *is* calling you to do something countercultural — something that causes people to take notice, not of you, but of God. How will you respond? ♦

PRAYER

Lord, for me to live counterculturally, I need to ...

SPIRITUAL THIRST

When a Samaritan woman came to draw water, Jesus said to her, "Will you give me a drink?" (His disciples had gone into the town to buy food.) . . . Jesus answered her, "If you knew the gift of God and who it is that asks you for a drink, you would have asked him and he would have given you living water."

JOHN 4:7–8, 10

In John 4, Jesus has a remarkable conversation. After traveling for a long time, Jesus is exhausted and thirsty. He sits down at the town's well and asks a woman for a drink. She is shocked because she is a Samaritan. The people of Israel viewed the Samaritans as religiously and ethnically impure.

This isn't Jesus' attitude. Jesus continues to talk, asking if the woman knows about a special kind of water that will satisfy every thirst, no matter how deep. Jesus calls it "living water." Eventually Jesus reveals that he knows about her deeper thirst and her serial relationships.

This woman was spiritually eager, but she had a block—an inappropriate sexual relationship. Often a sinful relationship keeps people from truly experiencing God.

In a recent survey by Willow Creek Community Church of more than 250,000 Christians, nearly 20 percent said one of the reasons they stalled spiritually was because of an inappropriate relationship that pulled them away from God.

If you want a breakthrough in your relationship with God, perhaps you need to determine whether God is most important to you. If so, you may need to break off with that person who is holding you back. It could mean losing a relationship—but you'll get God. And Jesus insists that trade is always worth it. Do you thirst for him? ♦

PRAYER

Lord, I'm thirsty . . .

NOTHING TO FEAR

He who vindicates me is near. Who then will bring charges against me? Let us face each other! Who is my accuser? Let him confront me!

ISAIAH 50:8

It was a stormy summer day in Germany in the year 1505. A young man was returning to university on horseback when suddenly a bolt of lightning struck the ground nearby. The man was terrified. Gripped by his fear of death and divine judgment, he cried out to God, vowing to serve him for the rest of his life as a monk. That man was Martin Luther.

In *Luther the Reformer*, James Kittelson explains that Luther made good on his vow and entered a monastery. Yet he fell deeper into spiritual despair. In seeking to find peace with God through his own acts of devotion, he found only slavery to fear. "I lost touch with Christ the Savior and Comforter," he wrote, "and made of him the jailer and hangman of my poor soul."* He was a miserable man, unable to hide from the accusations of the Devil or from his own guilty conscience.

Then he met the true Christ. In searching Scripture, he came to realize that it was only through Christ's finished work on the cross that he could be made right with God. Like the lightning bolt from years before, that truth struck with brilliant intensity, this time infusing him with a peace he had never known before.

In the Bible we are told that Satan accuses us before God day and night (Revelation 12:10). Yet Christ has faced the accuser and won! Now he stands at the right hand of God interceding for us (Romans 8:34). If we are in Christ, we have nothing to fear! ♦

PRAYER

Take away all fear, Jesus, as I hide myself in you ...

---

*James Kittelson, *Luther the Reformer* (Minneapolis: Fortress, 1986), 79.

ON DAD'S SHOULDERS

About Benjamin he said: "Let the beloved of the LORD rest secure in him, for he shields him all day long, and the one the LORD loves rests between his shoulders."

DEUTERONOMY 33:12

No matter what time you woke up today, regardless of what tasks you face, God wants you to rest in him. You may have all kinds of concerns. Perhaps you're out of work. Maybe your marriage is on the rocks. It could be that you've messed up big-time in a relationship. Remember this: You are called beloved of God, and you can rest in the security of a love that never fails, a love that is not dependent on your attitude or your success.

The picture we are given in this verse is that of a father hoisting his son onto his shoulders. From that vantage point, not only can the child rest, but he can also look at life from a different perspective — a higher perspective.

As men, we like to act tough; we like to think we have it all together and can do everything on our own. But Jesus said this to his disciples when they were acting macho and arguing about greatness: "Truly I tell you, unless you change and become like little children, you will never enter the kingdom of heaven" (Matthew 18:3).

Yes, God wants us to grow up; he wants us to mature and act like men. But as far as our trust in him is concerned, he desires that we be infant-like.

As you face life today, take a deep breath and ask your heavenly Father to pick you up and carry you through the day, perched high atop his strong and loving shoulders. ♦

PRAYER

Father, may I rest in you . . .

FAMILY REUNION

For the Lord himself will come down from heaven, with a loud command, with the voice of the archangel and with the trumpet call of God, and the dead in Christ will rise first. After that, we who are still alive and are left will be caught up together with them in the clouds to meet the Lord in the air. And so we will be with the Lord forever. Therefore encourage one another with these words.

1 THESSALONIANS 4:16–18

Class reunions can be fascinating events as friends reconnect after many years. Some have to be reintroduced to each other because of changes in appearance. But many take up as though no time has passed. Former best friends reunite with smiles all around.

At family reunions, no one has to be introduced, except in the case of a new spouse or child. And close families celebrate each individual, and the days are filled with joyful hugs and stories.

Eventually, all believers will enjoy a great family reunion in heaven. This truth brought hope to Paul's readers who were suffering, persecuted, and martyred for their faith. Paul challenged them (and us) to "encourage one another" with this message: Jesus will return and take all of his followers to be with him forever. What a great promise! And what an encouragement.

When you are being hassled and hurt for being a Christian, remember your Lord.

When you experience reversals and wonder about the future, remember his promise.

When you struggle to live for Christ in a world that is falling apart, remember that this world is not your home.

When you grieve at the graveside, remember that you will see your beloved again.

When you feel trapped with no way of escape, look up. ♦

PRAYER

Dear Father, I long to be . . .

ANCHORMAN

God did this so that, by two unchangeable things in which it is impossible for God to lie, we who have fled to take hold of the hope set before us may be greatly encouraged. We have this hope as an anchor for the soul, firm and secure.

HEBREWS 6:18–19

If you've ever fished on a lake during a windy day, you know the importance of an anchor, especially if you want to stay where the fish are. Otherwise, you'll be blown away.

These days, hurricane-like forces conspire against us—the winds of change, pressure from peers, temptations, stress from physical problems, uncertainty about the future. We long for a deep foundation, a place to stand secure. Without an anchor, we simply respond to the forces pushing against us and drift back and forth and away from where we need to be.

The writer of Hebrews asserts that we have "an anchor for the soul" in these "two unchangeable things": God's nature and the fact that he will do what he says. God is always the same; he never changes. We can count on him to be with us wherever we are and in whatever we experience.

God also always tells the truth and keeps his promises. One of his most personal promises is eternal life to all who trust in Christ as Savior ... for sure!

When you begin to feel adrift and pushed this way and that, drop anchor into these truths and take hope. You will be able to weather any storm. ♦

PRAYER

The winds are strong, Lord, but you ...

POP QUIZ

Remember how the LORD your God led you all the way in the wilderness these forty years, to humble and test you in order to know what was in your heart, whether or not you would keep his commands.

DEUTERONOMY 8:2

This is a test. Those words bring a twinge of anxiety. A teacher clears her throat, and the combination of goose bumps on your arm and a nauseous feeling in your stomach predicts what she is going to say: "Please take out a blank sheet of paper for a pop quiz." A period in our lives when we feel like God has forgotten us can seem like a test too. A test is a difficult experience through which a person's true values, commitments, and beliefs are revealed. *Test* is a very important word in the Old Testament. A test was to prove or to demonstrate the character and faith of God's people. The depth of one's love will be measured by their willingness to follow Christ in difficult and trying circumstances. By the way, a test was always reserved for people of faith, never for the ungodly. Even though tests are painful and unwelcome, they are an act of love. Tests prove *our* faith and *God's* goodness.

While times of testing are not necessarily pleasant times, they are learning times. During our times of testing, our spiritual muscles are stretched, our faith is strengthened, and our character is forged. God's tests are designed to develop us into men and women of strong spiritual resolve. Let's face it. Our spiritual roots grow deeper when the winds assault and the storms assail. Take away the tests, and we become spiritual wimps.

Our tests—physical, financial, emotional, or vocational—have a spiritual component. Each test will determine if we trust God. Will we depend on God's unfailing love, understand his perfect salvation, and experience his wonderful goodness? ♦

PRAYER

Lord, help me to depend on you when ...

USE IT TO THE FULLEST

In Christ we, though many, form one body, and each member belongs to all the others. We have different gifts, according to the grace given to each of us.

ROMANS 12:5–6

It's often said, "If you want something done, ask a busy person." Are you one of those busy people to whom everyone goes whenever something needs to be done? As Christians we're called to use our abilities to help others. You may have the gift of public speaking. Maybe your talent is teaching, or leading the worship team. If being front and center makes you uncomfortable, maybe your gift is more behind the scenes in service or as a prayer warrior.

Whatever it is, you should use your gift to the fullest. But this doesn't mean you have to say yes every time you're asked to do something.

Many men think of themselves as superheroes. We relish the times people come to us with problems or needs and we have the solution. But even if we can provide the answers, it may not be our place to do so. Sometimes God just wants us to encourage others to develop their gifts by doing the work or solving the problem on their own.

When we are called to do something, let's aim to please God, not people. We are not superheroes; we can't do it all. Let's focus today on using the gifts God gave us in the situations to which he has called us. Remember, our being overextended, overworked, and exhausted is not in God's plan. Working within his will doesn't result in burnout. It's OK to say no. You may be allowing someone else to develop their God-given gifts when you do. ♦

PRAYER

Help me, Lord, to do what you have called me to do . . .

LET FREEDOM RING

So if the Son sets you free, you will be free indeed.

John 8:36

Christians should never envy the "freedom" of sinners. They have jumped from the plane of immoral freedom only to discover their chute won't open. The smile on their faces is the smile that comes just before they slam into the unforgiving earth.

Christian freedom is freedom *from* sin, not freedom *to* sin. In the Christian sense, true freedom is not doing whatever you dream of doing or acting on every wild idea; it is choosing to do what God approves of because you love him and you know to do so will bring you the greatest happiness today and the deepest joy in eternity.

Freedom is not the absence of restraint that can lead to anarchy. Freedom is the privilege and power to become all that God wants you to become. Freedom is the opportunity to fulfill your potential to the glory of God.

We are born with tremendous potential. We are free in Jesus Christ, not to do whatever we want to do, but to be all that God wants us to be. While Jesus was free from sin, we aren't. We break his laws; we fail him; we fall short of meeting his requirements. We may attempt to cover up our sins, but God says we can't get away with hiding our sins.

Jesus came along, the man who knew freedom from sin, and took the penalty for our sin. Because Jesus accepted the sentence of death we deserved, in Christ we are free from the penalty of sin.

While we are free from the consequences of sin when we die, we often live under the power of sin while on this earth. Sin creates horrible bondage. Bondage is life controlled by lies and motivated by selfishness. Freedom is the result of a living relationship with Jesus Christ—walking with him, talking with him, and learning from him. He is the only one who can set us free. ♦

PRAYER

God, help me to appreciate my Christian life . . .

BOLD DISPLAY

The heavens declare the glory of God; the skies proclaim the work of his hands. Day after day they pour forth speech; night after night they reveal knowledge.

PSALM 19:1–2

Go to the country on a clear, dark night, away from the light pollution of homes, streetlamps, office buildings, factories, stadiums, and vehicles. Look up and be overwhelmed by the heavens' light show—innumerable illuminations spread as far as the eye can behold. In that situation, a person will either focus on how small we humans are in relation to the universe or, as David did, on how amazing our Creator is.

Whirling galaxies, sparkling-diamond stars, and shiny planets move in ordered paths across the vast universe. Who can say there is no God, that there is no evidence for his existence? "The skies proclaim" it! All one has to do is look ... and listen. Do you want a glimpse of what God is like? Look at the skies and see his glory.

God created everything in the vast reaches of space, but he also created the subatomic particles in every living creature on earth—another well-ordered universe. But even more glorious than the power displayed in creation is the fact that this awesome God, creator of all things big and small, is interested in us, his insignificant, finite creatures. The Creator actually loves *us*, the created.

Whenever you need a refresher course on God's might and power, look at the skies. The heavens declare, and the skies proclaim! ♦

PRAYER

I am overwhelmed, Lord, by ...

PRECIOUS THOUGHTS ABOUT YOU

How precious to me are your thoughts, God! How vast is the sum of them! Were I to count them, they would outnumber the grains of sand—when I awake, I am still with you.

PSALM 139:17–18

Picture yourself on an ocean shore.

Scoop up a handful of sand from the beach and count the grains before they fall through your fingers. It's impossible because they are so small and so numerous. Take a wild guess. How many did you hold—a million? Ten million? Now look down the beach to your right and then to your left; multiply that number by the number of handfuls on that beach, only using dry sand and digging just one hand deep. Even with those limitations, the answer is not only impossible to determine; it is beyond imagination. That is how David pictures God's thoughts—beyond our understanding and even wildest guess. No human being could ever come even close to knowing the mind of God.

God's thoughts are precious to David, however, not just because of their number but because of their focus on God's great plan for the universe in general and for his creation in particular. David realizes that despite the fact that he cannot totally know or understand God, God knows and understands him.

God is thinking about you ... right now. Thank him for his unlimited knowledge and perfect plan, and turn your thoughts toward him. ♦

PRAYER

To think that I'm always on your mind, God, means ...

ON THE TRAIL

The LORD upholds all who fall and lifts up all who are bowed down. The eyes of all look to you, and you give them their food at the proper time. You open your hand and satisfy the desires of every living thing.

PSALM 145:14–16

Think of a father-son camping trip. They set off from their campsite in the early morning, each one carrying his own backpack loaded with supplies. By midafternoon on a warm day, with the trail narrowing and steadily inclining, the boy's load seems to be getting heavier, and his legs feel like lead. Each slow and painful step becomes a challenge. Then Dad stops, breaks out the energy bars, and quietly reaches over, removes the backpack from his son, and carries it as they continue their climb.

That's the picture in this psalm.

Some loads seem too heavy to bear. Guilt, sorrow, and daily responsibilities can weigh us down and nearly crush us. At times we feel too weak and burdened to continue. That's when we need to remember God's promise to care for us and to meet our deepest needs.

In this psalm, David praises God for his profound goodness and love, especially emphasizing God's compassion, mercy, and love. These attributes of the Father are seen in the splendor of creation and in his mighty acts.

When you feel overwhelmed by life, turn to the Lord for strength. He will carry your load, lift you up, feed you, and satisfy your desires. Look to him for strength on life's trail. ♦

PRAYER

Father, I need you . . .

july8

JUSTICE I AM

Yet the LORD longs to be gracious to you; therefore he will rise up to show you compassion. For the LORD is a God of justice. Blessed are all who wait for him!

ISAIAH 30:18

This world holds great injustice—no question. A child is murdered by a stray bullet in a drive-by shooting. An elderly couple lose their life savings through a clever scam. A teenage girl is date-raped by the boy she thought cared about her. A parent abandons spouse and children after an adulterous affair. An innocent person is sent to prison. A man loses his job because he dares to follow Christ in the workplace.

When we see evil in the world, the poor oppressed, the innocent condemned while evil and guilty ones go free, we wonder why. We can see that life is not fair and that often the "good guys" lose. But when we experience injustice firsthand, our questions become very personal, and we may be tempted to retaliate, to settle the score, to strike back.

That's the world's solution to injustice—fight; sue; get what's coming to you; get your way; get even; retaliate.

But God says to be patient, to wait for him. He, the perfect judge, in his perfect timing, will exonerate the righteous, punish the wicked, and right all wrongs.

Do you feel persecuted, misunderstood, oppressed, or unjustly judged? Don't take justice into your own hands. Take your concerns and questions to God, and wait for him—you will be blessed.

Don't despair at the evil in the world. Rejoice in God's justice. ♦

PRAYER

I admit, Lord, to feelings of . . .

july9

FORTRESS MENTALITY

But the LORD has become my fortress, and my God the rock in whom I take refuge.

PSALM 94:22

As a little boy, did you ever build a tree fort? Or did you have another place where you could hide out and feel safe? Those structures were probably pretty flimsy by today's standards, but you felt a measure of security when you were there.

Aren't there times when you just want a place to escape to and hide from the problems, pressures, and cares of this world—a place where you'll feel secure, safe from attacks, and shielded from harm? To that place you could retreat to find rest and restoration. As much as we'd like to run and hide, we know we have to face our problems and struggles—and in this world we'd never be totally safe anyway.

Psalm 94 tells of the onslaught of wicked people, arrogant and evil men and women in positions of power and authority, who continually threaten and attack. The psalm writer expresses anger, fear, and anxiety. Yet this writer concludes with stirring lines of hope and resolve. No fort or hideaway needed—God will be the strong rock "fortress" providing security and defense.

When you are under attack, especially from those in authority over you, find refuge in God and his Word. He will protect you. Go to him and take cover in his fortress of love, truth, and justice. ◆

PRAYER

Lord, hold me; protect me; hide me ...

NO CEILING

This is the confidence we have in approaching God: that if we ask anything according to his will, he hears us. And if we know that he hears us—whatever we ask—we know that we have what we asked of him.

1 JOHN 5:14–15

Maybe you've been at this point—sitting in church, driving in your car, lying in bed at night—wondering if your prayers are simply bouncing off the ceiling. Without hearing even a whisper back, holding a conversation with God can be tough. But God has told us to pray, to talk with him, to bring him our requests. And this passage says that he definitely "hears us."

God hears us when we pray because we belong to him. As his children, we can approach our loving Father with any confession, concern, problem, or request. God is never too busy to listen and never too preoccupied to pay attention. If what we ask for is good (that is, if it is in our best interests), he will give it to us. Asking "according to his will" means having the attitude that we want what *he* wants us to have, not demanding what we want regardless of the consequences to ourselves and others.

Don't be intimidated by God. Approach him with reverence and respect and with *confidence*, knowing he is listening carefully to "whatever" you (his child) ask and that he will give you only what you truly need.

Pray with confidence. ◆

PRAYER

I know you hear my prayers, Lord ...

WHAT ARE YOU BUILDING?

The carpenter measures with a line and makes an outline with a marker; he roughs it out with chisels and marks it with compasses. He shapes it in human form, human form in all its glory, that it may dwell in a shrine.

ISAIAH 44:13

Have you ever watched any "old school" carpenters at work? If you get a chance to see their craftsmanship, you'll notice that it's a thing of beauty. They learned their trade the hard way—without the aid of power tools or laser-guided measurements. They may take more time to build, but they take pride in their work and have a respect for the wood they use. The finished product is astounding.

No matter how good a carpenter is, however, they can only create out of that which has already been created. The beautiful cabinet, the stunning mantel— both came from the wood of a tree that God designed, both are only a reflection of the creativity and glory of God.

Through the prophet Isaiah, God told his people of the foolishness of making gods out of inanimate objects. Idolatry was rampant in those days. We may laugh at how people back then worshiped a piece of wood or a slab of stone, but idolatry can take many forms, especially today.

At times, it can take the form of our work, our accomplishments. Some of us are very skilled at our profession. In our pride, we might make a god out of that which we build. Let's not forget that the very abilities we have come from a generous and loving Creator. Any achievement is only accomplished by God's grace. May we keep our eyes on the Originator of life and give him the credit! ♦

PRAYER

Creator God, any ability I have comes from you . . .

july**12**

OUR GREATEST FIGHTS ARE WITH GOD

So Jacob was left alone, and a man wrestled with him till daybreak.

GENESIS 32:24

God is the divine intruder in our lives. He sometimes invades our lives, not to bring comfort, but to wage a war. As strange as it may sound, some of our greatest battles are with God. Often it is easier to say no to the Devil than it is to say yes to God.

Just ask Jacob. The night before the arrival of his brother, Esau, a most unusual thing happened. Thinking he was alone on a riverbank, Jacob was surprised by an aggressor, an attacker. Surprised from behind, Jacob was forced to retaliate and battle his unknown assailant. Who was Jacob's attacker?

None other than God himself. Alone at night, Jacob wrestled with God. And of all the fights that Jacob had experienced in his life, climbing and scheming to achieve success, his most difficult fight was with the Almighty. In fact, on that night, God changed Jacob's name to Israel, meaning "he struggles with God."

The toughest bout we will face is not saying no to a profitable career but saying yes to a divine prompting. It is not saying no to happiness but saying yes to holiness. It is not saying no to temptation but saying yes to righteousness. Please understand that God's desire is not that we be miserable and unhappy. He does want to give us the desires of our hearts. But saying yes to God's leadership can be a struggle, if not a downright battle.

Wrestling with God is the most difficult battle we will face. ♦

PRAYER

Lord, help me to say yes to your leadership, that I may ...

THE KEY TO A GOOD JOB

Preach the word; be prepared in season and out of season; correct, rebuke and encourage—with great patience and careful instruction.

2 TIMOTHY 4:2

Before painting walls, trim, bookcases, furniture, or even entire houses, you must first finish spackling, cleaning, and taping. These laborious and time-consuming tasks are about as exciting as watching grass grow. But they are necessary. The reason we go through the ordeal of sanding, scraping, and spackling is stated in bold letters on every paint can: *The key to a good job is preparation.* No truer words were ever written.

Think of all the preparation we do. We prepare for college, for job interviews, for retirement, and, hopefully, for death. Our lives are built on preparation.

A sturdy young man lacked self-confidence, but he asked a farmer for a job as a farmhand.

"What can you do?" inquired the farmer.

"I can do whatever has to be done, and I can sleep when the wind blows," replied the applicant.

Although mystified by the phrase "I can sleep when the wind blows," the farmer did not press the question but hired the young man.

Some nights later, a violent storm awoke the farmer. He got up and tried unsuccessfully to arouse the farmhand. With considerable annoyance, he then went out himself to see if all was well. He found the barn locked, the chicken coop properly closed up, a wagonload of hay covered with a tarpaulin securely battened down, and all else safely secured. Then the farmer realized what his new farmhand meant when he said, "I can sleep when the wind blows."

Few things are as needed for a job well-done as is adequate preparation. It's the key. ♦

PRAYER

God, help me to become better prepared for . . .

FINDING GOD IN THE DESERT

Now Moses was tending the flock of Jethro his father-in-law, the priest of Midian, and he led the flock to the far side of the wilderness and came to Horeb, the mountain of God.
EXODUS 3:1

God often appears when we are at our lowest.

Moses was eighty years old, minding his own business, far from the limelight, ready for retirement. Moses was in the desert. He had not come to the desert with a sightseeing tour or to collect rocks or to videotape the landscape. Moses had come to the desert to live. And, furthermore, he was on the backside of the desert. It was about as far away from anywhere as anyone could be.

His location wasn't very attractive. Neither was his vocation. He was a shepherd for his father-in-law, eking out his livelihood with a boy's job. He was about as far removed from civilization as anyone could be, as broken as anyone had ever been, and as lonely as anyone could imagine.

Our desert experience may not occur in a literal desert. Our wilderness experience might involve a stubborn physical condition that may never heal, an unfaithful spouse, a rebellious teenager, or countless other issues.

In our desert experiences, when we least expect it, God may be trying to get our attention.

There's nothing glamorous, colorful, or attractive about the desert. The desert is a better metaphor of the Christian life than the lush pastures of comfort and ease. The only redeeming value is that it is the place where we cannot live without the intervention of God in our lives.

We shouldn't curse the desert; instead, we should look for God. When we feel low, broken, and alone, it may just be God's burning bush in our lives. He is using your wilderness experience to get your attention. ♦

PRAYER

God, intervene in my life that I might do your will when ...

july15

WHAT FAITH BELIEVES

Though the fig tree does not bud and there are no grapes on the vines, though the olive crop fails and the fields produce no food, though there are no sheep in the pen and no cattle in the stalls, yet I will rejoice in the LORD, I will be joyful in God my Savior.

HABAKKUK 3:17–18

Faith believes that God is too wise to make a mistake. Even though it may not be easy to discern, God has a plan for our lives, and he is busy weaving it out in his time.

While it is occurring, we are unaware of why we are going through a tragedy. Only after we reflect on it does it strike us that God was in it all along.

Faith believes that God is too kind to be cruel. In the mathematics building of Princeton University there is a plaque that reads, "God is subtle, but he is not malicious." God is never malicious in his dealing with us. Whatever he does, he does for our good.

Faith believes that God always knows best and does best in his time. When we try to impose our timetable on God, we get into trouble.

We may want to short-circuit the maturation process during times of trial, but it is only in struggles that we obtain strength.

Faith believes that God is in control, and therefore we can rest easily if we so choose. It is our choice whether we will let the inevitable suffering and misfortune of life harden or soften us. We can decide whether we will be an optimist or a pessimist. It all depends on how we look at it, and we determine in which direction we look.

Faith believes that when we cannot trace the hand of God, we must trust the heart of God. Although life can feel like rough, uneven terrain, the Lord promises he will keep us on our feet as we travel the treacherous paths of life. He may not get us out of the troubles, but he promises to get us through. ♦

PRAYER

God, help me to trust in you when . . .

july16

WORD CHOICE

The soothing tongue is a tree of life, but a perverse tongue crushes the spirit.

PROVERBS 15:4

One mark of spiritual and emotional maturity is the ability to master our mouths. The inability to control our speech inflicts great harm on our relationships. The opposite is true too. Words can communicate great affirmation, comfort, and healing.

The proverbs utter much about controlling our words. In this passage, Solomon contrasts the effects of positive speech with the effects of negative speech. The outcome depends on our choice of words. In failing to control our tongue, we not only fail to give a blessing; we cause a bleeding that ruptures relationships. Words can wound.

Rabbi Joseph Telushkin of the Synagogue of the Performing Arts in Los Angeles is the author of *Words That Hurt, Words That Heal: How to Choose Words Wisely and Well*. He has lectured around the county on the powerful, and often negative, impact of words. He has asked audiences if they can go twenty-four hours without saying any unkind words about, or to, anybody. Invariably, a minority of listeners raises their hands signifying yes. Some laugh, and quite a large number call out, "No!" He responds, "Those who can't answer 'yes' must recognize that you have a serious problem. If you cannot go twenty-four hours without drinking liquor, you are addicted to alcohol. If you cannot go twenty-four hours without smoking, you are addicted to nicotine. Similarly, if you cannot go twenty-four hours without saying unkind words about others, then you have lost control over your tongue."

It can be extremely difficult to keep our tongues under control. A quick retort, no matter how unkind, is often respected and can become addicting. God calls us to build each other up. Try building up instead of tearing down. ◆

PRAYER

Lord, help me to affirm rather than condemn when . . .

THE TRANSMIT AUTHORITY

The word of the LORD came to me, saying, "Before I formed you in the womb I knew you, before you were born I set you apart; I appointed you as a prophet to the nations."

JEREMIAH 1:4–5

Competitions can be cruel. Usually only one contestant wins. For a culture wrapped up in winning, the runner-up is still a loser. But loss can feel like victory with a single word of an authority.

A student in architecture entered a nationwide contest for building design. Judged by a panel of architects, her design received Honorable Mention. She was utterly depressed. She believed hers was the best design. At lunch on the last day of the convention, she was hunched over her uneaten sandwich, staring at her creation. An old man was looking at it too. At last he remarked, not knowing who had designed the building, "This one, I think, is the best of the lot." Hearing this, the young student went home elated.

Why? The old man was Frank Lloyd Wright, a famous architect.

When the authority tells us something, we can count on it. God is the ultimate authority to whom we should be listening.

Jeremiah felt the emotions of being a loser, a second-rate prophet from a third-world country. He didn't feel like he could measure up to the assignment of being God's spokesperson. He was feeble, fallible, and flawed. But the authority (God) reminded him that he had a divine formation, a distinctive calling, and a chosen vocation. He was God's voice to God's people.

It helps to hear from the authority. Instead of entertaining the mockery of the multitude, the ridicule of the rivals, and the false accusation of your foes, listen to God. His voice is the one that really matters. And his is the one that speaks truth. ◆

PRAYER

God, help me to listen to your voice for assurance when . . .

GLOW IN THE DARK

The Word became flesh and made his dwelling among us. We have seen his glory, the glory of the one and only Son, who came from the Father, full of grace and truth.

JOHN 1:14

Glory is the manifestation of the divine nature of God. In the Old Testament, the glory of God was expressed through nature, theophanies (visible manifestations), and spectacular events. In the New Testament, God expressed his pure self in the fullness of his Son, Jesus Christ.

As the glory was manifested from God to Jesus, it has now been manifested from Jesus to all believers. We don't possess it, mind you. But we radiate it. When Moses went before God to intercede for the people (Exodus 33–34), he saw God's glory and returned to the camp beaming with holy light. Like a "glow in the dark" figure, Moses had no light of his own. But after standing near the most brilliant light in the universe, he glowed. His face was charged with the glory of God.

In like manner, God's glory affects our lives. We have been given the privilege of beholding God face-to-face in Christ. His glory in our hearts transforms us from within. God's glory is intrinsic to his nature. God's glory is evident throughout the world. But there are times when God wishes to demonstrate his glory through us by how we respond and react to difficulties. The reason, believe it or not, is that God can be glorified, so that a watching world will know that God is God, and so a fearful people can say, "What a God!"

The greatest problem with getting God's glory to the world at such impossible moments is that it has to go through us.

Not only is our reputation on the line, but God's is too. As odd as it may seem, God's reputation and his glory depend on our faith and trust. Let's not let him down. ♦

PRAYER

Lord, help me to exemplify you when ...

LET THE FIRE FALL

When all the Israelites saw the fire coming down and the glory of the LORD above the temple, they knelt on the pavement with their faces to the ground, and they worshiped and gave thanks to the LORD, saying, "He is good; his love endures forever."

2 CHRONICLES 7:3

Cliff Barrows, longtime associate of evangelist Billy Graham, tells of going with his dad to Yosemite National Park for a day. At the end of the day, the forest ranger who was leading their group took them to the ridge called Glacier Point. Darkness was falling. The ranger said that since early morning, men had been burning timber above the cliff, and the group could see huge piles of white-hot coals all along the rim.

The men high on the cliff began to shovel the hot coals over the side, and the coals burst into flames as they hit the cool night air. For several minutes this continued, and the group watched in wonder as a fiery wall over a thousand feet high and a hundred yards wide lit the night sky. Mesmerized, they watched the fire fall.

When the fire falls on our lives, whether personally or corporately, all we can do is fall to the ground and worship a holy and living God. Standing in awe, we are mesmerized by the sight of his consuming glory and grace. Worship is expressing our love to God for who he is, what he has said, and what he is doing. In genuine worship, the warmth of God's presence is felt; the cleansing of God's pardon is offered; the burning of God's purposes are revealed; the flame of God's power is displayed.

Worship occurs when people who have fallen in love with the God of the universe meet him in his consuming glory. Worship is a meeting between God and his people. It is a personal and collective encounter with the living God. Anything less is spiritual idolatry. ♦

PRAYER

Lord, help me to focus my worship more on you when ...

PUTTING IT OFF

Do not say to your neighbor, "Come back tomorrow and I'll give it to you"—when you already have it with you.

Proverbs 3:28

Most of us men could probably fill a book with a list of our good intentions. Some of us might even be able to fill a library! We've become adept at making promises we don't intend to keep.

> Sure, son, I'll play ball with you later.
> Yes, dear, I'll be home in time for dinner.
> You're right, Bill, we should get together sometime.

The thing about good intentions though is that they never benefit anybody. Good intentions may help soothe a guilty conscience, but they only cause more hurt and damage in the end.

You have something to offer others—time, money, abilities, service, love, or simply a listening ear. The question isn't about what you *plan on doing* with the gifts you've been given, but about what you *are doing today* with what has been entrusted to you.

It may be that you have been dreaming big. It may be that you have great plans to change the world. Be careful that your dreams don't snuff out your deeds and that your plans are followed by action.

What has God blessed you with? Health, wisdom, time, possessions, ability? Are you ready to give it away to benefit someone else? Or will you continue to procrastinate with plans and promises and great intentions that never make the journey from your head to the street? ♦

PRAYER

Father, I've been putting off ...

THE SECRET OF PEACE

Keep your lives free from the love of money and be content with what you have, because God has said, "Never will I leave you; never will I forsake you."

HEBREWS 13:5

Contentment lies not in what is ours but in whose we are. When we come into a relationship with God through his Son, Jesus Christ, we understand whose we are and what we have. Envy causes us to look horizontally at what others have—and so we are never satisfied. We pursue the God of money, thinking about what it can buy us. Contentment invites us to look vertically at God. When we look in his direction, we know he is enough.

Contentment is the secret to inward peace. It remembers the bare truth that we brought nothing into the world and can take nothing out of it, including our money. Life, in fact, is a journey from one moment of vulnerability to another. So we should travel light and live simply. The reality for most people is that we have enough—whatever enough is. We would be well-advised to be content with what we have.

Being content with less stuff and not envying those with a lot are tough challenges that require a dependence on and satisfaction in God. We must trust him and not money.

Too often we take our eyes off God and put them on earthly pursuits, with money most often being at the top of our lists. Money has the frightfully dangerous power of overshadowing God in our lives. The heart can only love one thing at a time. When we choose to love God, we will discover the marvelous benefit of contentment and the lack of satisfaction from money. Keep your focus, therefore, on God. He is enough. ♦

PRAYER

Lord, help me to keep my focus on you when ...

july22

TRUST IN GOD'S PLANS

"For I know the plans I have for you," declares the LORD, "plans to prosper you and not to harm you, plans to give you hope and a future."

JEREMIAH 29:11

Saying good-bye to anything is difficult. One thing we all look for and hope to find is our dream house, but what if after finding it we had to say good-bye to it?

Driving away, all you can see in the rearview mirror is that wonderful and cozy home. It was the place where you belonged.

But in the process of that move and relocation, there is a discovery to be made: "My security does not come from a house. Real security comes from trusting God. I will never grow if I always stay in my comfort zones. Spiritual maturity comes in learning to depend on God to meet my needs. Things should not be held too tightly—they can keep me from embracing what God has planned for me."

God's plan is the expression of his love. Never in our lives will God convey his plan except as an expression of his perfect love. God always has our best interests at heart. He'll take any situation people are going through, even if it is a terrible one, and will use it for a good overall purpose in one's life.

When God is at work, it always involves risks and changes and new ventures. We need to trust in God, not in a company; to find security in God, not in a home; to depend on God, not on friends and relatives.

God's plan is prosperous and hope-filled, one that will work for people's benefit. God desires that his people trust in his plan. He has not abandoned his people. He nourishes hope. He will satisfy life. He brings fulfillment. ◆

PRAYER

God, help me to depend on you when ...

july23

WE ARE BEING WATCHED

Whoever walks in integrity walks securely, but whoever takes crooked paths will be found out.

PROVERBS 10:9

Integrity is a high standard of living based on a personal code of morality that doesn't succumb to the whim of the moment or the dictates of the majority. Integrity is to personal character what health is to the body or 20/20 vision is to the eyes. A person of integrity is whole; their lives are put together. People with integrity have nothing to hide and nothing to fear. Their lives are open books. They say to a watching world, "Go ahead and look. My behavior will match my beliefs. My walk will match my talk. My character will match my confession."

Integrity is not reputation; it is not success. Integrity embodies the sum total of our being and our actions. It originates with who we are as believers in Jesus Christ—accepted, valued, capable, and forgiven—but it expresses itself in the way we live and behave, no matter where we are.

Unfortunately, integrity is in short supply and seems to be diminishing every day. All too frequently, our integrity is abandoned on the altar of fame or fortune. Sadly, what we want to achieve is more important than what we are to be. Integrity is lost when we focus on expedience more than excellence, on progress more than purity, on riches more than righteousness.

People are watching. They watch to see if our behavior matches our beliefs, if our walk matches our talk, and if our character matches our confession. In a word, they watch to see if we have integrity.

How genuine is your walk? ♦

PRAYER

God, help me to glorify you when . . .

july24

GRACE GROWTH

But grow in the grace and knowledge of our Lord and Savior Jesus Christ. To him be glory both now and forever! Amen.

2 PETER 3:18

New Christians are like babies: they are expected to move beyond that stage, to grow and mature.

That is precisely Peter's exhortation at the end of this brief letter, as he urges his readers to grow in the "grace and knowledge" of Jesus Christ. So the obvious question is this: How does someone do this? What does this mean?

A couple of centuries ago, the writer of "Amazing Grace," John Newton, said, "Although my memory is fading, I remember two things very clearly. I am a great sinner, and Christ is a great Savior." To Newton, growing in amazing grace meant gaining this clear understanding of who he was ("a great sinner") in relation to his Lord ("a great Savior").

We "grow in the grace and knowledge of our Lord and Savior Jesus Christ," therefore, by getting to know him better and better. This is the most important antidote to false teaching and the key to staying pure in a sinful world.

No matter where we are in our spiritual journey and no matter how mature we are in our relationship with Christ, our faith will be challenged. And we will always have room to grow. The more we learn about Jesus, the more we will love him. The more we understand his grace (his work on our behalf that we don't deserve and could never earn), the more we will live for him.

Every day, find some way to draw closer to Christ. Then you will be prepared to stand for God's truth in any circumstance. ♦

PRAYER

Lord, I need to continue to grow in ...

LIVING SACRIFICES

Therefore, I urge you, brothers and sisters, in view of God's mercy, to offer your bodies as a living sacrifice, holy and pleasing to God—this is your true and proper worship.

ROMANS 12:1

Most men understand the idea of giving an offering of money at church. We put our money or our check in an envelope and drop it in the plate. But we still need help with the idea of offering ourselves to God. After all, we can't put ourselves in an envelope.

Paul referred to this act of giving ourselves as "a living sacrifice." It sounds like an oxymoron, a combination of words that don't seem to belong together, like *jumbo shrimp.* Living means just that—*alive.* Sacrifice, by its very nature, means that if it is not dead yet, it is going to be dead soon.

Being a living sacrifice means giving our lives. Consider the aged pastor of a little Scottish church, who was asked to resign because there had been no conversions in the church for an entire year.

"Aye," said the old preacher, "it has been a lean year, but there was one."

"One conversion?" asked an elder. "Who was it?"

"Wee Bobbie," replied the pastor.

They had forgotten about a lad who had not only been saved but had given himself in full consecration to God. It was "Wee Bobbie" who, in a missionary meeting when the plate was passed for an offering, asked the usher to put the plate on the floor. He then stepped into it with his bare feet, saying, "I'll give myself—I have nothing else to give." Wee Bobbie became the world-renowned Robert Moffat, who, with David Livingstone, gave his life to healing the open sores of the continent of Africa.

What will you offer? ♦

PRAYER

Father God, today I offer you ...

BREAKING THE CHAINS OF DEBT

The rich rule over the poor, and the borrower is slave to the lender.

PROVERBS 22:7

The Bible doesn't prohibit borrowing; neither does it encourage it. Every biblical reference to borrowing money is negative. Up until the last century in the English-speaking world, failure to pay one's debts resulted in some form of slavery—a physical consequence. An entire family could become slaves to the lender, literally becoming his property. Another possible consequence resulted in "spending time" or even the rest of one's life in debtors' prison. And in Roman times, the creditors of a man who could not pay his debts broke up his workbench to make sure he did not start trading again. From the two Latin words that described this custom we get our English word *bankrupt*. So until recently, physical bondage resulted from failure to abide by biblical principles.

Nowadays, debtors' prisons are not made of stone and iron; they are made of plastic. And financial bondage is not physical, but mental—anxiety, sleeplessness, or stress. When we are in debt, we give away our personal power to lenders. Our debt robs us of the freedom of choice. It robs us of joy. It presumes upon the future.

Are you in financial bondage? Are your finances out of control? If so, there is help.

First, *seek God's control.* The controlling center of our lives should be not money but God. Next, *give away money.* Giving away money breaks the chains of the bondage that money has over our lives. Then *take time to budget.* The function of a budget is to tell your money where to go instead of wondering where it went. Finally, *live below your means.*

And then never become a slave to debt again. ♦

PRAYER

Lord, help me to manage my money when . . .

FLIRTING WITH DANGER

Reject every kind of evil.

1 THESSALONIANS 5:22

A young, newly married bank examiner was required to spend a lot of time traveling, often with a woman colleague. These work associates would often travel together, work together all day, eat dinner together, and then stay in the same hotel—all in a town where neither of them knew anyone else. This man knew this was a risk that could be detrimental to his marriage and asked not to travel alone with other women. His boss was able to accommodate him for a while, but soon it became impossible. The man, recognizing the potential danger and the consequences of flirting with danger, pursued another job.

Reduce the odds of temptation by controlling the circumstances that could cause you to fall.

Many affairs happen among couples who are close friends in the neighborhood, at church, or at work. A simple flirtation can lead to an innocent meeting that can lead to a dangerous rendezvous. A momentary indiscretion can yield a lifetime of regret.

Make note of the following suggestions and act on them to avoid temptation and to abstain from the appearance of evil: Do not visit someone of the opposite sex alone at home. Do not go to lunch alone with a member of the opposite sex. Do not kiss any person of the opposite sex or show affection that could be questioned.

One of the greatest threats to the marriages of many businesspeople is travel. Practice the following to avoid temptation and to abstain from the appearance of evil: If at all possible, travel with other men. Take family photos with you and place them where you can view them. Unplug the pay channels on the television set. Call your family every night. ♦

PRAYER

Lord, give me the strength to resist temptation when ...

HOME MANAGEMENT

He must manage his own family well and see that his children obey him, and he must do
so in a manner worthy of full respect.

1 TIMOTHY 3:4

The marketplace teaches us that success or failure in any venture depends on effective management. Effective management is not doing things right; it is doing the right things.

The same is true for families. And dads, the Scriptures inform us that managing your family is your responsibility. Before you tune out the apostle Paul as being hopelessly chauvinistic, you need to understand that the word *manage* means "to stand before; hence to lead, attend to (indicating care and diligence)." The use of this word in 1 Timothy 3:4 doesn't give a husband permission to be a dictator. It simply means that as a manager a husband is the one who will answer to the Lord for the home he and his wife have created. For good or bad, dads, we are the ones who are responsible for our homes — our families.

Most of us have had enough experience in the workplace to know the difference between good and bad management. Good managers lead by influence. They delegate but are available to help; they seek the input of others; they plan ahead. In contrast, poor managers lead by authority. They tend to control all decisions yet are uninvolved when problems arise; they resist the input of others; they tend to make decisions on the spur of the moment.

Dad, you are the leader, the manager, of your home. Serve in that capacity with all your heart. Your family hungers for it. Your wife and children will respect you for it. And God will be pleased when you stand before him to give an account of how you carried out your responsibilities. ♦

PRAYER

Father, help me to better manage my household when ...

HOW TO HAVE PERFECT CHILDREN

Start children off on the way they should go, and even when they are old they will not turn from it.

PROVERBS 22:6

Nothing in life is more rewarding than child rearing, yet nothing is more frustrating. When it is properly understood, Proverbs 22:6 contains a world of insight into the task of parenting.

To begin with, "start off" (Hebrew, *ḥānak*) was translated "dedicate" in the account of the dedication of the temple (1 Kings 8:63). This thought conveys the parental responsibility to give the child to the Lord. In essence, the child is the Lord's to begin with. The term also was used to describe a rope placed in the mouth of a horse to give it direction while the rider was breaking it. The parent has an awesome responsibility in directing the child in the things of God.

The writer of Proverbs goes on to state, "on the way they should go." The word *way* is used figuratively, referring to the makeup of a child—his or her unique characteristics and mannerisms. As parents, we must be careful to avoid two errors—first, rearing our children the way we were reared, mistakes and all; and second, applying the same approach of child rearing to each child.

The writer concludes this verse by declaring, "and even when they are old they will not turn from it." The word *old* in the original language means "hair on the chin." It suggests someone approaching adulthood, not approaching retirement. If the purpose is fulfilled and the process realized, then the result is a child who will not depart from the way in which they have been trained. The child will be perfect. No, not in the meaning you think, but in the biblical sense. The child will be mature and ready to face life. ♦

PRAYER

Father, guide my parenting and help me to do your will for my child when . . .

LEAVING A MARK

These commandments that I give you today are to be on your hearts. Impress them on your children. Talk about them when you sit at home and when you walk along the road, when you lie down and when you get up. Tie them as symbols on your hands and bind them on your foreheads. Write them on the doorframes of your houses and on your gates.

DEUTERONOMY 6:6–9

The greatest motivational principle in parenting is this: Children do what children see. This is why the Old Testament writer instructs that the commandments of God, namely to love God with all our heart and soul and strength and mind, are to be on our hearts. And we parents are to impress this truth on our children at all times. We are the teacher, the model, the example. Our talk and our walk reflect this value every hour of every day. Parents are never off duty and never wait for another time. The foundation that produces healthy, well-balanced, Christlike children begins to take shape when our walk matches our talk.

A former major league baseball superstar tells of the time when as a boy he and his friends and his father were out in the yard playing ball. They played there regularly, and the grass had really taken a beating as a result. It didn't look very good anymore—unless you were a child looking for a nice place to play baseball.

On this particular day, as the kids and the father were playing in the yard and having a great time, the neighbor called out across their fence, "Can't you guys find someplace else to play? You're killing the grass."

The father looked at the neighbor and answered, "We aren't raising grass; we're raising kids!"

Children are not things to be molded but people to be unfolded. They are unfolded through parental leadership, instruction, and modeling. When we fulfill the assignment, the foundation begins to take shape. ♦

PRAYER

God, help me to be a better parent when . . .

RECOGNIZING GOD'S PRESENCE

But the Lord stood at my side and gave me strength, so that through me the message might be fully proclaimed and all the Gentiles might hear it. And I was delivered from the lion's mouth.

2 TIMOTHY 4:17

Loneliness has been called the most desolate word in the world. Loneliness is no one's friend but everyone's acquaintance. Loneliness eats at one's inside. It brings a vacuum of emptiness. It causes a gnawing hunger of wanting to belong, to be understood, and to be loved.

Paul had a relationship with God but was feeling alone. He knew God was with him, even though others had deserted him. He knew God would never leave him. He was forever comforted by the presence of God.

Where is God when you are lonely? Right next to you. God said, "Never will I leave you; never will I forsake you" (Hebrews 13:5). God is a relational God, and more than anything else, he wants you to be in relationship with him. Here is a wonderful truth: If you are a believer in Jesus Christ, you are never alone. God is always with you. If you are feeling lonely, maybe God is nudging you closer to him. Loneliness may be a signal that it's time to become better acquainted with God.

Could it be that loneliness is not a curse but a gift? Loneliness weighs heavy on our hearts, leaving us empty and depressed. Anything *but* a gift. But maybe loneliness is God's way of getting our attention.

God's answer to loneliness is not a thing. God's answer to loneliness is wrapped up in a *person*—Jesus Christ. He is a friend—the only one who will never leave you or forsake you. Loneliness can be overcome through a personal relationship with Jesus Christ. Do you know him? ♦

PRAYER

Lord, help me to realize your presence in my life when . . .

august1

THORN IN THE FLESH

But he said to me, "My grace is sufficient for you, for my power is made perfect in weakness." Therefore I will boast all the more gladly about my weaknesses, so that Christ's power may rest on me. That is why, for Christ's sake, I delight in weaknesses, in insults, in hardships, in persecutions, in difficulties. For when I am weak, then I am strong.
2 CORINTHIANS 12:9–10

You've probably seen the strongest man competitions or celebrated victories and agonized over defeats in the Olympics—wrestling, running, jumping, weight lifting, cycling—and have been impressed by individual feats of strength. And at the gym, you've watched muscle-ripped specimens moving through the various weight machines as they work out. (Perhaps that describes you!)

Our society values strength, especially in men, and not just in muscles. We hear that "only the strong survive," and we are told that we must be tough and invincible in order to succeed in this world.

God's way is different. No hard-guy, tough veneer needed with him. Instead, he wants us to be humble and vulnerable in his presence. He also promises to use our "weaknesses" for his glory.

Paul struggled with many weaknesses—a "thorn in [his] flesh" (2 Corinthians 12:7), "hardships," "persecutions," and other "difficulties." Rather than allowing his struggles and problems to defeat him, Paul found his strength in Christ's power and perfection, allowing him to "delight" in his weaknesses.

Where are you weak? Rejoice! God can use your limitations and problems. And people will glorify God and be drawn to Christ when they see his divine power working in and through you, making you strong.

Be a strong weak person. ♦

PRAYER

Lord, despite my appearance and bravado, I am ...

FORGIVEN!

Blessed is the one whose transgressions are forgiven, whose sins are covered. Blessed is the one whose sin the LORD does not count against them and in whose spirit is no deceit.

PSALM 32:1–2

Imagine the relief of a husband whose wife has forgiven his infidelity, the hope of a man who has been rehired and given a second chance after blowing it on the job, and the joy of a defendant who has been declared "not guilty." Now imagine the absolute exhilaration of a former resident of death row who has just been pardoned by the governor. Condemned to death, he has been forgiven by the state and released. Instead of awaiting execution, he is free to leave and to live. He has turned from death to life!

Sin drives a wedge in our relationship with God. Our disobedience breaks fellowship and scars our souls. We sinners — all of us — stand guilty before our Judge, awaiting our deserved punishment. Like condemned murderers, we know that the just sentence is death.

But there is good news! We can be pardoned and set free. That's why in this penitential psalm, David exclaims enthusiastically that we are blessed. David knew this truth firsthand. After committing adultery with Bathsheba, he arranged to have her husband killed after she conceived a child. When God sent the prophet Nathan to confront David, David readily admitted his guilt. God blessed him with forgiveness (2 Samuel 12; Psalm 51).

If you have given your life to Christ and trust him for salvation, your sins are forgiven, thanks to the blood that Jesus shed on the cross. Thank God for his love and justice, and rejoice in your freedom.

Gulp the sweet air of freedom. You are forgiven! ♦

PRAYER

Heavenly Father, I acknowledge and receive your forgiveness for ...

BUSH LEAGUE

The angel of the LORD appeared to him in flames of fire from within a bush. Moses saw that though the bush was on fire it did not burn up. So Moses thought, "I will go over and see this strange sight — why the bush does not burn up."

EXODUS 3:2 – 3

Moses, the famous deliverer and receiver of the law, has one of the more famous encounters with God found in Scripture. It's called "the burning bush," but really, that's a misnomer. The bush wasn't burning, even though it was on fire! And that got Moses' attention — eventually.

How long do you think Moses watched the bush burn before noticing that it wasn't being consumed? Ten minutes? Think about that — ten straight minutes of sitting and watching a bush on fire. How boring, right? Especially in our world, where we want everything right away. We don't like to wait for anything — food, entertainment, information.

So consider this: Maybe God is trying to communicate with you, but you're so busy with a multitude of distractions that you aren't paying attention. What if God dropped a "burning bush" along your route to work or along your running path — would you even notice?

God is always there, but sometimes we need to slow down to notice him. ♦

PRAYER

Lord, open my eyes to your signs . . .

august4

WHEN YOUR SPIRITUAL TANK IS EMPTY

You, God, are my God, earnestly I seek you; I thirst for you, my whole being longs for you, in a dry and parched land where there is no water.

PSALM 63:1

Whenever we men drive our cars on empty, certain feelings are always present. We become stressed. Our palms become sweaty. Tension rises like a thermometer on a hot, sultry August afternoon. We fret. Driving, which often is pleasurable, becomes laborious. We fail to notice beautiful surroundings. We focus only on the needle and on how many miles we've traveled since the needle ventured into the dangerous area of red.

Spiritually, we occasionally run on empty too. During those times, we have no energy to engage in ministry. We find no enjoyment in reading the Bible. We have little peace and contentment. Our empty spiritual tank is an invitation to disaster; like a car out of gas, we cough and sputter and pull over to the shoulder, out of service, unable to go any farther.

Spiritual emptiness is one of the most serious threats to Christian health. We can overcome spiritual emptiness by adhering to some basic soul and body fueling and maintenance practices:

- Receive spiritual nourishment.
- Engage our spiritual gifts in service.
- Avoid overcommitment.
- Replenish our physical and spiritual resources.

The Christian life is not like a drag race. It is more like a cross-country road race. And to survive for the long haul, we need to constantly and consistently engage in those activities that keep the body, mind, and soul fueled and running in top condition. ♦

PRAYER

My tank is low, Lord ...

FUTURECAST

I pray that the eyes of your heart may be enlightened in order that you may know the hope to which he has called you, the riches of his glorious inheritance in his holy people.

Ephesians 1:18

At times we wish we could see ahead a few days, months, and years, especially when we are struggling with an important decision or wondering about the result of a certain course of action. But as finite human beings, we must live each moment, hour, and day without knowing for sure what will occur. Sometimes the future seems bright; at other times it appears bleak or threatening, with only bad news on the horizon. Whatever the case, it is unknown.

So reading God's promise of a glorious future for those who trust in him fills us with a new zest for life. Whether we live or die, become famous or remain unknown, have fragile health or great health, we can be confident that God has called us to his "riches." That gives us hope. This is our "inheritance," so it's guaranteed. God's riches include total forgiveness, strength for each day, satisfying peace, ultimate reunion with loved ones in our heavenly home, and joy unspeakable—all in the presence of our Savior.

You can't know the future, but you can know the One who does. Turn each day over to God, and live one day at a time by faith. You are heading home, and your future is bright. ◆

> **PRAYER**

Father, I know that my future is . . .

OWNER'S MANUAL

All Scripture is God-breathed and is useful for teaching, rebuking, correcting and training in righteousness, so that the servant of God may be thoroughly equipped for every good work.

2 TIMOTHY 3:16 – 17

The owner's manual for a new car is packed with helpful information and advice, everything from how to turn on the windshield wipers to how to change a tire. The manufacturer wants to be sure the owner has everything needed to operate and maintain this expensive and complex piece of machinery. Automobile owners who ignore the information in this manual do so at their own peril.

Infinitely more valuable and complex than automobiles are human beings, special creations of their loving Creator. In a confusing and dangerous world, they need care and guidance. God has provided just that in his "owner's manual," the Bible. Written by chosen, godly men as they were inspired by the Holy Spirit, this book, God's Word, contains everything we need to live right. It teaches us truth, shows us where we are wrong ("rebuking"), highlights the right life path to take ("correcting"), and trains us in holy living. Together, all of this thoroughly equips us "for every good work" — helping us glorify God through everything we think, say, and do.

The Bible is God's instruction manual, handbook, spiritual first-aid kit, and love letter. Read it; study it; learn it; memorize it; apply it. And thank God that he loved you enough to give you such a profound and personal book. ♦

PRAYER

Lord, as I read your Word, open my mind to . . .

TOUCHING THE SCARS

[Jesus] said to Thomas, "Put your finger here; see my hands. Reach out your hand and put it into my side. Stop doubting and believe."

JOHN 20:27

Doubt. Like a storm cloud on a summer afternoon, it can pop up out of nowhere and block out the light. Like an earthquake, it can shake the very foundation of our lives, threatening to topple us to the ground. To make matters worse, *doubt* is a dirty word among many in the church. Few want to talk about it. So what are we to do when faced with doubt?

We may be shaken and others may be appalled, but God is not disturbed by our doubts. Look at the way Jesus reached out to Thomas. He didn't *have* to cater to his unbelief. He didn't *have* to show up.

When faced with doubt, the first thing to keep in mind is that we're not alone. Plenty of Jesus' followers have struggled with it. Something else to remember is that doubts are often general in nature. It may be helpful to ask yourself what exactly is bothering you and what specific questions you would need answered in order to move forward in faith. Thomas knew what evidence he needed—to touch the scars on Jesus' resurrected body. Ask God to help you "put a finger on" your doubts. Ask the questions. Search the evidence. A number of good books have been written about the evidence behind the Christian faith.

In the end, however, faith always demands a choice on your part. Once God has shown you the evidence, he will tell you, as he told Thomas, "Stop doubting and believe." ♦

PRAYER

God, these are my doubts ...

august**8**

WHAT DID HE SAY?

When Jesus saw their faith, he said to the paralyzed man, "Son, your sins are forgiven."
MARK 2:5

Unable to get to Jesus, the paralyzed man's friends are emboldened. The crowd is too thick to get close to Jesus by going in on the ground floor. They come up with an idea—making a hole in the roof. Desperate times call for desperate measures.

Inside the house, Jesus is teaching, when suddenly a noise above him muffles his words. A shaft of light breaks through the ceiling. Someone has knocked a hole in the roof! Jesus stops, looks up, and smiles. Everyone else looks up, only to see four faces in the hole peering down at them. Slowly the four men lower a stretcher through the hole in the roof. On the stretcher a man lies silently. Even a casual glance tells you that he is suffering greatly.

A hush falls on the room.

Jesus doesn't immediately say, "Son, your body is healed." Instead, he declares, "Son, your sins are forgiven" (Mark 2:5). Don't you find that statement a little odd? This man who is coming for healing is first given forgiveness. Too often we want healing for the physical paralysis rather than the spiritual. Why does Jesus say, "Your sins are forgiven"? There is more than one kind of paralysis. There is the paralysis of the body caused by disease; there is also the paralysis of the soul caused by sin. This man was sicker than he knew. He was doubly paralyzed and didn't even know it.

We need what Jesus gave this man. Our deepest need is to have our sins forgiven. Without forgiveness, healing doesn't really matter. Healing touches the body, but it doesn't touch the soul.

Where there is forgiveness, there is grace and mercy and a future as bright as the promises of God. ♦

PRAYER

Lord, help me to seek your forgiveness when ...

august9

THE PROBLEM WITH PRIDE

One day as Jesus was teaching the people in the temple courts and proclaiming the good news, the chief priests and the teachers of the law, together with the elders, came up to him. "Tell us by what authority you are doing these things," they said. "Who gave you this authority?"

LUKE 20:1–2

Many of the conflicts Jesus experienced in his earthly ministry were instigated by the religious leaders. In Luke 20, we see fight after fight after fight with the Pharisees. The underlying reason for many of the brawls was the arrogance of these leaders. The Pharisees continually demanded that Jesus confirm the source of his authority. After all, in their eyes Jesus was just the upstart son of a carpenter. His popularity was a threat to them. Knowing this, Jesus always refused to give in to their demands.

Humble people don't usually fight among each other. Think about the humblest, gentlest people you know. Do they often get in big fights? No. And when they do, they're always quick to make things right.

Pride is insidious. It can start with an attitude, a look, or a belief about how we think circumstances should go. For example, when hard times come, we might question God, believing that he has "no right" to put us through such times. In a way, this is the same as the Pharisees questioning Jesus' authority.

Ever find yourself questioning God, demanding that he give an account to you of the whys of your life? If you acknowledge him as the Savior of your life, you also acknowledge his authority over your life. And that means he's earned the right to lead you.

Feeling the pull of pride? Why not seek God's solution — submit. ♦

> **PRAYER**

Heavenly Father, I submit to . . .

TOUGH OBEDIENCE

Noah was a righteous man, blameless among the people of his time, and he walked faithfully with God ... Now the earth was corrupt in God's sight and was full of violence. God saw how corrupt the earth had become, for all the people on earth had corrupted their ways.

GENESIS 6:9, 11–12

You may remember the classic comedy routine by Bill Cosby—the one that vaulted him to national prominence. It features a fabricated conversation between Noah and God about building the ark. Hilarious!

More recently, the film *Evan Almighty* tells the imaginative story of a modern-day Noah (played by Steve Carell) who is visited by God (Morgan Freeman) and given ark instructions.

In both cases, the point is well made: the task is daunting and must be completed despite doubts and opposition. Imagine what Noah's family must have thought! Surely they voiced doubts and concerns. We know his neighbors (and everyone else on earth) were nasty. The peer pressure must have been fierce. But the Bible simply reports, "Noah did all that the LORD commanded him" (Genesis 7:5). And because of Noah's obedience, his family (and the world) was saved.

The chances are slim to none that God will tell you to build a huge ship and gather all living creatures two by two to save humanity. But you may sense that God is asking you to do another daunting task—ask for forgiveness from someone you've wronged (your wife? your child?); confront a friend about sin in their life; leave your present job because of the company's illegal or immoral practices; admit your addiction to close friends and ask them to hold you accountable; tell your neighbor about Christ ... or something else. Remember Noah, and with God's power, do what God asks. ♦

PRAYER

Lord, please strengthen my will and ability to obey ...

YOUR SHADE

The LORD watches over you — the LORD is your shade at your right hand; the sun will not harm you by day, nor the moon by night. The LORD will keep you from all harm — he will watch over your life; the LORD will watch over your coming and going both now and forevermore.

PSALM 121:5 – 8

When do you feel most insecure, unsure, or downright afraid? During economic recessions or relationship crises? When you feel a sudden pain or receive a disturbing report from your doctor? In unfamiliar territory or a terrible storm?

The topic of this psalm is fear and safety, using familiar scenes to depict life-threatening situations in the writer's Middle Eastern environment.

Sun — scorching, searing, and unyielding — withers plants and burns and saps our energy. Without shade and water, we would perish quickly in the desert.

The night holds its own terrors, for that is when animals attack and thieves steal.

Using the sun and moon to illustrate his point, the writer highlights God's protection for his people. He is like an oasis in the desert, providing nourishment and rest; he is like a watchful sentry at night, allowing us to work in safety and sleep in peace. And God's care is not limited to just one place; he also watches over our "coming and going" — no matter where we are. It also is not limited to just "now"; he watches us "forevermore."

As you go about the business of living each day, remember that God cares about and for you. Turn to him in your time of need, and thank him for his tender care. God is watching, wherever you are and whatever you're going through. ♦

PRAYER

Help me, Lord, to rest secure . . .

august**12**

ASKING FOR DIRECTIONS

Trust in the LORD with all your heart and lean not on your own understanding; in all your ways submit to him, and he will make your paths straight.

PROVERBS 3:5–6

Men have the reputation of not wanting to ask for directions, even when we seem hopelessly lost. Perhaps that's because we are overly confident, or maybe it's a matter of pride and saving face—we don't want to appear weak. So we drive on, sometimes in the opposite direction from where we're supposed to be going.

This also happens in other areas of life, well beyond highways and country roads.

Knowing what direction to take, which way to go, what decision to make can be confusing at times. Life's roads seem crooked, with sudden twists, dips and rises, hidden intersections, and unfamiliar landscapes. In an effort to choose correctly, we analyze the situation and think through our options. Then we try plans A through Z. As a last resort, we may even "ask for directions" and request divine assistance.

But talking with God, asking for his insight and guidance, should be our *first* resort. Instead of leaning on our *own understanding*—knowledge, experience, intellect, and expertise—we should trust in the One who gave us our ability to think and reason, who knows us perfectly, and who knows the future. When we *submit* to him, the right path will be clear and straight.

God knows the way—follow him. ♦

PRAYER

I admit, Lord, that my pride and self-reliance . . .

august13

THE "AH" OF TRUST

Ah, Sovereign LORD, *you have made the heavens and the earth by your great power and outstretched arm. Nothing is too hard for you.*

JEREMIAH 32:17

"Ahhh"—that's what we say when we experience something satisfying and relaxing—sipping a cold drink during a break in a tough, physical project; diving into the lake or the pool on a miserably hot day; falling exhausted into bed after a long day.

"Ah"—what a great way to begin a statement about God that highlights his power and might. Jeremiah sounds as though he is falling back into an overstuffed easy chair, totally relaxing in this truth about God. Secure. At peace. Content.

God's sovereignty has a way of doing that—of building feelings of security and confidence. Knowing that our omnipotent God controls the heavens, the earth, and everything therein can relieve much anxiety and stress. We can rest in that knowledge.

In contrast, when we take our eyes off God and focus on our daily stresses and strains, problems and pressures, appointments and activities, we can feel hassled and confused and tired.

For what problems do you need solutions? What important decisions do you have to make? What struggles are you facing? For which questions do you want answers? Turn to your all-powerful Creator. Nothing is too hard for him. Fall back into God and find rest in him. ♦

PRAYER

Ah, Sovereign Lord, I know that you . . .

august14

YOUR MOVE

"I the LORD do not change. So you, the descendants of Jacob, are not destroyed. Ever since the time of your ancestors you have turned away from my decrees and have not kept them. Return to me, and I will return to you," says the LORD Almighty.

MALACHI 3:6–7

Many Christians look back with longing to when they first came to faith or attended a special retreat, conference, or church service and felt God's presence. They were confident of their faith and motivated to live for the Lord. But as life happened, things changed and distance grew in this most important relationship.

If that describes you, here's a news bulletin: If you don't feel very close to God anymore, guess who moved? Not God.

God doesn't change. He is consistent, faithful, and trustworthy. In fact, that's why he didn't destroy Israel (the "descendants of Jacob"), even though they had turned and moved far away from him. But God had promised to keep his promise (the covenant) to his people.

We move away from God when we stop reading his Word, stop talking to him in prayer, stop applying the Scriptures to our lives, and start living under our own power and direction, only for ourselves. That's when we rationalize our behavior and fool ourselves into thinking God has changed, that he doesn't really care how we live and would never judge us.

But God doesn't change. And he waits, as our concerned and loving Father, for us to return to him and to live close to him again.

Go back to God, "descendant of Jacob" (one of God's new covenant people), and he will return to you.

God waits for your return. ♦

PRAYER

Lord, I confess that I have ...

august15

AWESOME

Oh, the depth of the riches of the wisdom and knowledge of God! How unsearchable his judgments, and his paths beyond tracing out! "Who has known the mind of the Lord? Or who has been his counselor? Who has ever given to God, that God should repay them?" For from him and through him and for him are all things. To him be the glory forever! Amen.

ROMANS 11:33–36

In the last few chapters of his letter to the Romans, Paul is discussing in great detail God's sovereign plan for both the Jews and Gentiles. Suddenly overcome with emotion, Paul breaks into praise to God for who he is and for the wisdom of his plan.

We are finite, with very limited knowledge and perspective. Thus we can't begin to know God's thoughts and plans. We just know that he is all-powerful, all-knowing, and sovereign, and that he loves us ... and we trust him.

Although God's purposes, methods, and means are beyond our comprehension, we know he governs the universe and our lives in perfect wisdom, justice, and love. No one has fully understood the mind of the Lord, and no one has been his counselor. God alone possesses absolute power and wisdom. In the final analysis, all of us are absolutely dependent on him. He sustains and rules our world, and he works out all things to bring glory to himself. The all-powerful God deserves our gratitude and adoration.

Consider what God has done in your life and how his plan is working to perfection. And praise his holy name.

"From him and through him and for him"—praise God! ◆

PRAYER

Awesome God, I adore you ...

august16

LONELINESS: EVERYBODY'S ACQUAINTANCE, NOBODY'S FRIEND

Do your best to come to me quickly ... Do your best to get here before winter.

2 TIMOTHY 4:9, 21

Have you ever been lonely? You can have a million close friends and still be lonely. You can be surrounded by people and yet feel miles apart.

Loneliness knows no barriers. It affects the wealthy and the poor, the popular and the unpopular, the beautiful and the ordinary-looking, married and singles, the introverted and the extroverted, the famous and the not so famous. Everybody experiences loneliness at one time or another.

If you are wearing a face of loneliness, make an effort to spend quality time with a few people. The task at hand is not in meeting more people; it is in deepening the relationships we presently have.

Many suffer from loneliness because they have lost the sense of community. Numerous sociologists have observed that most Americans do not have a feeling of meaningful belonging or involvement in any sort of community. We often hear this expressed in the need for "home." People will say "I want to go home; I miss home." But what is home? Home is not a place but people. It is those people who care for you, love you, and accept you. These people may be related to you, but then again, they may not.

By the way, one would think the church fits that bill. But unfortunately church can be one of the loneliest places on earth. Churches can be filled with friendly strangers—people who are nice and cordial and welcoming—but there is nothing deep. It is all superficial. When you are lonely, you need people who will go deep with you. Find those people. ♦

PRAYER

God, help me to know who my home is when ...

august17

WHEN SOMEONE YOU LOVE IS HURTING

Your love has given me great joy and encouragement, because you, brother, have refreshed the hearts of the Lord's people.

PHILEMON 7

Do you know anyone who has "hit bottom" or "made a mistake," or who "took a wrong turn"?

The apostle Paul writes a letter about a hurting person. The letter is the only private letter we have of Paul's, in fact; it reads more like a postcard. Paul now has a converted slave on his hands in Onesimus. What should he do? He decides to send Onesimus back to Philemon, his master. But Onesimus is now a believer in Christ. He left as a rebel and now returns as a brother. Paul wants to make sure Philemon understands what has happened, and that's why he writes this letter.

This letter reminds us that Christianity has the power to heal hurting hearts and put those people back on their feet again. And we can be the link to that power. We can be a friend to those who are hurting.

A friend has been described in many different ways. A friend knows all about you and loves you anyway. A friend steps in when the whole world steps out. A friend is one who never gets in the way, except when you are on your way down.

What does a friend do? A friend refreshes the wounded. Philemon had that gift. Paul said of him, "Your love has given me great joy and encouragement, because you, brother, have refreshed the hearts of the Lord's people" (Philemon 7).

A friend comes alongside the hurting individual to offer support and encouragement. They help the struggler by assisting and comforting. They lighten their load of burden and pain. They remind the wounded of hope and of God. ♦

> **PRAYER**

Father, help me to be a better friend when ...

GIVE SOMEONE A FUTURE

Formerly he was useless to you, but now he has become useful both to you and to me.

PHILEMON 11

In the postcard letter of Philemon, we read about Onesimus, a runaway slave owned by Philemon, who comes into the company of Paul and as a result is converted to Christ. Now, Paul sends Onesimus back to Philemon, appealing for his acceptance and forgiveness of Onesimus. Philemon has Onesimus's future in his hands. By law he can have him executed. Or, as a believer, he can restore him to an exalted place of brotherhood and service. What will Philemon do? Paul knows that Onesimus has a great future. But that future is now dependent on Philemon's action.

When Paul wrote to the Galatians, "Brothers and sisters, if someone is caught in a sin, you who live by the Spirit should restore that person gently" (Galatians 6:1), he could have been writing to Philemon about Onesimus. The word *restore* was used to describe the mending of a fisherman's nets so that they could be used the next day. It is the idea of putting people back into workable and useful shape. It reminds people how valuable they are to God and to society. It is what Jesus did for the woman at the well, the woman caught in adultery, and the man with the withered hand. It is what Jesus has done for us who are believers.

A church father named Ignatius, writing fifty years later in a letter to the Ephesians, addressed their wonderful minister, their bishop. His name? Onesimus. In this letter, Ignatius refers to Onesimus as the one "who formerly was useless to you, but now he has become useful both to you and to me." He uses the very same Greek words that appear in Philemon 11.

Do you know someone who needs a friend? A second chance? A future? For many hurting people you may be the person who can help them turn their life around by offering them friendship, forgiveness, and a hope-filled future. ♦

PRAYER

God, help me to be a better friend to ...

LOVING OBEDIENCE

At that hour of the night the jailer took them and washed their wounds; then immediately he and all his household were baptized.

ACTS 16:33

When the Philippian jailer rose from his knees after believing in Jesus, he knew what was expected. He then entered a life of obedience. In obedience he began serving others, was baptized, and sought to bring others into a relationship with Jesus Christ.

In the New Testament, belief and obedience are not isolated concepts. Rather, the two ideas are united in the one word: *faith*. Belief impels a commitment to full obedience. Obedience, therefore, is not an option but a necessity.

A lifestyle of disobedience, in contrast, eats relentlessly at our faith. Disobedience often means taking the easy way out, relying on our own understanding rather than on God's. When we fail to obey, our trust muscles get little exercise and grow flabby.

When we obey, we discover on a deeper level that God is trustworthy. It is no longer head knowledge; it is heart and soul knowledge.

Interestingly, Jesus' typical exhortation to his disciples wasn't "believe me" but "follow me." He expected a loyalty based on love. Supreme obedience has always been translated as an expression of love. Christ loves us; we, in turn, love him.

Once the foundation of faith with Christ is laid, a whole new relationship develops. We become obedient to him not because we have to but because we want to. No longer do we fear the Master, but a loving affection emerges and grows.

Obedience is our response to what God has done for us in his Son, Jesus Christ. Acknowledging his love, a relationship develops and matures. ♦

> **PRAYER**

God, help me to obey you when ...

august20

GOD'S IDEA OF CHANGE

Then the man said, "Your name will no longer be Jacob, but Israel, because you have struggled with God and with humans and have overcome."

GENESIS 32:28

While we're content with superficial changes, God wants to make monumental changes. While we're satisfied with cosmetic surgery, God wants to perform radical surgery. God wants to reach down into the gut of our existence and change us into his image. He wants to reach down into the basement of our soul and perform a miracle. We want to work on the exterior of our charisma, while God wants to work on the interior of our character.

God wanted to change Jacob. If the name *Jacob* was significant in his past life, then the name *Israel* played a significant role in his new life. Israel means "he who struggles with God," or, literally, "God prevails." Jacob, the deceiver, had been changed from a deceiver of men to the prince of God.

After we have had a personal encounter with God, we can no longer be the same. God knew Jacob's potential; he saw beneath his exterior of trying to be a worldly-wise tough guy. God saw all of Jacob's weaknesses, but he also saw beneath the surface to what he could become. God saw the prince in Jacob, and the former cheater began to become the man for whom the entire nation of Israel was named.

In that one act of grace, God set Jacob free to be Israel. That's how God works in our lives too. God sees a person of character within us. He wants to set us free, like he did for Jacob. He will chisel and cut anything that's not right until he changes our cold lifeless existence to set us free to be the people he wants us to be. ◆

PRAYER

God, work in my life that my character may reflect you when . . .

ACT BRAVELY

For the Spirit God gave us does not make us timid, but gives us power, love and self-discipline.

2 TIMOTHY 1:7

One morning in December 1955, a bus driver told a seamstress and devoted Christian woman that she must leave her seat in the white section of the bus and move to the back where African Americans had to sit. In one of the most courageous choices of the twentieth century, she refused to move. The next Monday night, ten thousand people gathered together at her church to pray and to ask God, "What do we do next?" Because of that choice, a revolution started that was not easy. It had a high cost; many were beaten; many were imprisoned; some even died. But it changed the conscience of a nation — all because a mild-mannered, soft-spoken, Christ-following seamstress dared to act.

Action is a rarity. We are content to let the other person do it. We are apathetic about situations, causes, and problems. We have been sucked into the attitude that says my voice won't matter, so why bother. What if Jesus had displayed a similar attitude? Where would we be?

Chariots of Fire tells the story about two runners who were determined to win. Harold Abrahams was a Jewish student, and Eric Liddell was a Scot. Both won gold medals at the 1924 Paris Olympics. One scene in the movie depicts Abrahams as thoroughly discouraged and wanting to quit after he lost a race to Liddell. He blurted out to his friend, "I run to win. If I don't win, I don't run." To which he angrily replied, "And if you don't run, you won't win." He ran again. And won.

Inactivity never accomplished anything.

People who act become our heroes. They muster courage and inspire us to rise up and beyond our own inactivity and indifference. ◆

PRAYER

Lord, help me rise up and act when ...

august22

RESPONDING TO HURT

But just as he who called you is holy, so be holy in all you do; for it is written: "Be holy, because I am holy."

1 PETER 1:15 – 16

Have you ever been hurt? A friend betrays you. A girlfriend rejects you. Your wife walks out on you. Those closest to us hurt us the deepest.

What was your response? Did you want to hurt them back? Send incriminating letters to their boss and friends? Take out a newspaper ad that revealed their sins? The prevailing thoughts in the world system around us are about payback, getting even, taking revenge.

The Christians at Rome knew hurt. They were enduring the wrath of Emperor Nero, who accused the Christian community of starting a fire in Rome they did not start. They were on the receiving end of some painful attacks. Those early Christians probably wanted to attack their attackers, persecute their persecutors, slander the slanderers, and hurt the ones hurting them.

Peter informs them this is not the way a Christian responds. Two times, Peter commands the early Christians: "Be holy." The word *holy* means "distinct, separate, not the same, out of the ordinary, unusual." When the hurts come, and they will, a Christian responds in love, grace, humility, and forgiveness. In this way, we reflect the nature of Jesus. A holy person is not an odd person, but a different person. Just like Jesus.

Blaise Pascal said, "The serene, silent beauty of a holy life is the most powerful influence in the world, next to the might of God."

Believers in Christ have been commanded to live lives of holiness, even when people hurt us. ♦

PRAYER

Lord, help me forgive . . .

THE POWER TO BLESS

Esau said to his father, "Do you have only one blessing, my father? Bless me too, my father!" Then Esau wept aloud.

GENESIS 27:38

Paul Tournier, the late Swiss psychiatrist-theologian, discovered a recurring psychological problem called "the unblessed child" as he conducted his therapy. It had nothing to do with the ability of the child or the opportunities in life the child enjoyed. The children were not feeling approved by their parents, feeling they somehow did not measure up. Tragically, many people feel unappreciated and unaccepted, like Esau. The cry of every person is for approval. Giving approval and acceptance is what the Bible calls "a blessing."

Appropriate human touch plays an enormous role in the bestowal of a blessing—meaningful hugs, kisses, the shaking of hands. The arm of a parent around the shoulder of a child brings comfort, approval, and acceptance.

As a teenager, we often desired to please others. When we made mistakes, as we often would, the people closest to us would choose to teach and comfort rather than scold. The touch from someone we loved communicated acceptance in spite of disappointment.

Positive and edifying words also play a key role in communicating blessing. Even the toughest coach on a sports team will encourage the players with positive reinforcement. They may yell and scream during practice, but that will be followed by a pat on the shoulder or statement of praise. Encouragement, no matter what form it takes, is something we all need. We need to know that someone else besides us and God thinks we can accomplish great things.

When we look beyond another's rough exterior to see their potential, we point to the person's worth and value. In doing so, we have the power to set people free. We bless them. ♦

PRAYER

Lord, give me the insight to bless ...

KEEPING HIS WORDS

I have revealed you to those whom you gave me out of the world. They were yours; you gave them to me and they have obeyed your word.

John 17:6

Obedience to Christ is one of the most distinguishing marks of a Christian. Obedience is the gauge of our discipleship, the litmus test of his lordship, and the indicator of our spiritual maturity. As Jesus obeyed the Father, we are to obey Jesus.

Obedience begins with the attitude of the mind. Jesus prayed that we be given the word. This word is the stated facts or truths that have been clearly recorded in the Bible. This is the action of God toward us. He has given us the life we are to live. Here we *hear* the words.

Obedience continues with the affection of the heart. In a sense, everyone has been given the words of God. People are hearing the gospel, but not everyone believes. We are not to be merely hearers of the word; we are to *receive* the word. It is not enough to take the words into our minds; we have to integrate our hearts. While many hear the words, not all receive the words. The words of Jesus, the words of Scripture, only free us when we receive them into our hearts. Here we *apply* the words.

Obedience results in the action of the will. The whole direction of our lives is moving toward obeying Jesus Christ and all his demands on us. That is what characterizes a Christian. A Christian obeys *because* he is saved. Here we *appropriate* the words.

True obedience will never let mere listening substitute for action. Many believers are educated three years beyond their obedience. In other words, they have the training, the education, the knowledge of what needs to be done, but they don't act. ◆

PRAYER

God, help me to listen and obey . . .

august25

I NEED HELP

Blessed are the poor in spirit, for theirs is the kingdom of heaven.

MATTHEW 5:3

In the movie *Apollo 13*, Flight Commander James Lovell radioed back to planet Earth after observing smoke and debris emitting from the space craft, "Houston, we have a problem."

In like manner, we too have a problem. It is a problem as old as man and as destructive as any we have ever seen. There is no greater need than when we think we have no need. The Greeks called this arrogance *hubris*; the Bible calls it pride.

Whereas pride says we don't need help, Jesus declares the opposite: "Blessed are the poor in spirit, for theirs is the kingdom of heaven." Poor in spirit is the opposite of being rich in pride. The poor in spirit acknowledge their spiritual bankruptcy, their destitution before God.

The poor in spirit are like Peter, who when walking on the water toward Jesus takes his eyes off Jesus and sinks. He cries out desperately, "Lord, save me." The poor in spirit, realizing their need for God's intervention, cry out, "Lord, help me."

Can you imagine the number of problems that would be solved if people would seek help? Many are stuck in ruts because they are unwilling to cry out for help. God is willing and wants to help. All we need to do is ask.

We can't overcome our spiritually impoverished condition on our own; we need the help of Jesus. When we recognize our need and call on Jesus, God meets our poverty with his plenty. God delights to bring us to the end of ourselves, to expose our deficiency, so that his sufficiency might show forth.

Here's the catch: the only acceptable position for coming to God is humility. We don't brag; we beg. ♦

PRAYER

Lord, help me with ...

august26

WHAT MONEY CAN'T BUY

Honor the LORD with your wealth, with the firstfruits of all your crops; then your barns will be filled to overflowing, and your vats will brim over with new wine.

PROVERBS 3:9–10

Consider the following: Four out of five Americans owe more than they own. Forty percent borrow more than they can make monthly payments on. The average American family is three weeks away from bankruptcy. According to Social Security, eighty-five out of one hundred Americans have less than $250 in cash saved by age sixty-five.

Who wouldn't want a lot of money, thus believing that their needs would disappear? So how do we get this wealth? While many are hoping for a grand return on their investments or an inheritance from a family member or, God forbid, winning the lottery, a better way exists.

Solomon was the Warren Buffet of his day. He advised us to "honor the LORD with your wealth." The Hebrew word for *honor* means "heavy" or "weighty." When we say someone "carries a lot of weight," we mean they have a lot of clout. God is weighty; he has eternal influence. We should use our money to increase God's fame, to extend his reputation, to show he is first in our lives.

When we do, God honors us. God blesses those who bless him. If you esteem God by giving him the first portion of your money, "then your barns will be filled to overflowing, and your vats will brim over with new wine." Filled barns and overflowing vats are not a guarantee of financial wealth, but rather metaphors for a full life that has its needs being met. One lives confidently and comfortably. That's a great way to live. And money can't buy it.

Those who honor God, God will honor. ♦

PRAYER

Lord, I want to honor you by . . .

august27

BUT IT HURTS

My son, do not despise the LORD's discipline, and do not resent his rebuke, because the LORD disciplines those he loves, as a father the son he delights in.

PROVERBS 3:11 – 12

Baptist pastor Peter Lord once noted, "There is one attribute of God through which we are able to see all the other facets of him. It serves as the viewpoint or table from which we are able to view all the other facets of his personality. God is first and foremost, above and beyond anything else, a father."

God is the divine parent. His discipline of his children is no different from the correction we get from our loving earthly fathers. While the idea of punishment is certainly present, discipline primarily involves teaching or training. Similar to military training, the threat of penalty is present, but the main focus is to prepare and equip one for battle.

Discipline is a mark of love. Solomon reminds us "the LORD disciplines those he loves." If you are venturing down the wrong path, God loves you too much to allow you to keep going in the direction you are headed.

Discipline, therefore, is not God's way of getting even or his means of retaliating for the wrongs you have committed. When God disciplines you, he seeks to bring you away from what will destroy you and toward his likeness.

God, our Father, wants the best for you. Tom Landry, legendary head coach of the Dallas Cowboys, once said, "The job of a coach is to make players do what they don't want to do, in order to achieve what they've always wanted to be." That's what God does for us. God loves us just the way we are, but he refuses to let us stay that way. Don't take his discipline as anger toward you; take it as affirmation that you are his child and that he wants nothing but the best for you. ♦

PRAYER

God, help me to see your discipline as a way to grow when . . .

august28

FOR SURE

For, "All people are like grass, and all their glory is like the flowers of the field; the grass withers and the flowers fall, but the word of the Lord endures forever." And this is the word that was preached to you.

1 PETER 1:24–25

When Hurricane Katrina devastated New Orleans and the Mississippi and Alabama coastlines on August 28, 2005, rescuers remarked that the awful scene resembled the aftermath of a nuclear blast. Similar comments were echoed after tornadoes ripped through Kansas. Seemingly indestructible buildings had been pulverized or blown away, along with the homes and aspirations of thousands.

What is sure? What stands secure in this world? Nothing.

Fires destroy houses and lives; earthquakes reduce highways and bridges to rubble; hurricanes, floods, and tsunamis wash away dreams. Even the strongest athlete, the most powerful politician, the most glamorous celebrity, and the richest tycoon grow old and feeble and eventually die. And no one is promised even one more breath—life can change that quickly.

Only, says Peter, "the word of the Lord endures forever." Then he adds, "And this is the word that was preached to you."

In a world of instability and insecurity, we have the sure Word of God—the Bible. And we have the freedom to read it, interpret it, and apply it to our lives.

Do you want to know what God is like? Do you want to find the answers to life's most perplexing questions? Do you want to know how to live? Do you want a solid foundation? Study God's Word.

Life is temporary. God's Word stands forever. ♦

PRAYER

I love your Word, Lord . . .

LIVING AS ONE

I pray also for those who will believe in me through their message, that all of them may be one, Father, just as you are in me and I am in you. May they also be in us so that the world may believe that you have sent me. I have given them the glory that you gave me, that they may be one as we are one—I in them and you in me—so that they may be brought to complete unity.

JOHN 17:20-23

Knowing the end was near, Jesus prayed one final time for his followers. Striking, isn't it? With death breathing down his neck, Jesus prayed for our unity, so that we would fulfill his purpose. He prayed that we would love each other as we go forward to bring the world to him. He prayed for his disciples and for all those who would come to faith in Jesus Christ and become his followers. That means us. Is the answer to Jesus' prayer of unity just so that we will see harmony among the brethren, or is there a deeper purpose? Of all the lessons we can draw from these verses, don't miss the most important: *Unity matters to God.* When Christians stand together in unity, they bear living proof of the truth of the gospel. A unified church will convince people there is a God in heaven. Unity creates belief.

How can the world come to believe the gospel if those who already believe it are battling among themselves? When Christians splinter over frivolous and nonessential issues, observers have reason to doubt the validity of the gospel. Is it fair to say that one of the obstacles that keep people from being drawn into evangelical churches today is the way we treat one another?

One theologian has stated, "The proclamation of the gospel apart from the unity of the church is a theological absurdity." Unity is the evidence to the world that our faith is real. When unity is present, we fulfill Jesus' prayer. If unity isn't experienced, how must Jesus feel? ♦

PRAYER

Father, provide me with a greater ability to unify those around me when . . .

CONSIDER THIS — FIRST

Can a man scoop fire into his lap without his clothes being burned? Can a man walk on hot coals without his feet being scorched? So is he who sleeps with another man's wife; no one who touches her will go unpunished.

PROVERBS 6:27–29

A law of physics says that for every action there is an equal and opposite reaction. For every sin there is a consequence. The next time you are tempted to cross the line, rehearse the possible consequences of your actions.

Physical. You may contract a sexually transmitted disease and possibly infect your spouse or future spouse. You may cause a pregnancy and experience all the personal and financial implications of bringing a child into the world.

Mental. You will relive the experience in your mind over and over again. What you experience, especially sexually, is retained for life. Those memories and flashbacks could plague future intimacy with your spouse.

Emotional. You will venture down a path that may lead to addiction.

Personal. You may lose your self-respect. You will create a form of guilt that is difficult to shake.

Professional. You may lose your job. You may waste years of training and experience because of the need to change careers due to impropriety.

Relational. You will destroy your example and credibility with your family. You may lose the respect and trust of your spouse and family members.

Spiritual. You will grieve the Lord, who redeemed you. One day you will have to look Jesus in the face and give an account of your actions.

Periodically reviewing and rehearsing the consequences cuts through the fog of rationalization, filling our hearts with the healthy, motivating fear of God. ♦

PRAYER

Lord, give me the strength to fight temptation . . .

WISE UP

Get wisdom, get understanding; do not forget my words or turn away from them.

PROVERBS 4:5

Two women stand before the judge, each claiming that a living baby is hers. No witnesses are available, and blood tests and DNA tests haven't yet been invented. How can the judge determine which woman is the true mother?

He says, "Bring me a sword. I will cut the living child in two and give half to one and half to the other."

One of the women cries out, "Please, give her the baby! Don't kill him!"

This response reveals to the judge that she is the true mother. It reveals true wisdom. (Read the story in 1 Kings 3:16–28.)

Wisdom understands what is true and right. Sometimes it goes by its nicknames—good judgment, insight, perception, or understanding. It is the ability to make the right calls. Other words that fit under the umbrella of the concept of wisdom are discerning, judicious, prudent, and sensible. Not very glamorous words perhaps, but words you can build a life on.

Someone has said that knowledge is the ability to take things apart, while wisdom is the ability to put things together. Wisdom is the right use of knowledge.

In the end, we have to want wisdom. Wisdom comes to those who pursue it, like a thirsty deer searching for water or like a greedy man wanting to make more money. You have to go for it, want it more than nearly anything else. Then you will find it.

Those who arrange their lives around the goal of gaining wisdom will receive rewards that far exceed anything they can imagine. Nothing you desire can compare with wisdom. Seek and find wisdom. ♦

PRAYER

God, give me the wisdom to ...

september1

OVERFLOWING WITH HIS JOY

"I am coming to you now, but I say these things while I am still in the world, so that they may have the full measure of my joy within them."

JOHN 17:13

Joy has always been one of the most significant hallmarks of God's people. Joy is the product of a Christ relationship. Yet it remains conspicuously absent in many Christians. Why? Why does the fullness of joy elude even some of the most committed Christians?

Joy is the result of a relationship with the King of kings and Lord of lords. If Jesus is King and Lord—in other words, if he is in control—then what do we have to worry about? If joy is a flag that we fly, indicating that Jesus is in our hearts, can people tell that Jesus is in our hearts by the joy on our faces and the happiness in our voices? Jesus prays that we will have this disposition, this attitude, this confidence in our lives. He is praying for joy in our lives.

The question is this: Are you experiencing Jesus' joy? If not, here's how to get it.

Live in close contact with Jesus. Have you ever noticed that certain people bring an energy, a happiness, a joy to a room? Jesus is that kind of person. We have been led to believe that joy is found in possessions; but the reality is that joy is found in a person and a relationship.

Joy comes through prayer, but don't be quick to ask for it when you pray. Joy comes in the presence of Jesus. So bask in his presence. We tend to be too quick in our prayers and too fast with our worship. Slow it down. It is in the time with God that we become joyful, and we see Jesus' prayer come to fulfillment. ♦

> **PRAYER**

God, give me your joy when ...

248

september**2**

NOTHING BUT THE TRUTH

He will use ... all the ways that wickedness deceives those who are perishing. They perish because they refused to love the truth and so be saved.

2 Thessalonians 2:10

Picture a courtroom. Now envision a woman standing before judge and jury, placing one hand on the Bible and the other in the air, and making a pledge. For the next few minutes, with God as her helper, she will "tell the truth, the whole truth, and nothing but the truth."

She is a witness. Leave it to the attorneys to interpret, the jury to resolve, the judge to apply. The witness simply speaks the truth.

We don't like the truth because it reveals something about our character, our performance, and our relationships. So we cover it up. We justify. We rationalize.

We've replaced truth with tolerance as culture's absolute. Tolerance has replaced truth as the cardinal virtue of our society. Tolerance used to mean that everyone had a right to their own opinions. Today, tolerance considers everyone's beliefs, values, lifestyle, and truth claims as being equally valid. So not only does everyone have an equal right to their beliefs, but also all beliefs are equal. The new tolerance goes beyond respecting a person's rights; it demands praise and endorsement of that person's beliefs, values, and lifestyle. We have cheapened truth. People are apt to say "Something may be true for you but not true for me" in the same way one person likes chocolate ice cream while another prefers vanilla.

Everyone may be entitled to their own opinion, but no one is entitled to their own truth. Truth can be received, ignored, or rejected, but it cannot be created by the likes of mere mortals.

Let's start today by telling the truth, the whole truth, and nothing but the truth. ◆

PRAYER

Lord, help me to tell the truth when ...

september3

YOUR SERVE

Be shepherds of God's flock that is under your care, watching over them — not because you must, but because you are willing, as God wants you to be; not pursuing dishonest gain, but eager to serve, not lording it over those entrusted to you, but being examples to the flock.

1 PETER 5:2–3

Service is at the heart of greatness. Too many people spend an entire lifetime focusing only on themselves, thinking that significance comes from success. To make a difference the focus must be turned outward first instead of inward, giving instead of getting, serving rather than being served.

Peter addressed the church leaders in his letter, a group of people who had given themselves to others. He instructed them to serve. They did enthusiastically and not for monetary gain, providing a model for all to follow.

We don't make a lasting impact by what money we make. That's secondary. We make a lasting impact by what we give. We tend to equate having money with having influence. Instead of focusing on how much you can get, focus on how much you can give. If you want to make a difference in your family, assist them; in your church, find a place to volunteer; in your community, give; in your world, help. Ask not what others can do for you; ask what you can do for them.

If you want to leave a mark on this world, then serve others. ♦

PRAYER

God, help me to give more when . . .

september4

THE WAY UP IS DOWN

All of you, clothe yourselves with humility toward one another, because, "God opposes the proud but shows favor to the humble." Humble yourselves, therefore, under God's mighty hand, that he may lift you up in due time.

1 PETER 5:5–6

In a collection of children's letters to God, Wayne, age eleven, wrote: "Dear God, my dad thinks he is you. Please straighten him out." We all need straightening out—for our own good—especially when it comes to humility.

While the world calls for upward mobility, the Bible speaks of downward mobility. The world says that one ascends into greatness. In contrast, the Bible reveals that one descends into greatness. As odd as it may sound, the way up is down.

Peter communicates that descending movement in the word *humility*, a word that comes from humus or soil. Let's be clear about what humility doesn't mean. A humble person does not have self-hatred or a lack of self-confidence. Furthermore, it is not a call to mediocrity and a substandard quality of life.

Humility is thinking true and realistic thoughts about God and ourselves. It is the habitual quality whereby we live in the truth—that we are created and not the Creator, that God is God and we are not. We, therefore, reflect the dignity and grace of God by understanding our proper role. Just as God humbled himself and became a man, so we should humble ourselves.

Humility is perhaps the most countercultural virtue in all of Scripture, especially for people grasping for the top. So instead of promoting yourself, advancing your cause, or pushing your agenda at the expense of others, humble yourself before God and others.

The path to greatness flows downward through humility. ♦

PRAYER

Lord, help me to be more humble . . .

WARM WORMS

Cast all your anxiety on him because he cares for you.

1 Peter 5:7

A recent survey of men asked this question: What worries you the most? The answers revealed their biggest concerns:

1. personal finances
2. weight
3. personal appearance
4. general health and fitness
5. relationships
6. job security
7. sexual problems
8. career prospects—promotion, etc.
9. state of the economy in general
10. getting older*

Worries are real. What do we do with them?

An old man came up to a young boy who was ice fishing and asked what his secret was to catching so many fish. The kid bent down and spit something out of his mouth. Wiping off his lips, looking up at the man, he said, "I keep my worms warm."

Similarly, some people believe they must keep their worries warm. Their anxieties occupy their minds like the worms occupied the boy's mouth. They fret constantly, are troubled, lose sleep, and lose hope. There is a better way.

The words *care* and *anxiety* mean "to strangle." Worry chokes the very life out of us. There may be greater sins than anxiety, but few are more debilitating and destructive.

Give your anxieties to God; let him carry the weight of worry. That is one of his jobs. God is willing to carry your anxieties. One of the greatest things about God is that he works for us before commanding us to work for him.

Worriers don't make much of an impact on this world because they are so busy fighting imaginary dragons that they don't have time to fight the real ones. ♦

PRAYER

God, help me to worry less about . . .

---

*Rod Collins, "Men's Biggest Worries,"
 www.rodcollins.com/wordpress/mens-biggest-worries-what-bother-men-the-most-top-10.

september**6**

THE BATTLEGROUND

Be alert and of sober mind. Your enemy the devil prowls around like a roaring lion look-ing for someone to devour. Resist him, standing firm in the faith, because you know that the family of believers throughout the world is undergoing the same kind of sufferings.

1 PETER 5:8–9

Lions in Africa prey on weak, unsuspecting animals who have wandered away from the protection of the herd. Likewise, the Devil prowls around to deceive and devour those unsuspecting, weak Christians who have wandered off from other believers. Believers who refuse to be accountable and protected by other believers find themselves isolated and defenseless—delicious prey for the crafty deceiver.

The Christian life is not a playground but a battleground. Every day, every hour, every minute we are under attack. We are in a war. It is an invisible, yet real, war. We are fighting a foe with highly organized strategies, tactics, and battle plans. If we do not understand these facts, we will lose the battle.

Peter informs us of three decisive actions: *be self-controlled*, which is actually Christ's control; *be alert* by always being on guard and watchful; *resist Satan*. Once we have Christ in control of our life and are alert to Satan's tactics, we resist him. Notice carefully that Peter *doesn't* say to resist temptation, which, by the way, the Scriptures never instruct. Oscar Wilde was right when he said, "I can resist everything except temptation." We are to *resist Satan* the Tempter, not the temptation. The failure to understand and employ this strategy is where many believers stumble and fall.

We can only resist Satan in the power and through the presence of Jesus Christ. We don't have to be clever or strong, but we must rely on the power and authority of Jesus Christ. ♦

PRAYER

Father, help me to resist the Devil when ...

september7

THE PLACE OF NO MORE

He will wipe every tear from their eyes. There will be no more death or mourning or crying or pain, for the old order of things has passed away.

REVELATION 21:4

John ran out of words to adequately describe heaven. So he was forced to describe, as we often do, what heaven is like by speaking of what won't be there. The number of truths about heaven stated in the negative is striking. Heaven is the place of "no more."

Consider this:

> There will be no more sickness, disabilities, injuries, poverty, or drugs.
> There will be no more crime, homelessness, violence, or hatred.
> There will be no more religious disagreements, separations, arguments, or theories.
> There will be no more learning, teaching, or reading.
> There will be no more fear, darkness, suffering, sadness, or pain.
> There will be no more sin.
> There will be no more good-byes, no more children growing up, no more long trips to go on, no more broken friendships and broken marriages, and no more family arguments.

Heaven is so indescribable that the only way to fully understand it is to go there. It's like trying to describe the Grand Canyon or Yellowstone National Park to someone who has never been there. Words fail you; pictures don't do it justice. Eventually, you have to say: "Well, you've just got to go there."

Once in heaven, earth will have lost its attraction. The thought will hit us, "Why did we spend so much time trying to make our stay on earth more comfortable and more extensive when we had the eternal ecstasy and indescribable delight of heaven awaiting us?" ♦

PRAYER

God, give me the strength to help others find heaven by . . .

september8

HANDLING SUCCESS

In everything [David] did he had great success, because the LORD was with him.

1 SAMUEL 18:14

David first appeared on the scene in the Bible to confront and defeat the giant Goliath. He led Saul's armies into battle with rousing victories. In fact, David was so successful that the people sang songs to him: "Saul has slain his thousands, and David his tens of thousands" (1 Samuel 18:7). It was David's success that drove Saul insane with jealousy and envy. Without a doubt, David was successful.

We learn from David that one can be successful and still have a heart for God. But to keep success from crowding God out of the heart, it must be kept in check. The antidote is humility. Humility is not lowliness or being humiliated or abased. One does not have to be a doormat to humankind to be humble. Humility is simply recognizing the grace and mercy of God. When it comes to success and accomplishment, humility recognizes where these things come from.

The arena of politics or sports or business or even the religious community teaches us that success and humility often don't mix. Like water and oil, they seem to dispel the other. But in so doing, a fall is certain. In a prayer, David said, "You save the humble, but your eyes are on the haughty to bring them low" (2 Samuel 22:28).

Perhaps the ultimate test of a heart for God is seen in this question: How do you handle success? The greatest test of our character is not adversity but prosperity. When things are going well, do you pray as often? When you are enjoying promotions and bonuses, do you recognize God as the ultimate source of those blessings? ♦

> **PRAYER**

Lord, help me to be humble when ...

THE COMMON THREAD

You intended to harm me, but God intended it for good to accomplish what is now being done, the saving of many lives.

GENESIS 50:20

Taking a bad situation and making something good out of it is not uncommon. The pages of history are lined with individuals who encountered negative setbacks only to make something positive out of them. As a boy, Thomas Edison received a blow on his ear that impaired his hearing. Later he felt his deafness was a blessing, for it was a tool by which he was saved from distractions, thus allowing him to invent great things.

Victor Hugo, a literary genius from France, was exiled from his country by Napoleon and later birthed his most creative works. When he returned home in triumph, he asked, "Why was I not exiled earlier?"

Helen Keller, born blind and deaf, faced obstacle after obstacle in her life. However, on more than one occasion she confided, "I thank God for my obstacles, for through them I have found myself, my work, and my God."

George Frideric Handel was being threatened with debtors' prison and had become paralyzed on the right side of his body when he composed *The Messiah*, hailed as one of the greatest musical pieces in history.

Joseph responded to difficult crises with a positive attitude. He discovered in his defining moment that when life is unfair, God is still good. His life and attitude can be summarized by his own words: "You intended to harm me, but God intended it for good" (Genesis 50:20).

The fiber that ties Edison, Hugo, Keller, Handel, and Joseph together is that they saw their misfortunes and bad luck not as dilemmas but as opportunities to grow and develop in ways that otherwise would have been impossible.

What the world means for evil, God intends for good. ◆

PRAYER

Lord, help me to see your good intentions in ...

september**10**

DEALING WITH CHANGE

The LORD has done it this very day; let us rejoice today and be glad.

PSALM 118:24

The only thing constant in this world is change. Mastering change is the ability to learn, adapt, and apply what we learned to other circumstances. Here are three suggestions:

1. *Acknowledge the past.* God has been faithful in the past, and that truth gives us security for the future.
2. *Accept the present.* Life is lived one day at a time. The Serenity Prayer contains great wisdom: "God, grant me the serenity to accept the things I cannot change, courage to change the things I can, and the wisdom to know the difference."
3. *Anticipate the future.* We can ignore the changes that will come, react to them, or, better yet, anticipate the changes and adapt our strategies to address them.

A five-year study of ninety-seven active, productive people over one hundred years of age conducted by Dr. Leonard Poon of the University of Georgia found that there are four common characteristics that influence resilience:

1. optimism: they had a positive view of the past and future.
2. engagement: they were actively involved in life.
3. mobility: they stayed active physically.
4. adaptability to loss: they had an extraordinary ability to accept change and loss.

We have a choice:

- to resist or to acknowledge that change happens.
- to fear or to accept the present and God's accompanying presence.
- to resent or to anticipate, adapt, and move forward.

Change is here to stay. We can't always control the circumstances, but what we can control is our perspective about change. ♦

PRAYER

Father, help me to adapt to change . . .

september**11**

COURAGE TO WALK (ON WATER)

Take courage! It is I. Don't be afraid.

MATTHEW 14:27

We men try to construct manageable lives with some security and predictability to maintain the illusion that we are in control. We desire to stay in the boat of our making because it is convenient, safe, and warm. And then something happens—like the tragedy of September 11, 2001—that shakes everything up. And we are left with the options to fear the events of this world or to focus on the Savior.

Don't you want to be like Peter? Don't you want to walk on water, look beyond the tragedy, move past the fear? We have to start by getting out of the boat. And we have to focus on the Savior. Only then do we have the courage to take the first step.

When we focus on the Savior, we are given courage. Courage is not the absence of fear but the ability to walk on in spite of it. Courage is the muscle of character that flexes to give individuals, families, and nations strength to continue in the midst of overwhelming odds.

Courage kept firefighters and rescue workers searching for bodies in the wreckage of the World Trade Center and the Pentagon. It gave federal agents the resolve to apprehend possible assassins. It enabled our military personnel to face a cowardly enemy that had no regard for human life. It was the strength that surfaced in victims' families to face another day without their loved ones.

It is impossible to survive the storms and calamities of life without courage. It is the coat of character that we wear into the storm. Exterior supports may temporarily sustain us, but only inward character creates courage. ♦

PRAYER

I'm taking a step today, Jesus, and I'm focusing on you . . .

september**12**

THE PRINCIPLE OF RECONCILIATION

All this is from God, who reconciled us to himself through Christ and gave us the ministry of reconciliation.

2 CORINTHIANS 5:18

When two or more people come together, the potential for disagreement is always there. Even the best of relationships will have some degree of conflict. How do we deal with it?

One couple had been arguing about everything for years. They were tired of living in a perpetual state of conflict. Finally the wife tipped off her husband about the prayer she was lifting up to God. She said, "I've been praying for God to help us stop all this arguing by taking one of us to heaven. When he answers my prayer, I'm moving in with my sister."

A bulldog can whip a skunk, but it's not worth it. Most of the time, however, ignoring conflict is like ignoring termites. Eventually it will bring down the house.

Here is a principle to practice. God is a lover of truth. As such, he naturally encourages us to love truth as well. *The key to reconciliation is truth.* The truth is that you're not going to agree with everything your wife is going to say because she is her own individual. She's not you.

Even dating relationships should start out truthful. Lying about who you are in the beginning gives a false representation of who she is falling in love with.

Truth is your termite bomb. If you truly love one another, do not fear truth; embrace it. Tell each other everything immediately, all the time. Trust in one another implicitly. Conflict happens; lies never should.

Without reconciliation, no future, no freedom, no hope, and no healing exist. But where reconciliation is present, grace and mercy and a future as bright as the promises of God are prevalent. ♦

PRAYER

Lord, help me to reconcile by telling the truth . . .

KNOW THE ENEMY

... in order that Satan might not outwit us. For we are not unaware of his schemes.
2 CORINTHIANS 2:11

During World War II, while General George C. Patton's troops and tanks were engaged with General Erwin Rommel's German forces, Patton shouted over the din, "I read your book, Rommel!" In Rommel's book *Infantry Attacks*, the famed "Desert Fox" carefully detailed his military strategy, and Patton planned his moves accordingly.

God has fully exposed our enemy's tactics in the Bible. Shrouded with a mysterious veil of camouflage, the Devil must be unmasked if we are to win the spiritual war. The more an army knows about the tactics of its enemy, the more effective it will be in combat.

In his book *Spiritual Warfare,* Jerry Rankin observed, "Missionaries are aware of manifestations of Satan and demonic activity. Believers in the West also encounter Satan's activity in their lives and society every day. But we seldom recognize it because it is cleverly disguised and is discounted by our rational worldview."* We accept so much worldly and selfish living as the norm instead of recognizing it as Satan's anonymity. Sometimes his work is open and blatant, but his greatest successes are worked out in secret. C. S. Lewis wrote in the introduction to *The Screwtape Letters* that we're often guilty of two equal and opposite errors: we disbelieve in the existence of Satan, and we have an excessive, unhealthy obsession with him. Skepticism gives Satan free reign to influence our thoughts and behavior, and an unhealthy obsession with Satan attributes to him power he does not have.

To be ignorant of Satan's schemes and devices is to be defeated by the Devil and conformed to this world. As Jesus and Paul were aware of Satan's tactics, so should we be. But unfortunately, the Christian is often unaware of Satan's schemes and becomes easy prey. ◆

PRAYER

God, help me to be aware of Satan's deceptions ...

---

*Jerry Rankin, *Spiritual Warfare* (Nashville: Broadman and Holman, 2009), 7.

september**14**

LIVE COURAGEOUSLY

Be strong and very courageous. Be careful to obey all the law my servant Moses gave you; do not turn from it to the right or to the left, that you may be successful wherever you go … Have I not commanded you? Be strong and courageous. Do not be afraid; do not be discouraged, for the LORD your God will be with you wherever you go.

JOSHUA 1:7, 9

It takes courage for a man to be committed to his convictions even in the hard times when it would be easier to cheat and to cut corners. It takes courage to start over when life has blindsided you—through a lost job, a failed marriage, or a bankrupt business.

Courage is the inner resolution to go forward in spite of obstacles and frightening situations. Courage is hanging on. The courageous act bravely. They do what is right.

Until the fifth century the great coliseum in Rome was filled to capacity with spectators watching human beings battle against wild beasts or against one another to the death. When Honorius was emperor of Rome in AD 404, a Syrian monk by the name of Telemachus leaped onto the floor of the coliseum. Telemachus stood before a stadium full of blood-frenzied fans and cried out, "This is not right! This must stop."

The spectators became enraged at this courageous man. They mocked him and threw objects at him. Caught up in the excitement, the gladiators attacked him. A sword pierced him, and the gentle monk fell to the ground dead.

Suddenly, the entire coliseum fell silent. For the first time the people whose bloodthirstiness had been insatiable recognized the horror of what they had once called entertainment. Telemachus kindled a flame in the hearts and consciences of thinking people. History records that because of his courageous act, within a few months the gladiatorial combats began to decline and then passed from the scene. Why? Because one man dared to speak out for what he felt was right. ♦

PRAYER

Lord, give me the courage to speak for you …

DEATH: MONSTER OR MINISTER

For as in Adam all die, so in Christ all will be made alive.

1 CORINTHIANS 15:22

The essence of death is the unnatural separation of the body and the spirit. Imagine driving up to a five-star hotel where a valet parks your car and a doorman opens the door and escorts you in. Your car is like your body that transports you through this world that is not your home. Your soul has to have a body to get around. But at death, your body is parked in a cemetery—the underground garage—and put to rest, while your spirit is escorted to the gates of heaven. The gate is opened by the doorman, Jesus, the one who paved the way and paid the price for you to enter in. By the way, he doesn't just meet you on the other side. He also walks with you on this side and through the journey of death.

You will die. But while death at first seems to box you in, it actually frees you to go to God to experience the luxuries and amenities of an out-of-this-world resort (heaven). Death is often referred to as a departure, when for believers in Jesus Christ it is actually an arrival. Death is the doorway by which you can leave the limitations and pains of this existence to enter into the heavenly realm, made completely and perpetually alive. Only death can free you for the gift of eternal life.

The grave is an entrance not to death but to life. Have you made preparations for the journey? ♦

PRAYER

Father, help me to make preparations for my journey to you by ...

september**16**

THE INWARD THREAT

Nevertheless, I have this against you: You tolerate that woman Jezebel, who calls herself a prophet. By her teaching she misleads my servants into sexual immorality and the eating of food sacrificed to idols.

REVELATION 2:20

The biggest threat to the church is from within. It is the people who appear loyal to the church but instead are undermining it through these sins:

1. the sin of tolerating sin, which says, "I know they are living in sin, but they mean no harm. No one is perfect."
2. the sin of selective authority, which says, "Who are you to tell me what to do? I'm a member of this church. I pay my tithe."
3. the sin of personal preference, which says, "I want everything in the church to be done my way."
4. the sin of catered needs, which says, "The church is to look after me and to take care of my wants."
5. the sin of inward focus, which says, "Before we go out to bring new people in we need to take care of our own."
6. the sin of limited evangelism, which says, "That person seated there is not our kind."
7. the sin of closed fellowship, which says, "We don't want our church to get too big. If we get too big, we won't know everyone."
8. the sin of silent apathy, which doesn't say anything.
9. the sin of cultural Christianity, which says, "Your parents are Christians; you are good and decent. You're in."
10. the sin of partial obedience, which says, "I'm doing my part, but I can't tell others about Jesus." ♦

PRAYER

Lord, help me to be more proactive in my church and help others . . .

WHAT'S YOUR ONE THING?

One thing I do: Forgetting what is behind and straining toward what is ahead, I press on toward the goal to win the prize for which God has called me heavenward in Christ Jesus.
PHILIPPIANS 3:13 – 14

What is the one thing that is most important to you? It goes by many names. You can call it your purpose, your goal, your controlling center, your passion, your vision, your mission. It is the reason for your being, your answer to the question, "What gets me up in the morning?"

What makes this one thing important is not what it is called but what it does. Your one thing provides drive.

Do you know your one thing?

The apostle Paul did. He wrote, "One thing I do" (Philippians 3:13). Here was Paul, the greatest defender and propagator of Christianity, using the imagery of running a race to describe his "one thing" of carrying the message of Christ into the world. In spite of beatings, imprisonments, and attacks, he was passionately consumed with the one task of communicating God's message of hope and love to a lost and dying world.

Notice again that Paul said, "One thing I do," not, "These many things I dabble at."

In the Billy Graham Training Center in Asheville, North Carolina, is a small museum dedicated to the life and ministry of Billy Graham. A framed copy of the articles of incorporation is on the wall. Sealed on September 17, 1950, the stated purpose of the Billy Graham Evangelistic Association is "to spread and propagate the gospel of the Lord Jesus Christ by any and all ... means." Simple. Concise. One thing.

What is your one thing? ◆

PRAYER

Help me to understand that one thing you call me to do in my world ...

september**18**

EXTREME MEASURES

*Then an Israelite man brought into the camp a Midianite woman right before the eyes
of Moses and the whole assembly of Israel while they were weeping at the entrance to the
tent of meeting.*

NUMBERS 25:6

The sin of Zimri, the "Israelite man" referred to in Numbers 25:6, was deeper
than just giving himself over to his sexual passions. This issue had a spiritual
component. Moses had lectured for hours about the kind of community that God
wanted the Israelites to become. Zimri knew full well that his behavior went
directly against the commands of God. He just didn't care.

Zimri was shockingly unrepentant in his attitude. He wasn't slinking around,
hiding in shame. He brought this woman with him to the meeting of leaders for
everyone to see. It was a slap not only in the face of the leaders—who were at
that very moment weeping about the destruction that behavior like Zimri's was
bringing to Israel—but also in the face of God.

That kind of attitude is toxic. Phinehas, the grandson of Aaron the high priest,
knew something drastic had to be done.

There is a little bit of Zimri in all of us. Desires rise up; temptations call to us.
And to give in to them would be to spit in the face of all that we know is right.

Jesus says, "If your right hand causes you to stumble, cut it off and throw it
away" (Matthew 5:30). Sin is so destructive to our lives—and to the people around
us—that we have to take extreme measures. Jesus' metaphor is perfect. Getting
rid of sin is like cutting off our hand. It's painful because we have to be honest
with ourselves and about ourselves before God. Are you ready to take that step? ♦

PRAYER

Lord, reveal the Zimri-like attitudes within me . . .

september19

A CHOSEN ONE

Therefore, as God's chosen people, holy and dearly loved, clothe yourselves with compassion, kindness, humility, gentleness and patience. Bear with each other and forgive one another if any of you has a grievance against someone. Forgive as the Lord forgave you.
COLOSSIANS 3:12–13

An adopted child can look at his situation from a negative point of view, that he was unwanted and given away by his birth parents, and feel bad about himself. But if he looks at the other side, he will realize the truth: *that he was wanted.* His new adoptive parents had a place in their lives that only that little boy could fill. They chose him.

The Bible uses the same picture to illustrate our relationship with the Father. In the Old Testament, we read of Israel as God's "chosen" people (Deuteronomy 7:6). Here Paul uses that description for believers. We were orphans, cut off, and alone, but then God himself chose us—his adopted sons and daughters—and gave us a fresh start.

In this passage, Paul affirms the relationship and describes this new life— what it means to live as God's children. He says that we are to be compassionate, kind, humble, gentle, patient, forgiving, loving, peaceable, and thankful (see also Colossians 3:14–15).

When you feel insignificant or lonely, cut off from love and acceptance, remember your Father and the amazing truth that you belong to him. He chose you and loves you. Then live in such a way that befits a member of God's family. ♦

PRAYER

Father, thank you for choosing me...

september**20**

WITH GREAT JOY

To him who is able to keep you from stumbling and to present you before his glorious presence without fault and with great joy — to the only God our Savior be glory, majesty, power and authority, through Jesus Christ our Lord, before all ages, now and forevermore! Amen.

JUDE 24–25

Picture this: While hiking with your dad, you approach a rough, uneven stretch, strewn with branches and rocks of varying sizes, some larger than your seven-year-old feet. As you begin to take a tentative step, Dad grasps the shoulder straps of your backpack and says, "Don't worry, son; I've got you!"

That's the picture here — God holding us, keeping us from falling. Of course, the stumbling mentioned in this passage is far more significant than tripping over rocks on a trail. And God's hold is infinitely securer and stronger.

What a marvelous promise — God will keep us from stumbling! We don't have to worry or try to cling tightly to God, because *he is holding us.* And his purpose is to bring us to himself "without fault." All this is possible through our Lord Jesus Christ. He died on the cross in our place, taking the penalty for our sin. Then he rose from the grave, defeating sin and death, and now he lives to intercede with the Father on our behalf. When we trust Christ as Savior, we are forgiven of our sins — past, present, and future — and we enter a secure relationship with God. Hallelujah!

This doxology and benediction by Jude is a profound hymn of praise to our glorious God, who has all glory, majesty, power, and authority. Make this your daily song. ♦

PRAYER

Heavenly Father, I know you are with me ...

ANXIETY ANTIDOTE

Do not be anxious about anything, but in every situation, by prayer and petition, with thanksgiving, present your requests to God. And the peace of God, which transcends all understanding, will guard your hearts and your minds in Christ Jesus.

PHILIPPIANS 4:6–7

Life is filled with worries—at home, at school, on the job, even at church. We can feel financial stress and wonder how we will be able to pay the bills. We can have health concerns when certain symptoms appear. We can fear for the safety and security of our loved ones.

In reality, we can become anxious about virtually everything. These days, just as when Paul wrote this letter, anxiety and stress can eat us alive.

Here Paul presents the antidote to anxiety. In a word, it's *prayer*. Realizing that God is in control, that he loves us, and that Christ is making intercession for us, we can turn our worries into prayers. This means talking to God about *everything*, turning every concern, decision, and relationship over to him. We will feel anxiety melt away as we lean on our loving Lord. And we will know his peace.

God's peace is not found through positive thinking, conflict resolution, or emotional release. It comes from knowing God and from trusting him, and it reaches into the very depths of our being.

Instead of worrying, pray—and experience God's peace, which "transcends all understanding." You can rest in his peace. ◆

PRAYER

Lord. I give all my concerns to you ...

september22

WHAT'S YOUR STATUS?

Live in harmony with one another. Do not be proud, but be willing to associate with people of low position. Do not be conceited.

ROMANS 12:16

From the time we toddle into day care or walk through the doors of preschool, we start building superficial status groups. Granted, it may not be too obvious early in life, but the older we get, the more defined our groupings become. It's a worldwide phenomenon. From the historical caste system in India to the economic stratum we have in our own culture, we have a penchant for position and rank.

As followers of Christ, however, we are supposed to break the mold. Prejudicial partitions have absolutely no place within the body of Christ. James, the half brother of our Lord Jesus, cautioned believers against showing favoritism. Christ is our example. He allowed himself to be born to a peasant woman, placed in a manger, surrounded by the smell of animal manure. Although he was visited later on by "important" dignitaries from foreign lands, his birth was first announced to lowly shepherds. As a man, Jesus associated with the rich and the poor, the "righteous" and the sinners. In God's eyes, man-made distinctions count for nothing.

With whom do you spend your time? How do you choose your friends? Choosing to associate with those outside your status group would be a radical decision. But then, isn't our world in need of a radical status change? ♦

PRAYER

Flush out, Father, my attitude toward status ...

september23

THE WRONG CROWD VERSUS THE RIGHT CROWD

Was it not because of marriages like these that Solomon king of Israel sinned?... Must we hear now that you too are doing all this terrible wickedness and are being unfaithful to our God by marrying foreign women?

NEHEMIAH 13:26–27

Several times in the Old Testament, God specifically commands his people to avoid associating too closely with foreign people. This is especially confusing when you consider that in other places in the Bible, God tells us to love everyone, regardless of our differences. How do these two ideas fit together?

Perhaps it makes more sense from a parent's perspective. When you were a kid, chances are your parents warned you about hanging out with the wrong crowd at school. Why? Because parents know you are who your friends are.

From this perspective it makes a little more sense that God wouldn't want his people forming close alliances with people whose value systems were entirely opposite of what God wanted. All the surrounding foreign nations worshiped many gods. Many had rituals in their religious ceremonies that were immoral. These were things God specifically wanted his people *not* to do.

And just like a parent guiding his adolescent through the stormy waters of peer relationships, God reminded Israel to stay focused on him. The same is true for us. God wants us to form our closest friendships with people who will encourage spiritual growth—people who love God and can help us love him better.

How are you doing with this? Is there a friendship you have that's dragging you down spiritually? You can begin to invest in some friends who share your beliefs. Initiating deep friendships with other men who love Christ is never easy. But the gain is always worth it. ♦

PRAYER

Examine my friendships, Lord ...

september24

THE NEED TO PERFORM

I write these things to you who believe in the name of the Son of God so that you may know that you have eternal life.

1 JOHN 5:13

In business deals and daily decisions we expect others to perform. When we compete, we expect a good performance from ourselves and those around us. Men often get frustrated and lose faith if the performance is subpar.

The weight of performance is heavy on a man's shoulders; it's how we've been raised in society. It's difficult to be consistent and even harder to be consistently successful. We need something that is constant, true, and real all the time.

God fills that need and empowers with life. We can have confidence that he gives life to those who are faithful, to those who believe in him. There is no falling back, no loss of what you thought was gained, no desertion when times get difficult and human understanding is at a premium.

Life will get difficult. Performance will not always be optimum. We will feel lonely at times because of the nature of who we are. But God is forever faithful to those who believe in his Son. He loves us—win or lose. In him we find life, truth, and reality. In him we find true success. ♦

PRAYER

Help me to rest assured, Lord, that I have life in you . . .

september25

LEGACY OF FAITH

And now, LORD, let the promise you have made concerning your servant and his house be established forever. Do as you promised, so that it will be established and that your name will be great forever. Then people will say, "The LORD Almighty, the God over Israel, is Israel's God!" And the house of your servant David will be established before you.

1 CHRONICLES 17:23–24

King David prayed, reminding God of his promise and asking for God's blessing and for God to glorify himself through David and his descendants. Although David was praying about himself and his family, his main focus was on God — that God's name would be "great forever." David wanted his children and all of the future generations to be true to the Lord and to be blessed by him.

Parenting can be scary — no guarantees. We've seen compliant children morph into rebellious teenagers almost overnight. And we've seen juvenile delinquents turn into upright citizens. In truth, all parents are amateurs. At the birth of a son or daughter, we aren't given a set of instructions explaining exactly what to do when, to ensure an exemplary child. So Christian moms and dads parent by faith — praying like crazy, doing what they think is best, and trusting God for the outcome.

That's what King David did. More than anything, he wanted his progeny to live for their Lord.

What do you wish for your family? What do you ask God to do for them? May your prayers focus on God's good work in your children's lives, that they may honor him and enjoy his blessings forever and that God will be praised because of them. Claim God's blessings for your kids! ♦

PRAYER

Heavenly Father, I claim . . .

FOR GOODNESS SAKE!

The LORD is good, a refuge in times of trouble. He cares for those who trust in him.

NAHUM 1:7

Remember the short prayer you repeated before meals as a child? It went something like this: "God is great. God is good. And we thank him for our food." You probably didn't think much about what you were saying, but these simple phrases have profound meaning.

The middle sentence echoes the first line of this verse in Nahum—"God is good." We may repeat these words as a child would, easily and without thought, but we need to hear their truth: The Lord is *good*, not evil or neutral. The fact that God is good means that he wants nothing but the best for us, and he will never lead us down the wrong path.

And God isn't aloof. Goodness isn't passive—he "cares for those who trust in him," actively looking out for their best interests. This implies protection, direction, empowerment, rescue, and sustenance.

When you feel surrounded by violence and hatred and the world seems to be falling apart, remember that *God is good*. When you feel lost, abandoned, and adrift in a sea of anxiety, remember that *God is good*. When you experience gut-wrenching loss and pain and the "Why?" tears at your soul, remember that *God is good*. And he will be your safe refuge.

God is good! ♦

PRAYER

My great and good God, thank you for ...

TOUGH TIMES? REJOICE!

Though the fig tree does not bud and there are no grapes on the vines, though the olive crop fails and the fields produce no food, though there are no sheep in the pen and no cattle in the stalls, yet I will rejoice in the LORD, I will be joyful in God my Savior. The Sovereign LORD is my strength; he makes my feet like the feet of a deer, he enables me to tread on the heights.

HABAKKUK 3:17–19

Habakkuk looked at the world and saw evil and injustice permeating every level of society. Even worse, the wicked seemed to be flourishing in their evil deeds, reveling in greed, flaunting laws, and oppressing the righteous and poor. With dismay and anguish, Habakkuk complained to God, crying out, "Why do you tolerate wrongdoing?" (1:3)

God answered by reminding Habakkuk that he, the Lord, was holy and just and the judge of all the earth, and that at the right time, he would punish the wicked. Until then, the righteous (including Habakkuk, of course) should live by faith (2:4).

Hearing God's answer, Habakkuk responded with this strong word of courage and joy—declaring that regardless of the circumstances (no figs, no olives, "no food," "no sheep," and "no cattle"—pretty bleak, to say the least), he would "rejoice in the LORD" and continue to live for him.

When you feel beaten down, see no relief in sight, and wonder "why?" and "how?" and "how long?" remember that the final chapter has not been written—God's justice will prevail. Rejoice in who God is, and live by faith in your strong, loving, and holy Savior. He will lift you up and make you as sure-footed and swift as a deer. ♦

PRAYER

Lord, I admit that I have questions about ...

september28

TO TELL THE TRUTH

"Salvation is found in no one else, for there is no other name under heaven given to mankind by which we must be saved." ... Peter and John replied, "Which is right in God's eyes: to listen to you, or to him? You be the judges! As for us, we cannot help speaking about what we have seen and heard."

ACTS 4:12, 19–20

Taking a stand for Christ was risky business. In fact, Peter and John had just been arrested and jailed for "teaching the people, proclaiming in Jesus the resurrection of the dead" (Acts 4:2). But emboldened by the truth and empowered by the Holy Spirit, Peter and John courageously proclaimed that the only way to find forgiveness and salvation was through "Jesus Christ of Nazareth" (Acts 4:10). And when they were ordered by the rulers and elders to stop, they replied that they were compelled to speak because they had to obey God.

Many people don't like to hear the fact that God has provided no other way to be forgiven and destined for heaven. But it's true. Christians should be open-minded on many issues, but not on how to be saved from sin. No other religious teacher could take the penalty for our sins; no one else came to earth as God's only Son; no other person rose from the dead. No other name or way to heaven has been provided. Let us boldly proclaim the truth to the world.

Whenever you feel threatened for or embarrassed about sharing your faith in Christ, remember the words and example of Peter and John. Then tell the truth. ♦

PRAYER

I know the truth, Lord ...

september29

NEW LIFE FOR OLD

Therefore, if anyone is in Christ, the new creation has come: The old has gone, the new is here!

2 CORINTHIANS 5:17

New! Improved! The latest! Just in! State of the art!

Advertisers use these words and their synonyms because they are effective with consumers. They work. "New and improved" sells. Can you imagine an ad touting "same as before," "old," or "nothing different"? Not very effective. People want bigger and better and what is fresh, current, and "now."

Beyond the products they buy, in their deepest longings most also desire a new life—a transformation. They know that the old way doesn't satisfy and isn't working. They feel empty and weighed down by guilt and regret and want answers—new and improved, a fresh start.

That's exactly what Jesus Christ offers. In him, old things are gone and forgotten, and everything is new. And this newness isn't superficial, like a fresh coat of paint on an old car. Instead, God recreates each person, changing them on the inside. The price is amazing too—totally free, by grace through faith!

Christ gives . . .

   . . . new outlook and perspective
   . . . new desires and motives
   . . . new thoughts
   . . . new direction and purpose
   . . . new destination

It's true. Spread the news. Christ offers new life for old! ♦

PRAYER

As I reflect on my life, Lord, I'm amazed by . . .

september**30**

A FRUITFUL LIFE

I am the vine; you are the branches. If you remain in me and I in you, you will bear much fruit; apart from me you can do nothing.

JOHN 15:5

The purpose of an apple tree is to yield apples. The purpose of a cherry tree is to supply cherries. The purpose of a grapevine is to produce grapes.

Christians are also expected to bear fruit—love, joy, peace, forbearance, kindness, goodness, faithfulness, gentleness, self-control (Galatians 5:22–23)—and souls won to Christ (John 15:16).

Here Jesus says he is the "vine," and believers are the "branches." The disciples would have appreciated this metaphor, being familiar with vines and the process of growing and harvesting grapes. Certainly, a detached branch is good for nothing except as firewood; it certainly cannot produce fruit on its own.

In the same way, the secret for us to bear fruit is to stay attached to the vine. Jesus' point is that we are totally dependent on him. Just as we could not become God's children through our own efforts but only through faith in Christ, so, too, we cannot yield fruit by wishing and hoping for it or by working hard to "bear much fruit" on our own. Instead, we must allow Christ to produce his fruit through us. The secret is in "remaining."

We remain in Christ by communicating with him, doing what he says, living by faith, and relating in love to the community of believers.

So stay close, be nourished, and bear fruit. ♦

> **PRAYER**

I submit to you, Lord . . .

october1

FEAR AND TREMBLING

Therefore, my dear friends, as you have always obeyed—not only in my presence, but now much more in my absence—continue to work out your salvation with fear and trembling, for it is God who works in you to will and to act in order to fulfill his good purpose.

PHILIPPIANS 2:12–13

The believers who lived in Philippi found that living for Christ was relatively easy when Paul was with them. The great missionary apostle and teacher shared the good news, taught from the Word, modeled courageous faith, answered questions, and explained theological subtleties. He also held the believers accountable for their beliefs and actions. But with Paul gone, doubts, quarrels, and discouragement could arise, and they could be tempted to fall back into sinful habits. So Paul wrote of the seriousness of the Philippians' commitment to Christ—they should continue to think through their faith and live like followers of Christ, "with fear and trembling." But Paul also told them that they would not be alone in the battle—God was working "in" them, changing their desires and then giving them the power to obey him.

Who is your spiritual mentor—a parent, pastor, older Christian friend, or evangelist? Who holds you accountable for what you believe and how you act? Don't take your faith for granted; take it seriously, "with fear and trembling." Yet realize that your spiritual growth depends not on *your* work but on *God's* work in you. Stay in touch with him. He is changing you from the inside out! ♦

PRAYER

Thank you, Lord, for ...

october2

YOU'RE ADOPTED

He predestined us for adoption to sonship through Jesus Christ, in accordance with his pleasure and will.

EPHESIANS 1:5

One of the most amazing things about adoption is that choice is involved. Think about it. Although we men love our biological children dearly, we didn't get to choose them, did we? But in adoption, the child becomes part of a new family by the adoptive parents' conscious choice.

So it is with God. Scripture tells us that God knew us before we were born and that he had already made the conscious decision to adopt us into his family. That choice wasn't made out of obligation. God didn't think, "Well, I created this guy, and even though he's messed up his life, I guess I'm somewhat responsible to help him out." No way! Ephesians tells us that God's adoption of us is not only his will but also his *pleasure*!

Adoption isn't cheap either. It is costly. Any dad who has ever adopted can testify to the strain it puts on the pocketbook. Our adoption by God was the costliest in history. He paid for us with his very life! On top of that, he is forever patient with us in our times of confusion, bitterness, and rebellion.

God knew you before you were born. He chose you long before you knew he even existed. And he loved you enough to pay the price of adopting you as his son. ♦

PRAYER

Father, thank you for choosing me ...

CHRIST'S LETTERS

You show that you are a letter from Christ, the result of our ministry, written not with ink but with the Spirit of the living God, not on tablets of stone but on tablets of human hearts.

2 CORINTHIANS 3:3

When you are applying to a university or submitting a résumé for a new job, what do you need? Letters of recommendation. Why? Because your school or your future employer wants to hear from somebody else that you have what it takes.

Who do you go to when you need that kind of letter? Did you know Christ offers to write one for you? But it's not going to come sealed in a crisp, white envelope. It will be in the form of normal, faulty people with whom you rub shoulders as you go through your everyday life.

You see, God doesn't use pen and ink, nor does he shoot off any e-mails. His writing tablets are human hearts, and he gives us an opportunity to be involved in the stories he is writing in the lives of the people around us. Maybe it's a son who needs a little encouragement or a daughter who wants to hear her dad tell her she's doing a great job at school. Or perhaps it's a coworker we've hurt who needs an apology. It could be a child stricken by poverty in a country far away, or it could be someone as close to you as the woman you married.

The more we affect others for good, the more God writes in their lives. They become living, walking letters of recommendation that anyone can read. What letters do you have? Will God be writing any more for you today? ♦

PRAYER

Use me today, Jesus . . .

october4

WHEN EVERYTHING CRUMBLES

"Though the mountains be shaken and the hills be removed, yet my unfailing love for you will not be shaken nor my covenant of peace be removed," says the LORD, who has compassion on you.

ISAIAH 54:10

A job lost, a marriage failed, a tragedy encountered, a house foreclosed, a prognosis received, a dream forgotten. Everything we've worked so hard to build can come crumbling down around us in an instant—but not God's love.

God's love for us stands like an impenetrable fortress in which we can hide while the world around us crashes to the ground. His covenant of peace with us is like a safe house in the midst of the raging battles of life.

As men we like to feel we're in control. We like to think life is predictable. Lost in an illusion, we build towers of glass—stunning and brilliant—only to watch them shatter at the impact of a single, well-aimed rock. Stunned, we try to pick up the pieces but cut ourselves on the shards.

In that moment, beaten down and bleeding, to what do we turn? Some of us seek solace at the bottom of a bottle; others of us trade our integrity for cheap love; some of us just check out of life altogether. Yet after our self-made towers have crumbled down, we are able to see—perhaps for the first time—that God's love is indestructible and always predictable. How do we know? He showed us on a cross with outstretched arms as the ground around him trembled and the veil in the temple was torn in two.

God's love was present then. It is here now. And it will be there tomorrow. ♦

PRAYER

Father, at the bottom of life, I need you ...

october**5**

CHOOSING PEACE OVER PROSPERITY

So Abram said to Lot, "Let's not have any quarreling between you and me, or between your herders and mine, for we are close relatives. Is not the whole land before you? Let's part company. If you go to the left, I'll go to the right; if you go to the right, I'll go to the left." . . . So Lot chose for himself the whole plain of the Jordan and set out toward the east.
GENESIS 13:8–9, 11

As Abram and his nephew Lot lived and traveled together, interpersonal conflict arose between their respective herders. Whether or not any of the grievances were valid, Abram chose to defuse the situation, to make peace. An obvious solution: each man and his entourage should go their separate ways. Anticipating a potential area of disagreement, Abram allows Lot to choose and says that he will go in the opposite direction and take, in effect, the leftovers.

Remember when you and a sibling could split a piece of cake or another treat? Your parent, heading off conflict, whining, and claims of "that's not fair," probably said something like, "One person divides the cake, and the other one gets to choose first." In this situation, Abram was saying to Lot, "You cut the cake and choose your piece."

True to form, Lot chose the best land, the fertile and irrigated plain of Jordan. And Abram, true to his word, went in the opposite direction. It takes a big man to do what Abram did. Actually, it takes a godly man.

Every day presents opportunities for similar choices. Our natural tendency is to mimic Lot and think only of ourselves, choosing the best and leaving the rest. But God's way is the opposite. Jesus highlights this truth in a story about a wedding feast. His punch line is, "All those who exalt themselves will be humbled, and those who humble themselves will be exalted" (Luke 14:11).

Leave a "lot," and humbly choose the least. ♦

PRAYER

Father, help me, instead, to live your way . . .

october**6**

OUR REFUGE

The LORD is a refuge for the oppressed, a stronghold in times of trouble. Those who know your name will trust in you, for you, LORD, have never forsaken those who seek you.
PSALM 9:9–10

The oppressed in society are often those who are poor, disadvantaged, naive, and needy. Slum landlords exact high rent for substandard housing; domineering employers exploit workers; ruthless dictators demand total allegiance from their subjects while lining their own pockets with tax revenues; adults without conscience abuse children for pleasure and profit. Oppressors have one common trait: they have power; the oppressed have none. Those who oppress desire to keep people down, in their place, out of the way.

Believers are often numbered among the oppressed. Many are people of faith who live for Christ in their difficult situations, especially in countries where believing in Jesus is illegal. There believers pay the price socially, economically, and physically—often with their lives. They are persecuted and oppressed simply because they follow the Master.

Others work in Christ's name in those difficult places, relieving suffering, bandaging wounds, feeding, comforting, and teaching.

Whatever the case, this passage rings with hope for all who are ground under an oppressive heel—God promises to be their refuge. They can find safety and comfort in him.

You may not live in a society that outlaws your faith, but you still can feel the sting of rejection and oppression. At those times, remember that the Lord has never forsaken those who seek him. God is your refuge! ♦

PRAYER

Dear Father, help me to trust you ...

PRESS ON!

Not that I have already obtained all this, or have already arrived at my goal, but I press on to take hold of that for which Christ Jesus took hold of me. Brothers and sisters, I do not consider myself yet to have taken hold of it. But one thing I do: Forgetting what is behind and straining toward what is ahead, I press on toward the goal to win the prize for which God has called me heavenward in Christ Jesus.

PHILIPPIANS 3:12-14

Paul pictures a race in which runners expend every bit of energy to win the prize. You've been there and know the feeling. Whether running a race of a mile or a marathon, having the goal in sight is a tremendous motivator. With eyes on that goal, nothing matters but finishing the race and finishing well.

Life certainly mirrors a long-distance race. When aches, blisters, and exhaustion come, so do doubts and discouragement. That's when we must remember our goal and who is running with us.

Paul's goal was to know Christ, to be like Christ, and to be all that Christ had in mind for him. He had reason to forget what was behind—he had held the coats of those who had stoned Stephen (Acts 7:57–58) and had pursued Christians to their imprisonment and death. If he had wallowed in the past or even in present difficulties, Paul could have given in to discouragement. But he looked forward and kept running.

Everyone has committed shameful acts in the past, and we live with the present tension between what we have been and what we want to be. But because our hope is in Christ, we can let go of the past and look ahead to what God will help us become.

Don't let anything take your eyes off your goal of knowing Christ. With the focus of a dedicated athlete, lay aside everything harmful and anything that might distract you from winning God's prize. ♦

PRAYER

Help me keep my eyes on your prize, Lord...

october8

A SENSELESS BURDEN

When the LORD has fulfilled for my lord every good thing he promised concerning him and has appointed him ruler over Israel, my lord will not have on his conscience the staggering burden of needless bloodshed or of having avenged himself.

1 SAMUEL 25:30–31

His good friend Samuel had just died, and although he had already been anointed king, David was still a fugitive hiding from Saul. While in the Desert of Paran, David and his men helped protect the flocks of a very wealthy man named Nabal.

One day, David caught word that it was sheep-shearing time, and he sent over some men to ask Nabal to share some of his bounty during the festive occasion. The men returned empty-handed. Not only had Nabal refused; he also ridiculed David and his men.

David was furious. Immediately he set out with four hundred armed men to bring vengeance on Nabal and his household. Fortunately, Nabal had a very wise and noble wife named Abigail. As soon as she heard what was about to happen, Abigail set out with a peace offering. Her kind gesture and tactful words kept David from taking matters into his own hands and made it possible for him to one day claim the throne with a clean and guiltless conscience. About ten days later, Nabal fell dead, but not by David's hand.

Revenge comes naturally to all of us. Since childhood, we have all possessed a keen sense of justice—and woe to the one who would try to wrong us or those we love. Yet God is clear that we are to leave vengeance in his hands.

May God protect us today from the weight of a guilty conscience. ♦

PRAYER

God, may I not play the judge ...

october**9**

CHANGE OR DIE

I tell you, no! But unless you repent, you too will all perish.

LUKE 13:3

Jesus is saying simply, "Change or die." He is saying that if you continue on the path you are on, you will die. It is time to make an about-face and move in the right direction.

That's our problem, isn't it? We don't want to change.

A recent medical study reveals just how difficult change is for people. Roughly 600,000 people undergo heart bypass surgery a year in America. These people are told after their bypasses that they must change their lifestyle. The heart bypass is a temporary fix. They must change their diet. They must quit smoking and drinking. They must exercise and reduce stress.

In essence, the doctors say, "Change or die."

You would think that a near-death experience would forever grab the attention of patients. You would think the argument for change is so compelling that patients would make the appropriate lifestyle alterations. Sadly that is not the case.

Ninety percent of the heart patients do not change. They remain the same, living the status quo. Study after study indicates that two years after heart surgery, the patients have not altered their behavior. Instead of making changes for life, they choose death.

In the same way, the majority of churches choose not to change. They would rather die. Tragically, in most churches, the pain of change is greater than the pain of death.

Change or die? This is the question that dying churches have to answer. ♦

PRAYER

Lord, give me the strength to help my church change if . . .

286

MODELING BALANCE

But Daniel resolved not to defile himself with the royal food and wine, and he asked the chief official for permission not to defile himself this way.

DANIEL 1:8

One of the many gifts Daniel possessed was his ability to demonstrate balance in his life. Daniel had been taken captive and deported to Babylon by Nebuchadnezzar in 605 BC. He was not selected by accident. He was chosen for his outstanding qualities. Daniel excelled in six areas of his life. These provide a framework for the areas we are to keep in balance.

1. The physical dimension. This would entail exercise, proper rest, and sufficient nourishment.
2. The mental dimension. This area encompasses learning and studying.
3. The relational dimension. Our relationships need to be fine-tuned and balanced.
4. The spiritual dimension. Often in a person's effort to make the most out of life, they neglect God's role in their life.
5. The vocational dimension. This is the one area that often throws the other dimensions out of balance. Most of us have to work to provide for our family, but it must always be kept in proper perspective with the other dimensions.
6. The family dimension. Closely related to the relational dimension, room in a person's life must be provided for their family.

These dimensions would best be displayed in a pie shape, not a list. Each sector should not be drawn with equal portions but with the correct and proper portion allotted to keep all of life in balance. As you examine the basic components of your life, how do you measure up? Do you find that you are overemphasizing one? Are you concluding that you have neglected an essential area? ♦

PRAYER

Lord, help me live a balanced life by excelling in . . .

october11

IS GOD FIRST?

You shall have no other gods before me.

Exodus 20:3

God not only declares, deserves, and desires first place; he demands it. He will not share his place with anyone or anything. The words *before me* mean "in preference to me." The central thrust of this commandment can be summed up in one word—*priority*. God wants to be first, not a close second.

In her book *My Memories of Ike*, Mamie Eisenhower states that one of the reasons General Dwight D. Eisenhower was such a great leader and had such ability to inspire others was his deep love and loyalty for his country. After they had been married for about a month, Ike was given a new assignment. He put his arms around Mamie and said gently, "Mamie, there is one thing you must understand. My country comes first and always will; you come second." Mamie said it was quite a shock for a nineteen-year-old bride who had been married only one month to hear, "You come second."

For a person who obeys the first of the Ten Commandments, God must come first. Does God really have first place in your life?

Here are two simple tests to determine whether God has first place.

1. The love test. Origen from the third century stated, "What each one honors before all else, what before all things he admires and loves, this for him is God."

2. The trust test. Martin Luther noted, "Whatever thy heart clings to and relies upon, that is properly thy God." So what do you trust or cling to? "To trust anything more than God is to make it a god," declared the Puritan Thomas Watson.

Are you passing both tests? ♦

PRAYER

Lord, help me to put you first in . . .

october**12**

WHAT MAKES GLUTTONY DEADLY?

Put a knife to your throat if you are given to gluttony.

PROVERBS 23:2

Contrary to popular opinion, gluttony is not about overeating on Thanksgiving Day. Gluttony is not about appearance; it is an attitude. It is not about being overweight; it is overindulgence. Gluttony is misdirected hunger. It is the mad pursuit of the bodily pleasures that never completely satisfy. We connect it with the craving for food and this has been its primary expression. But the person who drinks or smokes too much is as gluttonous as the person who overeats — not to mention the person who watches television excessively or surfs the Internet into the wee hours of the night.

What is so bad about a little food gluttony, anyway? It's not one of the bad sins, like adultery or stealing. All gluttony does is make you soft and huggable. It's the cute sin. So what is the problem? The problem with gluttony is that it seeks to feed the soul with the body's food. It can cause a person to become so full in their stomach that they lose their appetite for God. The gluttonous not only have a misdirected hunger; they have misplaced God. They pay homage to their appetites; their conspicuous consumption is their extravagant act of praise. They no longer eat to live; they live to eat.

One of the crueler tricks of gluttony is that it exacts painful dues while failing to deliver the promised pleasure. In its clear and seductive way, it imposes the very opposite of what was promised. People caught within the throes of gluttony know all about the prison walls it establishes. They want to break free, but they can't. Their appetite is too strong. It demands too much. It must be satisfied. ♦

PRAYER

Father, help me to control myself . . .

october13

FORGIVENESS — A HEART MATTER

Bear with each other and forgive one another if any of you has a grievance against someone. Forgive as the Lord forgave you.

COLOSSIANS 3:13

Forgiveness is a work of the heart—first, foremost, and forever.

Beginning in the heart, forgiveness reflects a decision made on the inside to refuse to live in the past. This is critical. You can't move forward if you are still holding on to the past. It would be like looking at something on one side of the room and, without turning your head, trying to see something on the other side of the room.

In dealing with people, you may have heard someone say, "I just can't get over it" or "I can't let it go." These people have not forgiven. The old adage is true: You don't hold a grudge as much as a grudge holds you. Booker T. Washington gave voice to a profound insight: "Holding a grudge doesn't hurt the person against whom the grudge is held; it hurts the one who holds it." He also said, "I will permit no man to narrow and degrade my soul by making me hate him."

Forgiveness is letting go of the past and releasing the people who hurt us. Archbishop Desmond Tutu declared, "Without forgiveness, there is no future."

Forgiveness does not deny the pain or change the past, but it does break the cycle of bitterness that binds us to the wounds of yesterday. Forgiveness allows us to let go and move on.

Forgiveness is like salvation—it is a gift that is freely given; it cannot be earned. We can forgive without saying, "I forgive you," because forgiveness is a matter of the heart.

Not forgiving costs your heart. In time your heart will become cold, dark, and lifeless. The grudge you hold holds you in the end, petrifying your heart. ♦

PRAYER

Lord, I need to forgive . . .

october**14**

SECURITY MEASURES

Whoever dwells in the shelter of the Most High will rest in the shadow of the Almighty.
PSALM 91:1

Have you noticed that the more emphasis we place on security, the less secure we feel? Not only do we feel insecure on a national scope because of terrorism and crime, but we also feel insecure on a personal level. The psalmist invites us to snuggle up close, to feel the warmth of the One he is writing about, and to share in the protection he offers. A news report highlighted a rescue device used on the oil rigs in the Gulf of Mexico during a hurricane. In case of fire or (in this case) hurricane, rig workers scramble into the bullet-shaped "bus" and strap themselves into their seats. When the entry port is shut, the vehicle is released down a chute and projected away from the rig. The seat belts protect the occupants from impact with the water. The capsule then bobs in the sea until the rescuers come to pick it up.

That's an image of what God does for us. He is the One who protects us. The term *dwells* in Psalm 91:1 implies that we live in conscious fellowship with and draw daily strength from God. He is our defense shield, our alarm system, our protective coating. He is everything we need to feel secure in an insecure world.

This verse reminds me of a security blanket. Just as many children will not let their security blanket out of their sight, keeping it always in their grasp, so are believers to be constantly in touch with their security source. Live, therefore, constantly and continually in God's presence.

Every person craves security. Real security is not found in things but in the person of Jesus Christ. ♦

PRAYER

God, bestow on me your protection that I may feel more secure when . . .

october15

WHEN GOD PUTS YOU TO THE TEST

I the LORD search the heart and examine the mind, to reward each person according to their conduct, according to what their deeds deserve.

JEREMIAH 17:10

God often puts us to the test. A test is a difficult experience through which a person's true values, commitments, and beliefs are revealed. *Test* is a very important word in the Old Testament. A test was to prove or demonstrate the character and faith of God's people. Even though tests are painful and unwelcome, they are an act of love. Tests prove our faith.

While tests are not necessarily pleasant times, they are learning times. During our times of testing, our spiritual muscles are stretched, our faith strengthened, and our character forged. God's tests are designed to develop us into men and women of strong spiritual resolve. Let's face it, our spiritual roots grow deeper when the winds assault and the storms assail. Take away the tests, and we become spiritual wimps.

What do we do when we are put to the test?

Here's our choice: grumble or go to God. Grumbling is our response to pain or problems in life—in other words, to our tests. We grumble because we think we should experience pleasure rather than pain, prosperity rather than adversity. The problem with grumbling is that it distorts the facts. It causes us to focus on what we don't have, causing us to look at ourselves rather than God. And worst of all, grumbling repudiates God's ability to provide.

Going to God recognizes his sovereignty and his power in our lives.

Often when we face a test, we have a tendency to go to everyone but God. God says we should come to him first. ♦

PRAYER

God, shape me by testing me so I may be better prepared when ...

THERE IS GOD

In the beginning was the Word, and the Word was with God, and the Word was God.
JOHN 1:1

When Jesus became a man, he showed that God was not merely a principle but a person. Not a myth, but a man who was God at the same time. Not a figment of someone's imagination, but a living presence. Jesus was not an idea of God, not a picture of God, but God himself in human form.

Two young men on a battlefield in World War II made it to the safety of a foxhole in the midst of enemy fire. As they looked out before them across the battlefield, they perceived the horror of dead and dying men. Some men lay lifeless; others cried out for help. Finally one of the men yelled, "Where in the hell is God?" Soon they noticed two medics, identified by the red cross on their arms and helmets, carefully making their way across the perilous scene. As they watched, the medics stopped and began to load a wounded soldier onto their stretcher. They then began to work their way to safety. As the scene unfolded before them, the other soldier now boldly answered his friend's question with these words: "There is God!"

When Jesus came, it was his way of saying, "Here is God! Here is God!" He came in the midst of the loneliness and the horror of a world gone mad. Yet in the chaos and confusion, Jesus announced that God is here. Where in the world is God? God is here in Christ. Christ has come among us to show us who and what God is. Jesus showed us God in a way that we can understand. In a way that renews us. In a way that gives us hope. In a way that demonstrates compassion. ◆

PRAYER

Lord, help me to be more compassionate toward others when ...

october17

WHEN GOD SEEMS ABSENT

Why, my soul, are you downcast? Why so disturbed within me? Put your hope in God, for I will yet praise him, my Savior and my God.

PSALM 42:5

Sometimes we don't sense God being anywhere near us, no matter how faithfully we worship or how fervently we pray.

The psalmist had this thought and experience often. He felt separated from God. He felt sadness. He felt forgotten.

The psalmist in Psalm 42 experienced what one man has termed the "dark night of the soul." That time when one feels completely and utterly alone, abandoned by God. The psalmist, like us, questioned God. "I say to God my Rock, 'Why have you forgotten me? Why must I go about mourning, oppressed by the enemy?' My bones suffer mortal agony as my foes taunt me, saying to me all day long, 'Where is your God?'" (Psalm 42:9 – 10). The psalmist's words sound similar to the darkest moment for Jesus on the cross when he cried out, "My God! My God! Why have you forsaken me?" In speaking to God, we ask, "Why?" And God seems to not hear us. The psalmist is greeted with silence and separation.

In such situations, most people give up. Feeling as though God has abandoned them, they turn the tables and abandon God. They have no desire to worship a God who seems strangely distant when they need him most.

While faith belongs more to the mind, and love to the heart, hope concerns itself with the soul. Stephen King's character in *Shawshank Redemption*, Andy Dufresne, writes in a letter to his friend Red, "Hope is a good thing, maybe the best of things. And no good thing ever dies." On the poster for the movie a tagline stretches across the top: *Fear can hold you prisoner. Hope can set you free.* God will always be there to give you hope and freedom from your fears. ♦

PRAYER

Father, help me to remember you are with me . . .

october**18**

PARENTS, TELL YOUR CHILDREN

After that whole generation had been gathered to their ancestors, another generation grew up who knew neither the LORD nor what he had done for Israel.

JUDGES 2:10

Judges 2:10 is one of the saddest verses in the Bible. Joshua had died, along with the elders who had seen the Lord's great miracles in giving them their new home. The new generation did not know the Lord or remember his miracles. It was not that the Lord was unknown among them, but they did not know him in relationship. Religion was a secondhand experience.

This begs some questions for consideration: What responsibility do we presently bear for the next generation? Have we grown comfortable and complacent, failing to press spiritual issues on our children? Have we forgotten to tell our children about the wonders and works of God?

To avoid certain demise, the older generation bears the responsibility to instruct their children and grandchildren in the ways of the Lord. A failure to do so or the younger generation's refusal to submit to those teachings leads to disobedience and sin. When we parents allow our children to grow up without the knowledge of God, we not only foster their ignorance and unbelief but also promote their destruction. We parents have the responsibility to see that our children think correctly about God. ♦

PRAYER

God, give me the passion to tell my children about you . . .

october**19**

FOLLOW THE LEADER

Follow my example, as I follow the example of Christ.

1 CORINTHIANS 11:1

Great preaching requires an audience that will listen well. Great coaching necessitates players who will execute the plays consistently. Great parenting involves children who will obey instruction faithfully. And great leadership demands volunteers who will follow decisively. Isn't it interesting, however, that leaders are taught to lead well, but comparatively little affirmation or instruction equips the majority of us to follow well? Our culture, even our churches, places a limited value on following. We celebrate the great leaders but dismiss the many loyal followers.

All leaders are followers, but not all followers are leaders. And many followers resist being placed in a leadership role. Their mantra is, "I will follow anyone; just don't ask me to lead." They understand their role, and it is not out in front.

While we may never be invited to a class on how to follow, here are a few recommendations on following well:

1. Find a leader who follows the Lord.
2. Don't seek to compete with the leader, but complement them. Leadership is participatory. Leaders and followers exist in a mutually beneficial relationship in which each adds to the effectiveness of the other.
3. Stand in the gap. Leaders need loyal and dedicated people to fill the gaps in their efforts.
4. Take initiative. Leaders provide the overall plan, the vision, but followers execute. Good followers know what to do without being told.
5. Pray for your leader. The leader you follow faces murderous enemies—the world, the flesh, and the Devil. Pray that your leader will be faithful when tempted, steady when attacked, firm when needed. ♦

PRAYER

Lord, help me be your kind of follower . . .

HE IS COMING BACK

"Men of Galilee," they said, "why do you stand here looking into the sky? This same Jesus, who has been taken from you into heaven, will come back in the same way you have seen him go into heaven."

ACTS 1:11

In 1996, George Tulloch led an expedition to the spot where the Titanic sank in 1912. In his search, Tulloch realized that a large piece of the hull had broken from the ship and was resting not far from the vessel. Tulloch immediately saw the opportunity to rescue part of the ship itself.

After raising the twenty-ton piece of iron, a storm blew in and the Atlantic reclaimed her treasure. Before Tulloch left, he descended into the deep, and with the robotic arm of his submarine he attached to a section of the hull a strip of metal that read, "I will come back. George Tulloch." At first glance, his action is humorous. It's not like he has to worry about a lot of people trying to steal his piece of iron. Not only was it two and a half miles below the Atlantic's surface; it was also a piece of junk. Two years later, George Tulloch returned and rescued the piece of iron. He kept his promise.

Jesus also made a promise: "I will come back" (John 14:3).

Belief in the second coming has always been considered one of the fundamental truths of our faith. More than three hundred separate prophecies relate to it in the Bible, making it one of the most important doctrines in the Bible.

The second coming of Christ will bring an end to this age and usher in the kingdom of Christ. His return will bring us the final stage of our redemption, the culmination of all God has promised to those who love his Son.

Jesus Christ is coming back to the earth. It may be soon. Maybe today. ♦

PRAYER

Lord, help me to be prepared for your return ...

october**21**

REAL HOPE

We have this hope as an anchor for the soul, firm and secure.

HEBREWS 6:19

C. S. Lewis embraced the Christian faith and used his talents to influence people in a noble direction. Lewis lost his wife to cancer. He grieved severely but later emerged from his sorrow with renewed strength and unspeakable joy derived from God, the One in whom his hope was grounded. Lewis had the resources of a living God to see him through.

Lewis's life revealed, in contrast to a secular view, a hope that is not in us, in what we can do or achieve, but rather a hope that comes from beyond ourselves. God is both the inspirer and the object of hope.

Outside the Bible, especially in our society, hope consists of a halfhearted optimism with no secure basis. It has no anchor. It freely trusts in one ideology after another, from Marxism to capitalism, materialism to idealism, religiosity to secularism. Or its hopes are more clearly focused—but on objects that cannot satisfy hope: a career, business opportunities, money, a new home, and so on.

Real hope is based on God. That's why a believer can sing, "My hope is built on nothing less than Jesus' blood and righteousness. I dare not trust the sweetest frame, but wholly lean on Jesus' name. On Christ, the Solid Rock, I stand; all other ground is sinking sand, all other ground is sinking sand."

At those moments when we are overwhelmed by disillusionment, discouragement, depression, or even despair, we must never forget that God is our hope.

Your situation may appear hopeless. You may be agreeing with the critics who question, "Where is your God?" But hold on—or better to say, hope on. God is not dead. God is not distant. God is present. ♦

PRAYER

Lord, give me hope today for . . .

THE CHURCH'S FINEST HOUR

David also said to Solomon his son, "Be strong and courageous, and do the work. Do not be afraid or discouraged, for the LORD God, my God, is with you. He will not fail you or forsake you until all the work for the service of the temple of the LORD is finished."

1 CHRONICLES 28:20

This verse contains three sentences. The first sentence speaks of the *power*: "Be strong and courageous." It always takes a great deal of strength and courage to lead a people. The next sentence speaks of the *presence*. Fear may be our constant companion, but we have something even stronger—God's presence. The third sentence speaks of the *promise*. For he has promised and is faithful to be with us. He is not going to leave us or forsake us; he will bring to completion all that he has been working in us.

During the flight of Apollo 13 a mechanical malfunction caused the commander, Jim Lovell, to radio back to earth, "Houston, we have a problem." While landing on the moon was now not an option, the task before the team on earth and in the injured spacecraft was to get the three astronauts back home alive. As the men in mission control were weighing the odds, two men were talking in hushed tones, indicating that the odds were slim that the three astronauts on board Apollo 13 would return home. Then one of those men, a flight director, said, "This could be the worst disaster NASA has ever faced." The mission commander, Gene Kranz, overheard the men talking. With a stern and resolute face, he replied, "With all due respect, sir, I believe this is going to be our finest hour."

We have God's power, his presence, and his promise. But we have a role to play too. David gave Solomon the blueprint for the temple, the financial resources to build it, and even the workers to complete the project. But they had to go to work. They had a role to play, and it became their finest hour. ♦

> **PRAYER**

Lord, give me the will to see things through . . .

october23

ME, GENEROUS?

Command those who are rich in this present world ... to be generous and willing to share. In this way they will lay up treasure for themselves as a firm foundation for the coming age, so that they may take hold of the life that is truly life.

1 TIMOTHY 6:17–19

Did you know that generosity is the most talked-about value in the entire Bible? The word *give* or *giving* is used 2,285 times in the Bible. The Bible talks more about giving than about any other topic. Why? Because giving is the expression of faith, hope, and love.

Robert Allen, bestselling author of *Nothing Down* and *The One-Minute Millionaire*, didn't always tithe. But after he lost everything, he learned the value of tithing while he worked his way back to prosperity. As he became a dedicated tither, he became more grateful for what he had, and new opportunities started flowing to him. Now he inspires others to tithe.

He recalled one woman who approached him and complained, "My husband and I can't tithe. We can barely make our mortgage payment."

Bob admonished her, saying, "You don't tithe because you want to get something. You tithe because you've already gotten it. You're so blessed already that there's no way in the world you'll be able to repay it. You tithe out of the gratitude you feel for the unbelievable blessings and lifestyle you have."

What is it that holds you back from being a generous person? Fear of the future, not knowing what it may hold? The future is uncertain for all of us. The real issue is one of *trust*.

Sooner or later we have to decide, "Do I trust God more than money?" God says, "You give because you have been blessed. And when you give, then I will bless you more." ♦

PRAYER

Lord, fill my heart with generosity as an encouragement to give ...

WHEN SIN SEEMS VICTORIOUS

If you, LORD, kept a record of sins, LORD, who could stand? But with you there is forgiveness, so that we can, with reverence, serve you.

PSALM 130:3–4

Many low points have occurred in human history, yet could there be any lower point than the Holocaust of Nazi Germany that exterminated six million Jews? Or any places as wretched as the concentration camp at Dachau? This death camp revealed both the depth of man's inhumanity and the indomitable spirit that some people brought to Dachau. In 1967, the Protestant Church in Germany built the Church of Reconciliation on the site of this former concentration camp. Engraved on the wall of a corridor that leads up with a shining light to signify hope are the first five verses of Psalm 130.

This psalm reminds us that we have a personal problem as serious, as damning, as hopeless, and as destructive as what occurred at Dachau.

The truth about us is that *we all are sinners*. We all suffer from human brokenness and imperfection.

Our greatest problems are spiritual, not physical. If we are honest with ourselves, we see the terrible predicament we are in. What we want, what we need, is to experience pardon for our sin.

God does not delight in punishing our sin. He offers forgiveness. We cry to God. He hears us and comes, not with judgment, but with forgiveness.

Once we are forgiven, our slate is wiped clean. When we truly understand the cost of God's forgiveness in sending Christ to the cross, we are thankful to the God of love and mercy. This psalm teaches us that we can never fix ourselves because we lack the inner resources to solve our sin problem. God provides the solution; we in turn should acknowledge and worship him for his grace and mercy. ♦

PRAYER

Lord, thank you for forgiving my sins ...

THE LIFE

Jesus said to her, "I am the resurrection and the life. The one who believes in me will live, even though they die; and whoever lives by believing in me will never die."

JOHN 11:25–26

Tragedy can intrude at any moment, moving us toward grief and depression. Even when death is expected, we mourn the loss of our loved one. In those dark moments, we can wonder about God's love and care. We may even cry out to God, "Why?" or "If you had only done something!"

That's how Mary and Martha felt as they stood at their brother's tomb and grieved their loss. They had sent for Jesus, but he hadn't shown up until it was too late. Martha questioned Jesus' timing: "'Lord,' Martha said to Jesus, 'if you had been here, my brother would not have died'" (John 11:21).

But Jesus is never late. Gently he reminded Martha of his awesome power and limitless love. "I am the resurrection and the life," he said. Then he called to Lazarus, the dead man, and commanded that he come forth out of the tomb. And Lazarus did, still wrapped in his burial clothes.

What loss threatens to unravel your life? As you stand among the gravestones, what questions or demands do you have for the Lord? Remember, Jesus is never late. In his infinite understanding, perfect timing, and deep concern, he will hear your cry, answer your prayer, and bring life. In the meantime, keep resting in his sovereignty and trusting in his love. Jesus brings life. ♦

PRAYER

Forgive me, Lord, for . . .

FOLLOW THE LIGHT

When Jesus spoke again to the people, he said, "I am the light of the world. Whoever follows me will never walk in darkness, but will have the light of life."

JOHN 8:12

Suddenly the lights go out, and the unfamiliar room is so dark that you can't even see your hand in front of your face. Black silence envelopes you. How do you feel? What do you do?

Darkness can evoke fear. Like a child imagining monsters in the shadows, we may begin to hear and see threats in the dark.

Darkness can discourage and depress. Closed off from light and hope, we may wonder if there is any way out.

Darkness can foster doubt. Unable to see the realities we knew in the light, we may begin to wonder if they even exist.

Darkness can cause us to stumble ... and fall.

Dark and light—the contrast is dramatic. Light illuminates, exposes, highlights, and points the way—flashlights, bonfires, headlights, reading lamps, torches, floodlights, neon signs, spotlights, fireworks, fluorescents, halogens, incandescents, and the sun.

Darkness comes in many forms—economic reversals, personal loss, devastating sorrow, crippling illness, incriminating sin, persistent opposition.

But Jesus is the light, the light of the world. His presence will brighten the day. His words will give understanding and hope. His sacrifice will bring forgiveness and eternal life. His promises and love will provide certainty and security.

Don't walk in darkness; follow the light. ♦

PRAYER

Open my eyes, Lord ...

LOVING HE GAVE

For God so loved the world that he gave his one and only Son, that whoever believes in him shall not perish but have eternal life.

JOHN 3:16

Without a doubt, this is the best-known verse in the Bible—at least the most publicized. We see it on billboards and on signs in the end zones of football games and at other major sporting events. Usually this is the first verse we memorize in Sunday school. We know the passage so well that we can miss its profoundly personal application (or think it only applies to people who don't know Christ). But read the verse out loud slowly, and consider God's love for humanity ... for you.

Before you were born, God had already decided to send Jesus for you. When you were at your worst, deliberately rejecting him and his Word, God still loved you and pursued you. Jesus came, and he still comes ... for you.

When you feel rejected, abandoned, or unloved, remember the truth of this verse. God loves the world, and he loves you. You know this because he sent Jesus, his Son, to die in your place, taking the punishment for your sin. And through Jesus' work on the cross, you now have new life, eternal life, because you have believed in him, accepting him as your personal Savior.

Think of the sacrifice that Jesus made for you. He literally became sin on that cross, enduring the agony of separation from his Father. You are loved—Jesus proved it.

Now how do you feel? ♦

PRAYER

I admit, Father, that often I forget that ...

october28

TRUE HONOR

All those who exalt themselves will be humbled, and those who humble themselves will be exalted.

LUKE 14:11

Have you ever noticed how some themes are repeated over and over in God's Word? As men, we don't like it when someone has to remind us over and over about ... well ... anything. But when the Bible does it, we should take notice. Some things bear repeating simply so we will not forget the importance of the message. The issue of humility comes up quite often.

Many men—missionaries, mentors, those who volunteer at nursing homes, homeless shelters, and countless other places—have given up opportunities of personal acclaim in obedience to God's call on their lives. But their sacrifice doesn't go unnoticed by God.

Most men who seek acclaim are thoroughly humbled along the way. If they learn something from the experience, then God has broken through to them. Conversely, most men who humble themselves are eventually honored. True, the honor might not come in this life. But this life isn't where we're supposed to store our treasures anyway, right?

God says he opposes the proud and raises the humble. Our goal should be committed service to the Savior. If we get a little—or a lot of—praise along the way, then so be it. We should accept it with grace, not a swaggering touchdown dance. Likewise, when we are humbled, we should learn from the experience. ♦

PRAYER

Lord, in every situation, help me to be humble ...

AT WHAT PRICE UNITY?

They said to each other, "Come, let's make bricks and bake them thoroughly." They used brick instead of stone, and tar for mortar. Then they said, "Come, let us build ourselves a city, with a tower that reaches to the heavens, so that we may make a name for ourselves; otherwise we will be scattered over the face of the whole earth."

GENESIS 11:3–4

Unity, teamwork—we've heard the pep talks from coaches and bosses. We have to work together to make progress, to achieve, to win. And that message rings true in those venues. In certain sports, for example, successful teams have players who faithfully fulfill their assignments and put personal glory aside for the sake of the team. A running back needs the quarterback to hand him the ball, the linemen to open holes in the line, and others to block downfield. Whether on offense, defense, or special teams, individuals who freelance according to their personal agendas cause chaos on the field and defeat for the team.

Sometimes, however, unity can be destructive. This chapter of Genesis tells the story of the Tower of Babel. Here we find the people unified, committed, and working hard to achieve a common goal. Unfortunately, they were focused on themselves and their advancement and headed in the wrong direction. So God stepped in and stopped them, causing disunity and confusion.

Maybe you can relate. You're part of an organization that's headed in a way you think is wrong, perhaps even unethical or immoral. Yet you're expected to be a team player, to go along, to pull together to reach questionable goals or to use questionable means. You may have to be the one to stand up and say "no" or "stop" or "count me out." It will be risky and take courage—but it's the right thing to do.

Being a team player is important, but doing what God wants should be nonnegotiable. ♦

PRAYER

Lord, give me the courage to …

october**30**

CANDY CORN NATION

Command those who are rich in this present world not to be arrogant nor to put their hope in wealth, which is so uncertain, but to put their hope in God, who richly provides us with everything for our enjoyment.

1 TIMOTHY 6:17

Paul wrote these words to Timothy when the young man was pastoring the church in Ephesus. This coastal city was the most important one in the Roman province of Asia. It had all the attractions—library, gymnasium, theatre, huge marketplace, and temples. In fact, Ephesus was home to one of the seven wonders of the ancient world—the great temple of Artemis. Ephesus was overflowing with wealth.

In today's economy, you may not think of yourself as "overflowing with wealth." But consider this. Each year Americans eat so much Brach's Candy Corn that, if placed end to end, the candy corn would circle the globe more than four times! Compare that to a developing country where many people are happy to get a meal a day. Wealth is relative!

Wealth is also temporary and uncertain. We have been made painfully aware of that fact over the past few years. Why, then, do we give so much weight to our wealth? It could be greed. It could be a lack of trust in God's ability to provide for us. It may be that we're so shortsighted that we would rather hoard things bound to decay than store up treasures that will last for eternity.

Whatever the case may be, let Ephesus be a warning to us. The city is now an archaeological site, and the great temple of Artemis, one of the wonders of the world, now lies in ruins. Today may we place our hope in the God who never fails! ◆

PRAYER

You provide all I need, Lord . . .

october**31**

A STRONG STANCE

Resist him, standing firm in the faith, because you know that the family of believers throughout the world is undergoing the same kind of sufferings.

1 PETER 5:9

In 1508, Martin Luther began teaching that one could receive forgiveness of sins by simple faith in Jesus Christ as opposed to buying a pardon for sins. His disgust came to a head in 1517, when John Tetzel, a representative of the pope, came to Germany selling certificates already signed by the pope, offering a pardon of all sins to whoever procured one. On October 31, 1517, a trembling Martin Luther marched to the front doors of the Castle Church in Wittenberg, where he posted ninety-five theses, soon to become famous throughout the world.

Later, Martin Luther, father of the Reformation, was accused of heresy, and the pope demanded that he recant. Luther took the position that recanting was impossible for him because he believed, on the basis of the Scriptures and "evident reason," that he was speaking the truth.

The fact is, unless we stand, we cannot withstand. Unless we stand for something, we will fall for anything. As believers in Christ, our faith must be firmly grounded in the truth of God's Word and in the person of Jesus Christ. His Word needs to be planted in our hearts so we can give a reason for our faith whenever anyone asks. We must know what we believe and why we believe it.

Begin today to know what you stand for and why. ♦

PRAYER

Lord, I determine to stand for your truth . . .

november1

PRAY AND TURN

If my people, who are called by my name, will humble themselves and pray and seek my face and turn from their wicked ways, then I will hear from heaven, and I will forgive their sin and will heal their land.

2 CHRONICLES 7:14

Anyone can easily name and number the ills of our land: crime, abuse, family disintegration, racism, sexual immorality, terrorism, greed, corruption, violence—the list goes on. Just watching or listening to news reports with their stream of terrible stories can lead to discouragement and depression. We are painfully aware of our nation's problems.

Much more difficult is finding positive news and, infinitely more important, a cure.

Yet in every election cycle, we hear grand promises with proposed solutions, including political reforms, new legislation, better security, harsh sentences for lawbreakers, increased government spending, improved education, and other programs. These all sound good, but they've met with limited success, especially in terms of long-term solutions. We are wounded and need help.

In this passage, God explains the only sure route to healing—humility, repentance, and faith. God promises to cure our sin-caused disease if we, his people, turn away from our selfish insistence on making "us first," turn away from our sin, and turn toward him. Notice that although the results are national, the application is personal. Often we expect someone else to do the work, to bring about the change. But it has to happen with us; that is, we—individually and collectively as God's people—need to change. The prescription seems simple enough, but it is profound—and it is guaranteed. And the humbling, seeking, and repenting must begin with us.

Take God at his word and pray for the healing of our land. God will hear, forgive, and heal. ♦

PRAYER

God, please bring healing ...

november2

THE SECRET

I know what it is to be in need, and I know what it is to have plenty. I have learned the secret of being content in any and every situation, whether well fed or hungry, whether living in plenty or in want. I can do all this through him who gives me strength.

PHILIPPIANS 4:12–13

A few years ago, Tim Tebow, arguably the greatest collegiate quarterback to ever play the game, wore a headband under his helmet with "Phil. 4:13" on it—a simple reminder that he could achieve much through God's strength. He didn't complete every pass, and he fumbled a time or two, but he played every down with confidence.

You probably aren't facing three-hundred-pound defensive linemen these days, but do you face an impossible task, a formidable foe, or an insurmountable obstacle? Paul certainly faced many during his life—communicating the gospel to Jews, Greeks, Romans, army officers, slaves, and rulers; dealing with jealous religious leaders, hateful pagans, and corrupt politicians; surviving beatings, stonings, lashings, imprisonments, and shipwrecks; beginning churches in the most unlikely locales; training young men to be leaders in the church. Paul could do all this and more because of what Christ was doing *in* him. He had learned God's "secret of being content"—relying on the Holy Spirit's strengthening power.

What has God called you to do? You can do it—not in your own strength, but through Christ, who will give you everything you need. Depend on it, and move out in faith.

You can do all things through Christ! ♦

PRAYER

I'm facing some challenges, Lord . . .

november3

LOOKING AHEAD

The wisdom of the prudent is to give thought to their ways, but the folly of fools is deception.
PROVERBS 14:8

Bill Walsh, the former head coach of the San Francisco 49ers, was considered to be eccentric because of how extensively he planned his plays in advance of each game. Walsh wanted the game to respond to him. Walsh won a lot of Super Bowls with his "eccentric," proactive approach. He was a coach who looked into the future in advance.

As we learn from Bill Walsh, the key is to create our own actions in advance so that our lives will respond to us. What are the benefits of such a proactive pursuit?

1. *Looking ahead gives direction.* It's like using a highlighter on a road map. The highlighted road map not only provides information for where you are going; it also suggests where you are not going.
2. *Looking ahead helps us to create rather than react.* Each step along our journey we are faced with a choice either to create or to react. Many people spend all their days reacting. A better way involves making choices and following plans.
3. *Looking ahead saves time.* One hour of planning is said to save three hours of execution. We only have 24 hours in a day and 365 days in a year. If we don't use them wisely by looking ahead, we will forever forfeit those gifts.
4. *Looking ahead reduces crisis.* Our daily lives have two controlling influences: plans and pressures. If we fail to look ahead, we will spend our days in crisis mode.
5. *Looking ahead gives energy.* Failing to look ahead, we squander our energy on less important matters. We waste our time on the trivial.

Be wise, and look ahead. It may be eccentric, but it's well worth the effort. ♦

PRAYER

Lord, help me to look ahead more often . . .

november4

FRET NOT

But seek first his kingdom and his righteousness, and all these things will be given to you as well. Therefore do not worry about tomorrow, for tomorrow will worry about itself. Each day has enough trouble of its own.

MATTHEW 6:33–34

In the Sermon on the Mount, Jesus is teaching his disciples and the assembled crowd about worry. And he begins by saying, "Therefore I tell you, do not worry about your life, what you will eat or drink; or about your body, what you will wear" (Matthew 6:25).

Anxiety is epidemic. Just about anything and everything can cause us stress. We can worry that we don't have enough. Then we can stress about security, keeping all our stuff safe. These days, people are worried about what they have and what they don't have, about what they did and what they didn't do, about the past and about the future. And if that isn't enough, a single newscast can fill our minds with enough worries to last the whole day!

Instead of being anxious, we are told by Jesus to trust, to turn everything over to him. If we put him at the center of our lives, he will give us everything we need — now and in the future. So we have no need to worry.

What consumes your thoughts, fills your daydreams, and keeps you awake at night? A relationship? Money? Your career? Perhaps you're worrying so much because that person, plan, or possession holds the place of highest importance for you. Replace it with Christ, and let him reorder your life. Then take a deep breath and relax. ♦

PRAYER

Too often, Lord, my thoughts are consumed by . . .

JESUS REMOVES OUR DEMONS

... and from Jesus Christ, who is the faithful witness, the firstborn from the dead, and the ruler of the kings of the earth. To him who loves us and has freed us from our sins by his blood ...

REVELATION 1:5

In Florence, Italy, the Accademia Gallery displays many of Michelangelo's great works of art, the most famous of which is the statue of David. Four other works by him are unfinished. Originally they were intended to be used in a massive monument on the tomb of Pope Julius, but midway through the project, Michelangelo changed his mind; as a result, four partially finished figures remain. Nearly everyone who sees these works senses the turmoil, the struggle, embodied in these figures. It is as though they are trying to break free from their marble prison.

No matter how hard we try to set ourselves free, we never can quite pull it off. Like those figures of Michelangelo, we cannot break the chains that bind us and experience the fullness of being. We cannot achieve for ourselves the completion that was in the mind of the Creator when he brought us into being. We need the hand that will free us and restore us.

Jesus, the liberator, strips the chains from our ankles and wrists and makes us free to understand the good news. Jesus has accepted us; now we need to accept his acceptance. To hear the liberating word would be like a deaf person hearing a symphony for the first time.

Christianity's most basic truth is that Jesus Christ has already paid for all of our sins—sins past, sins present, sins future. All we need to do is accept that Jesus died on the cross. That's how Jesus frees us—releasing our sin and removing our guilt. Ultimately all sin is against him. Because of Jesus' sacrifice on the cross, he forgives our sin and removes our guilt and frees us to live again. ♦

PRAYER

Lord, help me to remember that you can take away my sin and guilt when I ...

november6

EXPERIENCING GOD'S PRESENCE IN WORSHIP

Exalt the LORD our God and worship at his footstool; he is holy.

PSALM 99:5

It is safe to say that true, life-changing encounters with the living God are missing from many of our churches. We desperately need a life-changing glimpse of the greatness and the loving-kindness of the God we serve.

The word *worship* conjures up all kinds of images in people's minds. The word *worship* comes from an old English word that means "worthship." With that definition in mind, we don't worship God for what we get out of it, but we worship to give God the honor that is due him, recognizing his worth, his value, his place in our church, and his claim on our lives.

Worship occurs when people encounter the God who loves them and desires a relationship with them. Worship is a meeting between God and his people.

When we worship God, whether on our own or in church, we come with an agenda—to meet with God. And as important as this is, we need to remember that God has an agenda as well—to meet with us.

God promises to manifest his presence in a special way when we worship. In corporate worship, God desires to remove our blindfolds and give us an extraordinary, breathtaking glimpse of divine radiance.

It is this extra glimpse of God that most of us need. Do you realize that you can experience God's grace without experiencing his presence? You can have an understanding that Jesus died for your sins; know facts and figures, dates and times about Jesus; and still never enter into the joy of his presence.

Look for God's hand at work in worship. Listen for God's voice. Open yourself up to new manifestations of God's presence. Be sensitive to the leadership of God's Spirit. ♦

PRAYER

Lord, help me to keep worship in perspective ...

november7

THE GIFT OF HOPE

Blessed are those whose help is the God of Jacob, whose hope is in the LORD their God.
PSALM 146:5

We know the word *blessed* means "happy." It occurs twenty-six times in the Psalms. It indicates a deep and abiding pleasure, a manifestation of joy. Whereas man disappoints and fails, God does not. God comes through again and again.

God is eternal; he stands outside of creation; he is not bound by it; he is sovereign over it.

We are faced with a choice: Where will we place our hope? Will we place our hope in God or in people?

It is a dangerous thing to place your hope in people, events, or circumstances. Why? Because with people there are no guarantees. Man is mortal. But if you place your hope in God, he stands behind his promise. God is immortal. He backs up his word. He has proven himself faithful over and over again. He always comes through in the clutch. He is a God who can be counted on. Apart from God, there is really no guaranteed hope.

Where is your hope? Is it in people, or is it in God?

When George Bush was vice president, he represented the United States at the funeral of former Soviet leader Leonid Brezhnev. Bush was deeply moved by a silent protest carried out by Brezhnev's widow. She stood motionless by the coffin until seconds before it was closed and then made the sign of a cross across her husband's chest. There, in the citadel of secular, atheistic power, the wife of the man who had run it all hoped that her husband had been wrong. She hoped there was another life and that Jesus might yet have mercy on her husband. ◆

PRAYER

God, help me to have hope when . . .

november8

MY PART IN THE SPIRITUAL GROWTH PROCESS

Therefore, my dear friends, as you have always obeyed—not only in my presence, but now much more in my absence—continue to work out your salvation with fear and trembling.
PHILIPPIANS 2:12

When we give our life to Christ, our eternal destiny is altered; there is a radical reorientation of priorities; there is a new life purpose; and there is the experience of the indwelling Holy Spirit. God has a role to play in our growth, but so do we, as the advancement toward spiritual growth occurs.

To work for something means to earn it, to deserve it, to merit it, which the Bible clearly rejects. Paul was not implying that we devise our own plan of salvation or that we work our way into a right relationship with God by our own efforts. *Work out* carries the meaning of "work to full completion." Today we use the words to describe physical exercise to accomplish fitness. Spiritual growth necessitates a "spiritual workout" or "spiritual training."

Spiritual growth is not about trying; it's about training. Merely trying to experience life change can never bring about life change. I will only be able to bench press 300 pounds by training to bench press 300 pounds.

Likewise, to become like Jesus, we don't try harder. We train. We do the things Jesus did in order to live like Jesus lived. To truly live a Christlike life, we have to order our lives around those activities, disciplines, and practices modeled by Christ to accomplish spiritual growth.

We pursue an intimate relationship with Christ, seeking to become more and more like him. Spiritual growth is highly relational. As we do our part and God does his part, in time the growth leads to a mature and faithful believer in Christ. ◆

PRAYER

God, help me to model my life around Christ by . . .

november9

UNANSWERED PRAYER

I cry out to you, God, but you do not answer; I stand up, but you merely look at me.

JOB 30:20

A Sunday school class wrote letters to missionaries informing them that they were praying for them. One missionary got a letter that read, "Dear Mr. Missionary, we are praying for you, and we don't expect an answer."

How many people pray without expecting an answer? They go through life wondering if God will ever answer their prayers. They are not alone.

Ask the twelve-year-old who says, "I don't believe in God anymore. Once I prayed for a trip to Disney World, but it never happened."

Nothing is more baffling than unanswered prayer.

Jesus' outrageous promises appear to be part of the problem. He promised, "Ask and it will be given to you; seek and you will find; knock and the door will be opened to you. For everyone who asks receives; the one who seeks finds; and to the one who knocks, the door will be opened" (Luke 11:9–10). He taught, "You may ask me for anything in my name ... I will do it" (John 14:14). Jesus' promises awaken an expectation that our prayers will be answered. This leads to profound disappointment when our prayers go unanswered. In addition, we are told that God is a Father who does not deny any good thing from his children. We think that if we are good and deserving, God will and should answer our prayers.

The fact is that God does not answer some of our prayers. Some of the reasons we'll never know on this side of eternity. Yet some of the reasons are quite obvious, if only we'll look. ♦

PRAYER

Lord, help me to remember to pray when ...

LOVE: SHOWING THE MARK

I have made you known to them, and will continue to make you known in order that the love you have for me may be in them and that I myself may be in them.

JOHN 17:26

As believers, we have a personal and intimate relationship with Jesus. We know God in order to make him known. Out of the knowledge of God comes the added benefits of an indwelling love and an indwelling presence. One of the clearest and most powerful ways of communicating our knowledge of God is through love.

Love is an important theme in John's gospel. John is known as the apostle of love. He uses the word *love* as a verb or noun fifty-six times. The word used for love is *agapē* — a beautiful word. This term became the standard, the mark, the distinguishing feature by which Christians were to love friend and enemy alike. Jesus showed us a new example of love (John 13:4 – 17) by washing the feet of his disciples. Jesus showed us what love looks like. Love is choosing to do someone's dirty work for them. Being the answer to Jesus' prayer is about getting on our knees and getting our hands dirty in the messes of life.

When we go into the world, we venture into dangerous and precarious territory. We can expect to be treated wrongly for doing right. We can expect to be persecuted for showing peace. We can expect to be hated for loving.

Love may be the most powerful apologetic in the Christian's arsenal. People need demonstrations of love and not just communications about God if God is to be known. When true love is demonstrated, people are changed. Love, hand in hand with truth, is the strongest persuasion any believer can give. Love is the most powerful message we can preach so people can know God. ♦

PRAYER

Lord, show me your love that I may show it to others when ...

november11

THINKING POSITIVELY

In your relationships with one another, have the same mindset as Christ Jesus.

When Jeff, a restaurant manager, was asked how he was doing, he would reply, "If I were any better, I'd be twins!"

One day he was asked, "How do you do it? I don't get it. You can't be a positive person all of the time."

Jeff replied, "Each morning, I wake up and say to myself, 'Jeff, you have two choices today. Each time something bad happens, you can choose to be a victim, or you can choose to learn from it.' I choose to learn from it. It's my choice as to how I will live life."

Jeff's positive philosophy was put to the test. One morning he left the back door to his restaurant open and was held up at gunpoint by three armed robbers. While trying to open the safe, his hand, shaking from nervousness, slipped off the combination lock. The robbers panicked and shot him.

Luckily, Jeff was found quickly and rushed to the local trauma center. In the eyes of the medical team, he read the message: *He's a dead man.*

A nurse asked if he was allergic to anything. "Yes," Jeff replied. "Bullets!" Over the sound of their laughter, he told them, "I'm choosing to live. Treat me as if I'm alive, not dead." Jeff lived, thanks to the skill of his doctors but also because of his amazing positive attitude.

Attitude is our response to life. It is our choice. One of the most significant decisions we can make on a day-to-day basis is choosing a positive attitude. The Bible teaches that the way we think determines the way we feel, and the way we feel determines the way we act. So if you want to change your actions, change the way you think. If you want to change your attitudes, change the thoughts you put in your mind. ♦

PRAYER

Lord, help me to view the world more positively ...

november12

BE PREPARED

Be on guard! Be alert! You do not know when that time will come.

MARK 13:33

The Boy Scouts' motto, "Be prepared," is good advice for any person and any occasion. Pack the right camping equipment so you will "be prepared." Assemble the right tools for the project so you will "be prepared." Put the right people on the job so you will "be prepared." Keep enough money in reserve so you will "be prepared." In this passage, Jesus seems to be giving his disciples the same message.

Jesus was about to leave these men with whom he had spent three intense years. He promised he would return, but he explained that, like his first, his second coming would be a surprise — no one would know the day or hour. Therefore, they should be prepared for this sudden and amazing event.

Jesus hasn't fulfilled this promise yet, but he could return at any moment. So his challenge from the first century still applies.

Months of planning go into a wedding, the birth of a baby, a career change, the purchase of a home, and a speaking engagement. How much more should we prepare for Christ's return! It is the most important event of our lives, with results that will last for eternity.

Preparing for the second coming does not mean selling everything and moving to the top of a mountain to look for Christ in the air. No one knows when he will come back, and he has work for us to do in the meantime. Getting prepared means studying God's Word and living for Christ every day. It means feeling the urgency of telling others about Christ.

Are you ready, on guard, alert? He's coming back. Praise the Lord! ♦

PRAYER

Jesus, I await your return with . . .

november13

TASTING DEATH

To the roots of the mountains I sank down; the earth beneath barred me in forever. But you, LORD my God, brought my life up from the pit.

JONAH 2:6

In a spiritual sense, we have to give up before we can be raised up. We have to get to that point where there is nothing more we can do except wait for God to intervene and save us.

When Jonah gave up hope of surviving and could sink no lower, God intervened and saved him. Jonah had to almost die before he could live.

If someone is drowning, often the rescuer will allow the victim to wail and flail to the point of exhaustion before they rescue the victim. It is only once the victim is near death or given up that the rescuer can safely save the victim.

Such was the case with Jonah. And such is the case with us.

In the highlands of Scotland, sheep often wander off into the rocks and get into places they can't get out of in pursuit of sweet grass. They may be there for days, until they have eaten all the grass. The shepherd will wait until they are so faint that they cannot stand, and then put a rope around the sheep and pull them up out of the jaws of death.

Why doesn't the shepherd go down there when the sheep first get in the predicament? For the same reason the lifeguard does not go at once to the drowning victim. The sheep are so foolish that they would dash right over the precipice and be killed if they did.

That is the way it is with us. God knows that sometimes we need to experience a little of death before we can enjoy the abundance of life. The Lord will come to our rescue the moment we abandon our attempts to save ourselves. ♦

PRAYER

Lord, help me to realize your desire to rescue me . . .

PRAYER BRINGS US TO GOD

If my people, who are called by my name, will humble themselves and pray and seek my face and turn from their wicked ways, then I will hear from heaven, and I will forgive their sin and will heal their land.

2 CHRONICLES 7:14

Prayer is the indispensable and vital function of a believer. No aspect of our Christian life is more essential and critical to our personal growth and health, and the church's growth and health, than spending time with God. We are never taller than when we are on our knees. We are never stronger than when we are confessing our weaknesses. We are never bolder in public than when we are quiet before God in private.

Prayer reminds us that we need God more than he needs us. That's why we are instructed, "If my people ... will ... pray." The essence of prayer is to join God, not to wait for God to join us. We ask what is on God's heart rather than telling God what is on our hearts. Prayer is the lifeline that saves the drowning soul. Prayer is the umbilical cord that provides nourishment to the starving spirit. Prayer is the channel by which God's life-giving presence flows to us.

Saint Augustine, the early church father and theologian, described prayer as being like a man in a hapless boat who throws a rope at a rock. The rock provides the needed security and stability for the helpless man. When the rock is lassoed, the man is not pulling the rock to the boat (though it may appear that way); he is pulling the boat to the rock. Jesus is the rock, and we throw the rope through prayer. ♦

PRAYER

God, help me to ask you for help through prayer when ...

november15

DO YOU OWN THE CROSS?

But we do see Jesus, who was made lower than the angels for a little while, now crowned with glory and honor because he suffered death, so that by the grace of God he might taste death for everyone.

HEBREWS 2:9

It took time for the Christian church to come to terms with the disgrace and horror of the cross. Church fathers forbade its depiction in art until the reign of the Roman emperor Constantine, who had seen a vision of the cross and had also banned it as a method of execution. Thus, not until the fourth century did the cross become a symbol of the faith. Strange as it may seem, Christianity has become a religion of the cross.

Despite the shame and sadness of it all, somehow what took place at Golgotha became arguably the most important fact of Jesus' life. And it can be the most significant event in your life.

We can't ignore the cross of Christ. The death of Christ is central in Christian history. All that precedes it is preparation. All that follows it is consequence. Jesus tasted what all men must taste—death. Jesus entered what all men must enter—the tomb. Jesus died for everyone. We can't look at the cross without seeing God's love. God can't look at the cross without seeing each of us.

The crucifixion was God's dramatic answer to the sins of all of humanity. The cross was raised in the sand of the first century, but its shadow falls on the entire length of calendar time. The cross was lifted to deal with the sins of every person.

Too many people see the cross and walk away from it unmoved. To own the cross is to see that Jesus experienced the worst of human suffering as he sacrificed his life so that you can receive forgiveness of your sins and victory over death. ♦

PRAYER

God, thank you for giving me victory over death. Help me to take full advantage of your gift when ...

SO MANY VOICES

"What shall I do, then, with Jesus who is called the Messiah?" Pilate asked. They all answered, "Crucify him!"

MATTHEW 27:22

Following Jesus requires listening for his voice. The problem is that we let too many other voices drown out Jesus' voice.

First is the voice of *compromise*. It says, "Everything is negotiable." With Jesus, however, there is no dealing. No negotiation. No compromise. With him it is all or nothing.

Second is the voice of *expedience*. It says, "I have other affairs to attend to, for I am a busy person." Our agendas are full. We are a people of pragmatism. Let's get on it and get it over with.

Third is the voice of *politics*. This voice asks the question, "Is it popular?" The voice of politics lacks the courage to stand up for what is right.

But finally, there is the voice of *God*. The still small voice speaks to the heart, saying, "Follow Jesus." It is the voice rapping on the door of our heart asking us to obey. It doesn't plead or demand or beg. It yearns, but it does not yell.

How many people do you think leave a church service in which the gospel is preached, knowing they should respond to Jesus but don't? Our hearts can become calloused. The more we refuse to listen to God, the harder our hearts become. Ignore the voice and fail to heed it, and eventually the voice of God can hardly be heard.

Pilate heard so many voices that day as he pondered what to do with Jesus. He heard the voice of compromise, the voice of expedience, and the voice of politics. So many voices. He even heard the voice of God. How could he not? Jesus was standing right in front of him.

So many voices. What voice will you listen to? ♦

PRAYER

Father, help me to hear your voice when . . .

THE WORD MEANS

In the beginning was the Word, and the Word was with God, and the Word was God.
JOHN 1:1

Jesus is God's Word to us. When God decided to give his greatest message to mankind, he didn't write a book that would come later. Instead, he sent himself and became that Word to us.

God has spoken. God is not mute but articulate. The Almighty is not speechless. Jesus is God revealing himself to us in a language we can understand.

Our words reveal to others our hearts and minds. They reveal what we are thinking. So Jesus is God's Word that reveals the heart and mind of God to us. If you want to get to know God, get to know Jesus. Jesus is the complete Word. Jesus is the embodiment of all we need. If you are looking for answers, they are found in the Word, Jesus.

There's a warning, however.

Jesus' words are difficult to follow. Why? The Word forces people to pick a side. With Jesus, it is all or nothing.

While there is a warning, there is also a benefit.

Jesus has the words of life. The Word embodies information, but that is not Jesus' main message. Jesus, the Word, brings life. In Jesus Christ we have the words of life and find the answers to the deepest needs of modern man. If you are looking for the answer to the question of life, his name is Jesus Christ.

As in a lot of conversations — especially heated and controversial ones — we know that the one who utters the last word usually wins. Jesus is the last word. God said it. That settles it. Whether we believe it or not, Jesus will have the last word.

What is he saying to you? ♦

PRAYER

Father, help me to hear you, to hear your every word . . .

AFTER THE BLAME DON'T FORGET TO THANK GOD

Sacrifice thank offerings to God, fulfill your vows to the Most High.

PSALM 50:14

There is an old story about a Jewish tailor who met a rabbi on his way out of the synagogue. "Well, what have you been doing in the synagogue, Lev Ashram?" inquired the rabbi.

"I was saying prayers, Rabbi."

"Fine, and did you confess your sins?"

"Yes, Rabbi, I confessed my little sins."

"Your little sins?"

"Yes, I confessed that sometimes I cut the cloth on the short side and cheat on a yard of wool by a couple of inches."

"You said that to God, Lev Ashram?"

"Yes, Rabbi, and more. I said, 'Lord, I cheat on pieces of cloth; you let little babies die. But I am going to make you a deal. You forgive my little sins, and I'll forgive your big ones.'"

Over the centuries, God has been accused of many big sins. He has been labeled cruel, unfair, sadistic, uncaring, and impotent.

Skeptics often ask, "If God is good, how can there be so much evil in the world?" To this we can respond, "If God is so cruel, explain how there can be so much good in the world."

The next time you are angry with God because of the injustices you see in your life, don't forget to look for the countless ways in which the goodness of God is manifested in your life. ♦

> **PRAYER**

Lord, thank you for being a kind and giving God; help me to see the goodness over the suffering when ...

november19

A CHAIN REACTION

Now I want you to know, brothers and sisters, that what has happened to me has actually served to advance the gospel.

PHILIPPIANS 1:12

A chain is a connected, flexible series of links, usually of metal, used for binding or connecting. Chains can pull cars out of ditches, measure distance, and restrain dogs on a leash or people taken captive.

Paul wanted to travel to Rome to conquer the capital of the empire for Christ; instead he arrived in chains. Yet he didn't whine or complain. Sitting there with an iron cuff and chain on one arm, bound to a Roman soldier, Paul wrote of his circumstances as having turned out for the progress and furtherance of the gospel.

Paul saw the guards not as enemies but as a captive audience. When guard members retired after twelve years, they were made leaders in Rome, which made them the perfect conversion goal for Paul. There could not have been a more strategic group with whom Paul could have conversed. As a result, the men guarding Paul were becoming Christians.

The guards who were chained to Paul came to realize that Paul was chained to Someone else. Paul may have been bound to the guard by one hand with a short chain, but his other hand was bonded to Christ.

And even in chains he spoke the word of God more courageously and fearlessly.

Sometimes God has to put "chains" on his people to accomplish an advancement of the gospel that could happen no other way. Chuck Colson was imprisoned because of his involvement with the Watergate scandal, but God used those "chains" to reach incarcerated men and women through Prison Fellowship, which Colson founded. The very chains we find ourselves in may be the means God desires to use to advance the gospel. ♦

PRAYER

God, help me to spread the gospel message today . . .

LA MOVIDA

You, my brothers and sisters, were called to be free. But do not use your freedom to indulge the flesh; rather, serve one another humbly in love.

GALATIANS 5:13

La Movida (from a Spanish word meaning "lively" or "hectic") is the term used to describe the period of time following the death of Spain's dictator Francisco Franco on November 20, 1975. For over thirty years, the country had endured the strict rules of Franco's regime. Life had been dull and bland. Conformity was the rule, and fear had held the people captive.

As the nation emerged from that bondage, many were overjoyed. The youth, especially, burst out of their cells of conservatism, eager to experience every kind of forbidden fare. In Madrid, bars and nightclubs were open all night. The city never slept but remained in a constant state of frenzy. Drugs, alcohol, and sex were all sampled to the greatest extent.

But the fun couldn't last forever. It wasn't long before people began to reap the consequences of their licentious actions. Diseases such as AIDS loomed like a dark cloud over the population. Drug and alcohol abuse began to take its toll. Young people discovered that the freedom they thought they had was only another form of bondage.

Christ freed us from the law. We no longer have to live under its tyranny. But Christ did not free us to sin; he freed us to serve. You see, our freedom is only found *in* Christ. It is by being bound to him (enslaved, if you will) that we are truly free. May we live out that profound paradox today! ♦

PRAYER

Lord, I define my freedom as . . .

november21

WHEN WE ARE WRONG

Surely the arm of the LORD is not too short to save, nor his ear too dull to hear. But your iniquities have separated you from your God; your sins have hidden his face from you, so that he will not hear.

ISAIAH 59:1–2

When our prayers aren't answered, whom do we blame? Most often, if we are honest, we blame God.

But let's face it, sometimes we are wrong. Sometimes we are *in* the wrong—an error in judgment, a poor decision, a thoughtless mistake. Sometimes when we're wrong with our praying, it stands in the way of our answers.

When we point our forefinger at God, laying the blame on him for not answering our prayers, we need to see the three fingers pointing back at us. We may be the reason our prayers are not being answered. God's "no" can be our own fault.

Over thirty times the Bible reveals instances when God didn't answer someone's prayer. Usually it was because of unrepentant sins. Some of those sins are broken relationships, husbands dishonoring their wives, pride, selfishness, and an uncaring attitude.

Make no mistake about it. Our sin can close the spigot of God's flow to answer our prayers. If you are tolerating sin and disobedience in your life, don't waste your breath praying unless it's a prayer of confession.

God answers the prayers, not of perfect people, but of repentant people. ♦

PRAYER

Lord, help me to realize when I am wrong so that ...

YOU'RE WORTH IT

As a prisoner for the Lord, then, I urge you to live a life worthy of the calling you have received.

EPHESIANS 4:1

In the epic World War II movie *Saving Private Ryan*, eight United States soldiers go behind enemy lines to save their comrade, paratrooper Private Ryan. In the process, many of the men lose their lives on their mission to save one man.

Toward the end of the film, in one of the most stirring scenes in the movie, the leader of the group, Captain Miller (Tom Hanks), is fatally shot. Ryan runs to him, and as he is dying, the captain looks at Ryan and says four words: "Earn this. Earn this."

What Captain Miller asked of Ryan is, of course, impossible. No man could ever live a life well enough to "earn" the sacrifice of the lives of six other men. But in that moment, Ryan realizes the high price that was paid for his life. And he realizes that because of this, he has an obligation.

In some ways, we are all like Private Ryan. A very high price was paid for us. Jesus was willing to give up his life so that we might have life and freedom. In many ways, our response can only be to live in such a way as to reflect our gratitude for what Christ has done for us.

But it goes deeper than that. The members of the team searching for Ryan often quarreled about whether Ryan was worth the risk. But when it came to you, Jesus had no doubt. In God's eyes, you were worth the price of his Son's life. So how can you respond to such a gift? Paul says, "Live a life worthy of the calling you have received." What will you do this week? ♦

> **PRAYER**

Jesus, for the gift of your life, I can only say . . .

november23

WHAT'S YOUR PROBLEM?

Some time later, [Samson] fell in love with a woman in the Valley of Sorek whose name was Delilah.

JUDGES 16:4

Tiger Woods was a child golf prodigy. He first broke eighty at age eight and dominated professional golf for years. He reached the pinnacle of his career, having accomplished everything a golfer would want to accomplish.

Yet on a November night in 2009, another side of his life emerged to the public. In the days and weeks that followed, it was revealed that he is a man with a large appetite for sex.

His story reminds me of another man who, having reached the pinnacle of his life, having accomplished everything a man would want to accomplish, in a series of events sank from the top right down to the bottom. His name—Samson. God had empowered Samson for a significant and specific purpose. He too was a prodigy. He too had it all.

But he too had a problem. Like Tiger Woods, he had a problem with women. He got involved in the wrong relationships. He toyed with temptation when he should have run from it. And it cost him severely.

Unless we deal with the real with regard to our problems, unless we get down to the level of "this is what I'm really like," until we do that, those problems will come back again and again and again. Step number one: Admit you have a problem. You'll never get better until you are willing to say, "I really need help in this area of my life." Unless we learn to deal with our problems now, we are going to deal with them later. They're going to come back to haunt us again and again.

And when they do, we risk falling prey to the Delilahs of this world. ♦

PRAYER

Lord, I need to talk about a problem I have . . .

WILL WE REMEMBER GOD?

I will give you thanks in the great assembly; among the throngs I will praise you.

PSALM 35:18

Someone once remarked that the worst of all possible moments for an atheist is to feel truly thankful and have no one to thank. Most Americans are not actual atheists, but they may be practical atheists. An actual atheist has no God to thank. A practical atheist has a God to thank, but he never thinks of doing it.

Thanksgiving became a national holiday at a time in American history when Americans were prone to see their rich country—and their good fortune to be born in it—as a direct gift from God. They spoke of the heritage of the Pilgrims, who gathered after the first harvest to thank God for the bounty that was theirs. According to tradition, their good friends, the American Indians, brought turkeys and venison and together they enjoyed a great feast in primitive Massachusetts.

Turkeys by the millions now die in November, and pudgy Americans (at least 76 percent of us are overweight) will snore with the television remote control rocking on their stomachs. But who received thanks for the good life?

America is proof that the blessings of God can immobilize us from remembering the necessity of God. Will we remember God this Thanksgiving? Will we thank him for who he is, what he has done, and what he has given us? ♦

PRAYER

I have so much to thank you for, Lord . . .

COME OUT OF HIDING

The man and his wife heard the sound of the LORD God as he was walking in the garden in the cool of the day, and they hid from the LORD God among the trees of the garden.

GENESIS 3:8

Robert Fulghum, in *All I Really Need to Know I Learned in Kindergarten*, writes about how he used to sit in his office and listen to the neighborhood kids playing hide-and-seek. Fulghum noticed a kid under a pile of leaves in the yard just under his window. He had been there a long time. Everybody else had been found, so Fulghum yelled out the window, "GET FOUND, KID!" He scared him so bad he wet his pants, started crying, and ran home to tell his mother. Fulghum writes, "It's hard to know how to be helpful sometimes."

Fulghum then tells of a doctor who discovered he had terminal cancer. He knew he was dying, and he didn't want to make his family and friends suffer through that with him. So he kept his secret and eventually died. His family and friends were angry that he didn't feel as if he needed them and didn't trust their strength. It hurt them that he didn't say good-bye. Fulghum writes that this man hid too well.

We have become a society that hides too well. We play an adult version of hide-and-seek. And when we don't get found, we can get mad.

How can we be found? When we admit our weaknesses. What if we were to take off our masks and admit our struggles?

We often think that if we open our hearts to others, it will repel them, when self-disclosure actually has the opposite effect. When we take off our masks, people are drawn to us.

If you are hiding, I offer this admonition: "Come out, come out, wherever you are." The game is over. ♦

PRAYER

Father, help me resist the urge to hide when ...

DEALING WITH THE CRITIC

But when Sanballat the Horonite, Tobiah the Ammonite official and Geshem the Arab heard about it, they mocked and ridiculed us. "What is this you are doing?" they asked. "Are you rebelling against the king?"

NEHEMIAH 2:19

The manager of the Cleveland Indians, Tris Speaker, said of Babe Ruth, "He made a great mistake when he gave up pitching." Jim Denny, manager of the Grand Ole Opry, fired Elvis Presley after a 1954 performance and said, "You ain't goin' nowhere, son. You ought to go back to drivin' a truck." The president of Decca Records said of the Beatles in 1962, "We don't like their sound. Groups of guitars are on the way out."

Whatever your feelings toward criticism, don't expect to miss out. No one is exempt. Well, maybe you can evade it, but there is a catch. Aristotle said, "Criticism is something you can avoid easily by saying nothing, doing nothing, and being nothing."

Maybe you face criticism at work, at home, or at school. Critics are a dime a dozen. They are everywhere. They resist change. They see change as a threat. Critics run with critics. Critics have a "herd" mentality. Critics hope to demoralize.

Since criticism is inevitable, we must measure the value or worth of the criticism. This step requires great self-control that helps keep us from becoming impatient and defensive.

Ask yourself if the criticism is true or false. Take an honest look at yourself. If the criticism is valid, do something about it. Sometimes the best course of action is to respond to criticism and learn from it. If the criticism is invalid, forget it. Sometimes the best course of action is to completely ignore it.

In the end, remember that they don't build monuments to the critic. ♦

PRAYER

Lord, help me to persevere through criticism ...

november27

FINDING TIME TO CONNECT WITH THE FAMILY

Unless the LORD builds the house, the builders labor in vain. Unless the LORD watches over the city, the guards stand watch in vain. In vain you rise early and stay up late, toiling for food to eat—for he grants sleep to those he loves.

PSALM 127:1–2

Often the missing ingredient in a family gone bad is time spent with each other. It is fundamental to understanding. And it is a prerequisite for love.

The number of hours spent at work has increased dramatically in recent years. And what gets lost? Time with the family, of course. Parents spend 40 percent less time with their children than they did twenty-five years ago, according to an analysis by the Family Research Council. In the mid-1960s, an average parent spent about thirty hours per week with a child. Today, the average parent spends only seventeen hours.

A man worked for a television studio, but unlike so many in the TV industry who seldom watch television themselves, he was addicted to it. He spent little or no time with his two children or his wife. Needless to say, his marriage was hurting. He and his wife decided to attend a Marriage Enrichment Conference, and that weekend literally changed his life. When he got home following the conference, he replaced the television with a family portrait. Next he shared his new set of priorities with his family and asked for their forgiveness. His twelve-year-old son interrupted him and said, "Dad, now that there is a picture of our family where the television used to be, does this mean we are going to be a family now?"

We must be diligent to screen out any attacks—vicious or otherwise—that would rob us from spending time with our family. Don't let your family be another victim that says, "I guess we never did have a very good family life." ♦

PRAYER

Father, open my eyes to anything I am putting before my family ...

THE INAPPROPRIATE REQUEST

Peter said to Jesus, "Lord, it is good for us to be here. If you wish, I will put up three shelters—one for you, one for Moses and one for Elijah."

MATTHEW 17:4

Have you ever had someone ask for a favor and as soon as the words were spoken, you knew you couldn't fulfill it? It was not that the request was immoral, unethical, or illegal. It was simply inappropriate. Likewise, some prayer requests, no matter how well-intentioned, are inappropriate. And God loves us too much to say yes to those requests.

For example, on one occasion the three closest disciples of Jesus accompanied him to a mountain. On that mountain God's glory descended on Jesus, and Moses and Elijah appeared beside him. Beholding Jesus' splendor, Peter, James, and John dropped back in awe. Then Peter came up with a bright idea. "Jesus, let me erect three memorials [sort of the Mount Rushmore of religion] on this mountain for you and Moses and Elijah. And I'll be happy to stay on the mountain and point you out."

Jesus' immediate response was an effective no—a thick cloud enveloped them, cutting off further conversation. The request was inappropriate because Jesus and the disciples had work to do down in the plains where people lived. Have you ever asked for safety, comfort, convenience? The Christian life is easy when we are on a spiritual retreat or having a mountaintop experience. If the disciples were capable of making inappropriate requests, so are we. Fortunately, God loves us too much to say yes to inappropriate requests. He will answer such prayers, but the answer is no.

If you have been praying diligently about a matter and have sensed resistance from heaven, I challenge you to review your request with this thought in mind: "If God were to grant this request, would it bring glory to him?" We must remember that some requests are inappropriate. And God loves us too much to say yes to inappropriate requests. ♦

PRAYER

Lord, help me to ask for the right things ...

THE FREEDOM OF SELF-CONTROL

Like a city whose walls are broken through is a person who lacks self-control.

PROVERBS 25:28

Greg took up golf. One day, when he was playing even worse than usual, he decided to explain his predicament to his teenage caddy.

"I took up golf to practice self-control," Greg said.

The youngster rolled his eyes and replied, "If that's the case, you should have taken up caddying."

The need for self-control is familiar to most of us. Sometimes we simply don't think at all; we react, ignoring our need for self-control. And where has it gotten us? In debt. Overweight and out of shape. Practicing immorality.

Self-control begins with our thoughts and attitudes. Our minds are mental greenhouses in which unlawful thoughts, once planted, are nurtured and watered before becoming actions. People seldom fall suddenly into gluttony or immorality. These actions are savored in the mind long before they are enjoyed in reality.

Retailer J. C. Penny often said, "Only the disciplined are free." Freedom is often defined as "living as one pleases." In reality, freedom is behaving as one should. Self-control liberates by enabling us to perform those activities that are essential and mandatory.

Self-control is always a matter of choice. When we say no to inappropriate concerns, we can say yes to what matters most.

At first we may not be able to see the fruits of delayed gratification, but if we keep on believing in and practicing self-control, they will become visible.

The payoff is worth the wait, and it beats caddying any day. ♦

PRAYER

God, help me to have self-control when . . .

november30

CHOSEN, COMMISSIONED, EMPOWERED

Have I not commanded you? Be strong and courageous. Do not be afraid; do not be discouraged, for the LORD your God will be with you wherever you go.

JOSHUA 1:9

Imagine that after playing four years of football, you graduate and go on to serve as an assistant coach. A week after the season, the head coach calls you into his office and says something like this: "I'm retiring, and I want you to take over for me as the new head coach. The administration has agreed that you're our man." After the initial shock, what would you think and feel? Now put yourself in Joshua's shoes.

After Moses died, God gave Joshua the awesome task of leading his people, the Israelites, into the Promised Land. Joshua must have been terrified at the prospect of taking over for Moses, a great leader and his mentor, to direct a whole nation. How could he be up for such a task, assuming so much responsibility and so quickly? And so God reminds Joshua of who is really in control and gives him the profound promise of his presence. Joshua will not be leading alone; God will be with him in every decision, meeting, and battle—counseling, guiding, encouraging, empowering. Joshua can be *strong and courageous*.

What battles loom on your horizon? What critical decisions do you have to make? What relationships need your attention? Who needs your decisive leadership? What's your God-given assignment? Take courage and draw strength from the fact that God is in control and is leading you. And *he will be with you wherever you go*. Remember, God is your commander. ♦

PRAYER

Lord, give me courage to ...

REST ASSURED

Come to me, all you who are weary and burdened, and I will give you rest. Take my yoke upon you and learn from me, for I am gentle and humble in heart, and you will find rest for your souls. For my yoke is easy and my burden is light.

MATTHEW 11:28–30

Ad agencies know how to sell products. They find a hole and promise to fill it; they find a need and promise to meet it; they find a problem and promise to solve it. Then with airbrushed pictures, polished actors, and glib celebrities, they make their pitch, with each product guaranteed to satisfy.

Fed a steady diet of Madison Avenue, we can easily build up immunity to their messages. And after dealing with a procession of products that fail to meet expectations, we can then take a cynical look at any new claim.

So when we hear, "Come ... you who are weary ... I will give you rest," we may turn it off in our minds. Certainly we are weary—from carrying heavy responsibilities and working to please God, ourselves, and others. But this claim, like many others, seems too good to be true.

Until we realize who is speaking. It is Jesus—God in the flesh, one of us, yet the Savior. Jesus tells the truth; he always comes through and lives up to his billing.

So are you tired of life's hectic pace, busyness, and demands, and of doing it all yourself? Throw off the burdens that weigh you down and give them to your Lord. Then live under his loving-kindness and direction, refreshed and renewed. ♦

PRAYER

I am so tired, Savior, and I need ...

december2

ACTION: THE EXPRESSION OF FAITH

Faith by itself, if it is not accompanied by action, is dead. But someone will say, "You have faith; I have deeds." Show me your faith without deeds, and I will show you my faith by my deeds.

JAMES 2:17–18

Faith is never passive or static, nor is it feeling a certain way. Real faith always embodies action. Dynamic faith rolls up its sleeves and gets to work.

Faith is best understood not as a noun but as a verb. When faith becomes a noun, it is dead. It becomes a religion that binds and restricts us from doing the will of God and experiencing the loveliness of Christ and the hope of the Holy Spirit. When faith is a verb, it gives us the means and the ability to actively reflect a distinctive life.

Consider three men standing beside a frozen river and contemplating how to cross over to the other side. The first says he doesn't believe the ice will hold, so he gives up and sits in the snow. The second says he'll step out in faith, then lies on the ice and crawls across, trembling the whole way. The third yells, "It'll hold!" He pulls up his dogsled and roars across the frozen river like a locomotive, passing the second man in a flash.

Who displayed faith that the ice would hold? The one who roared across and the one who crawled.

Who did not? The one who sat in the snow, right?

Who had the most faith? It appears that the third man did. But the last two both arrived at the same destination. True, one arrived faster and with less anxiety. But the difference lies between the person who possessed no faith and the ones who did. For those who expressed faith, the results were the same. ♦

PRAYER

Today, make my faith action filled . . .

THE ROCKS OF PRIORITIES

For what I received I passed on to you as of first importance: that Christ died for our sins according to the Scriptures.

1 CORINTHIANS 15:3

An instructor at a seminar placed a wide-mouthed gallon jar on a table, and one by one, he began to put as many rocks as he could into the jar, until the rocks inside were level with the top of the jar.

"Is the jar full?" The attendees said, "Yes."

Then the instructor dumped some gravel in the jar and shook it. The gravel invaded all the little spaces left by the big rocks. "Is the jar full?"

The attendees were uncertain.

The instructor next poured sand into the jar, filling in the gaps left by the rocks and gravel. "Now is the jar full?"

The audience roared, "NO!"

Then the instructor poured a pitcher of water in the jar until it ran over. At this point he stopped and said, "The point is this: If I hadn't put in those big rocks first, I would never have gotten them in."

Unfortunately, many people go through life stuffing gravel and sand and water issues into their life jar, leaving the rocks—the important things—outside the jar. Without taking charge of our lives and determining what is really important, we will never accomplish what we want.

Putting the rocks in first—determining our priorities—keeps us from falling into the trap of saying yes to everyone, assists us in managing our time, and helps us focus our energies.

Life places before us hundreds of possibilities when it comes to filling our jar. But each of us must decide, "What are my rocks? What is a priority to me?" ♦

PRAYER

Lord, help me to prioritize better ...

HOPE IN GOD

Why, my soul, are you downcast? Why so disturbed within me? Put your hope in God, for I will yet praise him, my Savior and my God.

PSALM 42:5

In the *Journal of the American Medical Association*, Jane McAdams told the story of her sixty-nine-year-old mother, who had lived a life deeply marked by the Great Depression of the 1930s. The only extravagance she had ever permitted herself, McAdams wrote, was a frilly nightgown kept in a bottom drawer—"in case I should ever have to go into the hospital."

That day had come. The daughter wondered, "Should I tell my mother about her chances with cancer? Is there, in fact, any hope?"

As she wrestled with these questions, McAdams realized that her mother's birthday was approaching. Perhaps she could brighten her mother's days by purchasing a new nightgown and matching robe. She did so, but her mother asked that the items be returned—exchanged for something she really wanted. An extravagant designer purse—a summer purse.

Jane's reaction was one of disbelief. Why a summer purse when she wouldn't be able to use it for several months? That's when Jane realized that what her mother really wanted was hope. She was going to live to use that purse. It would not go to waste.

Hope is a powerful tool in the toolbox of life. Without it, people give up on clinging to life and embrace death. Hope may be the best gift we can give to one another. Each day we are given the opportunity to dispense hope. How will you give hope today?

The gift of hope to a downtrodden person is the gift, not of a nightgown that announces death, but of a summer purse that says there is life after difficulty. ♦

PRAYER

God, help me to give hope wherever I can today...

december5

RECLAMATION BUSINESS

Jonah obeyed the word of the LORD and went to Nineveh. Now Nineveh was a very large city; it took three days to go through it.

JONAH 3:3

Disobedience to God doesn't automatically disbar us from later usefulness. David committed adultery and murder, but God renewed him to teach transgressors the divine way through beautiful psalms and hymns. Peter disowned Jesus not once but three times, but God reinstated him for service to his people as a great leader of the early church. John Mark, helper to Paul and Barnabas on the first missionary journey, defected along the way, but God reshaped his life—and he wrote the second book of the New Testament. Jonah rebelled, but God restored him for service.

We should reject the notion that if we turn away from God's will, we are forever disqualified. Satan likes to direct us into thinking we are beyond salvage, doomed to God's second-best. Don't believe it.

Reclamation is, quite simply, the process of "reclaiming" something. The word can be used of God. He is in the reclamation business as well. God never discards a repentant life. No matter what the disobedience, God wants to renew, reinstate, and reshape the life.

Perhaps you feel like you are on the scrap heap. You've made a mistake; you've willfully disobeyed. God is not through with you yet. Your life is not over. You are useful to God.

No matter how defeated you may feel, God cherishes in taking washed-up, used-up people and fashioning something beautiful out of them. That's what he does best. ♦

PRAYER

Father, turn my actions into something beautiful ...

december6

GIVE HIM YOUR BURDENS

Praise be to the LORD, to God our Savior, who daily bears our burdens.

PSALM 68:19

God our Savior "daily bears our burdens."

Daily—not just when he has time or feels like it, but as often as we bear them. Daily.

Bears—they are a weight on him, just as they are on us.

Our—ours, specifically ours. Maybe your burden seems petty next to your friend's burden (or vice versa), but he carries them both just the same.

Burdens—they're heavy and they have to be carried. They're not easy; they're not imaginary; they're not petty; they're not unimportant.

What is burdening you today? What weight bears down on your shoulders and your heart? What hurt causes your stomach to churn, your head to ache, your eyes to tear up?

It's easy to say "give it to the Lord," but not so easy to do. What does it really mean to "give" a burden to the Lord? What does it look like in reality? Is it even possible?

The best advice is to bring the burden to the Lord in prayer. Claim his promises. Grab on to your understanding that God will answer your prayer. Hold fast to what you know to be true about your heavenly Father. You may not be able to let go of your burden completely, but you can let go of your fear, your worry, and your stress when you know God is bearing your burden and has it all under control. ♦

PRAYER

I give you my burdens, Lord. Let's talk . . .

december7

THE HEART OF A VOLUNTEER

Each of you should use whatever gift you have received to serve others, as faithful stewards of God's grace in its various forms.

1 PETER 4:10

The movie *Pearl Harbor* is based on the historical events on and around that early Sunday morning, December 7, 1941, when Japanese warplanes screamed across the peaceful skies of Hawaii and jolted America into World War II. Following the Pearl Harbor attack, Colonel Jimmy Doolittle was asked to lead a daring air raid on Tokyo. In one scene in the movie, potential pilots were lined up in a single row facing the colonel. He asked them to take a look at the person on each side, telling them that one of them would not return from this mission. Then he asked those volunteering for this dangerous and potentially deadly mission to step forward. Without hesitation, all the men stepped forward.

Countless people step forward each day to volunteer at schools, hospitals, nursing homes, churches, and places of disaster to offer a hand and hope. While many volunteers are specifically trained in the areas they work in, such as medicine, education, or emergency rescue, others serve on an as-needed basis and in any way they can help.

Volunteering gives you an opportunity to change lives, including your own. It is a great way to cope with life, for it allows you to look at life from a different perspective. Sometimes it's easy to get consumed by worries. Volunteering lets you focus on others' needs to see that one's involvement in the world can be meaningful.

Back to the movie *Pearl Harbor*. In another scene after Doolittle's request of the young pilots, the men were aboard the ship that transported them closer to their launch point. Doolittle said to a fellow officer while watching the young pilots, "There is nothing stronger than the heart of a volunteer." ♦

Truly there is not.

PRAYER

Where can you use me today, Lord?...

december8

GIVE PEACE A CHANCE

You will keep in perfect peace those whose minds are steadfast, because they trust in you.
ISAIAH 26:3

Our lives are filled with peace stealers—concerns, worries, expectations, pressures, stress, busyness, emergencies, fears, and noise. We have bills to pay, agendas to keep, calls to return, e-mails to answer, appointments to keep, special events to attend, and goals to achieve. And our electronic "time-saving" devices seem to have compressed our schedules, demanding more during less time.

Not all of these are bad, certainly, but they seem to conspire to rob us of peace of mind and soul as we rush to the next activity, hurry to meet the deadline, and fight for sanity in a world that appears to be going insane.

Isaiah gives us the answer: The way to peace is a "steadfast" mind. *Steadfast* means "strong and focused," not allowing anything or anyone to distract us or move us off course. And where should our focus be? On trusting God, with our souls centered on him.

When the world seems to be falling apart, God can be trusted to keep you together. When the future seems bleak, God can be trusted to take you to his destination. When you are surrounded by pressures and problems and see no way out of your troubles, God can be trusted to lead you through. Trusting in our great and good God will bring you perfect peace. ♦

PRAYER

I need peace—your peace, Lord...

december9

HELP!

I lift up my eyes to the mountains — where does my help come from? My help comes from the LORD, the Maker of heaven and earth.

PSALM 121:1–2

When this psalm was written, idols were often situated in "high places" at the tops of mountains and hills. So during times of calamity, distress, famine, or war, people would look to the mountains for their rescue, relying on their false gods for salvation.

Today we don't build holy altars on hills, and most people don't worship wood and stone idols. But like people in the days of this psalm, we do look to a variety of places for help. We may depend on the government, a large corporation, money, family, or friends. No matter how powerful or influential, all of those forces and allies are impotent when compared to our awesome God. And if we're honest, we have to admit that those potential rescuers are our "high places," our idols. In reality, only the Lord brings us forgiveness and salvation.

The writer of this psalm rejects the notion that the "mountains" can help and turns instead to the Lord, the "Maker of heaven and earth." In effect, he is saying, "Lift up your eyes even higher — beyond the mountains to the heavens, to the Creator God!"

To whom do you turn? Never trust a lesser power than God himself. As the Creator of all there is, he can protect and rescue you. Don't look to the hills; look to your Maker. Your help comes from the Lord! ♦

PRAYER

Almighty God, I worship only you . . .

december10

CLEAN!

"Come now, let us settle the matter," says the LORD. *"Though your sins are like scarlet, they shall be as white as snow; though they are red as crimson, they shall be like wool."*

ISAIAH 1:18

Despite the advertised claims of many name-brand detergents, some stains remain in clothes, even after carefully following the washing instructions and using their soap. What has been the toughest stain for you to remove? Grape juice? Coffee? Grease? Mud? After soaking, scrubbing, and soaking some more, we often give up in frustration. It just won't come out, and the shirt, pair of pants, tie, or jacket is ruined!

The effects of sin run profoundly deeper than juice-soiled clothing, affecting all of life and staining the soul with real guilt and painful estrangement from God. And this sin-stain resists every human effort to remove it. No matter how hard we work or hope or even pray, the contamination remains.

The truth is that only God can remove sin's stain and make us truly clean. And he promises to do just that—through faith in Jesus Christ, his Son.

Are you struggling with guilt from transgressions and omissions—the whole spectrum of God-ignoring or God-defying attitudes and acts? You can be forgiven, released, and set on the path of righteousness. For a new start and a new life, confess your sins to God and trust in Christ. His stain remover works! You can be clean! ◆

PRAYER

Forgive me, Lord ...

december**11**

DRESS FOR SUCCESS

Be strong in the Lord and in his mighty power.

EPHESIANS 6:10

What is your definition of success? Today's Christian men are guaranteed success if they're dressed for it. "What do you mean by that?" you may ask.

If we fully commit ourselves to the Lord, we will enjoy all the spiritual blessings heaven has to offer and vanquish the enemy in every spiritual battle we encounter. Spiritual blessings and victories are guaranteed and can be expected without exception if we follow the Lord.

So how should a man dress for success? Ephesians 6:10–18 gives a full explanation of how we can be battle-ready from head to toe. Satan's primary tactic is deception. When we wear the full armor of God, we can stand against the schemes of the enemy.

Make no mistake, Satan wants you to fail. He wants you to mess up at work, disappoint your wife and kids, and let down your friends. The enemy appears as an angel of light when he is really a prowling lion (1 Peter 5:8), waiting to pounce and devour, robbing you of victory. But when you are covered in the righteousness of the One who claims victory over death and hell, you simply cannot fail.

When we are fully prepared for battle, we can emerge as victors. ◆

PRAYER

God, prepare me for any battle I may face today . . .

december12

THE GIVING

"The multitude of your sacrifices—what are they to me?" says the LORD. "... I have no pleasure in the blood of bulls and lambs and goats ... Stop bringing meaningless offerings! Your incense is detestable to me."

ISAIAH 1:11, 13

Picture this scene. Armed with a unique choice of ingredients from the pantry and refrigerator—cereal, orange juice, potato chips, bread, and ketchup—your child eagerly blends them together in a bowl in hopes of surprising you with "dinner."

How do you react? Despite the mess, both inside and outside the bowl, you express joy and gratitude for the sincere expression of love.

But what if your child thought the *gift* was more important than the motive and attitude behind the giving and continued to make similar presentations, year after year, in hopes of appeasing you and earning your love? Before long, you would undoubtedly say something.

Now check out the passage from Isaiah. God doesn't sound happy with the "gifts" of his people. Why not? Because they had confused the animal sacrifices themselves with the reason for making those sacrifices. So they worked hard at their religious works, and they missed the point. Did they really believe that God *needed* dead animals and blood? Didn't they know that he really wanted *their hearts*?

It's the difference between legalism and grace. And Christianity is all about grace.

Jesus came to earth to satisfy the demands of the law, to give himself as the ultimate sacrifice, to open the way for us to come directly to our Father (John 3:16–18).

Yet, sadly, we often continue to mix our potions and religious concoctions and miss the Savior. And all the while, like a loving parent, he is standing at the edge of the kitchen with arms open wide, extending the invitation: "Come to me, child. I want your love. I want your trust. I want *you*." ♦

PRAYER

Father, forgive me for thinking that I could ever earn your love ...

december**13**

GET UP! GET MOVING!

When they had gone, an angel of the Lord appeared to Joseph in a dream. "Get up," he said, "take the child and his mother and escape to Egypt. Stay there until I tell you, for Herod is going to search for the child to kill him." So he got up, took the child and his mother during the night and left for Egypt, where he stayed until the death of Herod. And so was fulfilled what the Lord had said through the prophet: "Out of Egypt I called my son."

MATTHEW 2:13–15

This small incident in the Christmas story, often overlooked and seldom portrayed in church pageants, looms large in the salvation narrative. Occurring immediately after what often is presented as the climax of the story—the visit of the Magi—Joseph has another nighttime encounter with an angel. This time, God's messenger tells him to flee with his family to Egypt.

They had just entertained Eastern celebrities bearing fabulous gifts for their child-king. Now, abruptly, they are to run for their lives—and the destination is Egypt.

The phrase "out of Egypt" appears nearly 150 times in Scripture. Egypt symbolized oppression and slavery, and God's people would remember that the Lord had freed them from that place. But here God tells Joseph to *go to Egypt*. What was Joseph thinking and feeling? His first encounter with an angel announced a "virgin" birth. Then the baby, born in a stable, was visited by shepherds and kings. And now this!

We don't know Joseph's thoughts, but we do know his actions. He obeyed. And Jesus escaped Herod's murderous wrath. And we celebrate Christmas.

"But," we protest, "we would obey too if we knew God was talking!" Really? He speaks to us daily, but do we listen?

Unlike Joseph, we have God's written Word, filled with direction and instruction. May we, with Joseph-like faith, obey and get moving. ♦

PRAYER

I am listening, Lord, and I promise to obey, to go out to do what you say. Speak to me ...

december14

THE GIFT

This is how God showed his love among us: He sent his one and only Son into the world that we might live through him. This is love: not that we loved God, but that he loved us and sent his Son as an atoning sacrifice for our sins.

1 JOHN 4:9–10

Christmas morning has arrived—her first *real* Christmas. Your toddler awakens and is soon immersed in the smells, music, lights, and excited chatter of the season. A gift is placed before her, and after some coaxing she begins to remove the wrapping paper and open the box. You help her pull out the toy, watching for her reaction. Then, with the camera recording every move, your daughter ignores the present and reaches eagerly for the sparkling paper and colorful ribbons.

We laugh at the scene and certainly get it. The little girl doesn't realize the difference between the wrapping and the gift. We also know that by the next Christmas she will understand and squeal with delight at getting "just what I always wanted!"

Yet we often replicate her actions in how we handle and value our Gift.

Christmas is about Christ, not about lights, lawn displays, hung stockings, red and green, Rudolph, bells, and bows—all wonderful traditions and treats. But in the excitement of the season, we can miss the Savior.

We should know better. After all, we've grown well beyond the toddler stage of Christian maturity ... right?

This year, go ahead and celebrate like crazy—sing, laugh, sip, trim, exchange, and feast. But dig deeper, beneath the wrappings and trappings. Unwrap the Gift. Discover Jesus. ♦

PRAYER

Jesus, my brother, my friend, my Savior—the Gift—thank you for loving us and giving yourself for us, for me ...

december15

A FAULTY PEDESTAL

Grow in the grace and knowledge of our Lord and Savior Jesus Christ. To him be glory both now and forever!

2 PETER 3:18

The young man had just completed his first semester of Bible college and was on his way to visit his grandfather in the hospital. His grandfather had spent a lifetime of service to God, with over thirty years on the mission field devoted to preaching the gospel in Africa.

When the youth entered the room, he saw the old man lying in bed, frail yet alert. He sat down and began to visit with him. He made sure he told his grandfather all about his accomplishments at college and about how he had been serving the Lord. Next semester he would even be visiting inmates in prison on a weekly basis!

The young man thought all this would impress his grandfather, but the old man looked at him with eyes full of love and asked him this simple question: "And are you growing in grace?"

The words cut deep into the young man's heart. With one question, the old man had gently torn down the pedestal of human effort on which this young man had been trying to build his faith. The focus of his life in Christ would be forever changed!

What's your focus? As men, we find it easy to place the emphasis on our accomplishments rather than on God's grace. May you experience afresh the grace — the unmerited favor and blessing — that Christ extends to you each day. May it overflow in your life and touch others in such a way that they see, not a great guy who gives so much, but a loving Savior who gave it all. ♦

PRAYER

Loving Savior, help me grow in grace . . .

december16

A CONTINUAL FEAST

The cheerful heart has a continual feast.

PROVERBS 15:15

Joy is strength (Nehemiah 8:10), and it is good medicine (Proverbs 17:22). Now we read that a joyful, cheerful heart is like enjoying "a continual feast." It surely sounds as though joy is a prescription for good health.

The picture here is of a heart overflowing with joy, with the result that everything in life is a cause for celebration—like having a great feast.

Often in Scripture, the picture of a feast is a picture of celebration. Nehemiah talked about joy being strength, and he told the people to "go and enjoy choice food and sweet drinks" (Nehemiah 8:10). David wrote in his well-loved psalm, "You prepare a table before me in the presence of my enemies. You anoint my head with oil; my cup overflows" (Psalm 23:5). Jesus compared the call of salvation in him to being invited to a great banquet (Matthew 22:1–14).

The picture of such celebration points to the ability to look at a blustery day and a sunny day and find the celebration in both. It's taking the difficult times and being willing to continually inwardly smile at what God is doing, at the feast he is preparing.

A continual feast means there is always a party going on in the heart. It's knowing that at the end of a tough time, a celebration is brewing—anticipating it as though it is already there.

A continual feast—always overflowing with good things and living life with not just a "glass half full" attitude but with an attitude overflowing with joy.

It's time to party! ◆

PRAYER

Lord, give my heart a continual feast of joy . . .

december17

STRENGTH AND SHIELD

The LORD is my strength and my shield; my heart trusts in him, and he helps me. My heart leaps for joy, and with my song I praise him.

PSALM 28:7

When darkness invades our lives, we "cry for mercy" (Psalm 28:6). Nothing feels darker than a time of silence from God—when prayers seem to go unanswered, when the heavens seem silent.

David, writer of this psalm, pleaded with God and asked him about dealing with wickedness and evil people who do evil things.

We may not find ourselves faced with purely evil people, but we may face situations that can only come from the evil one. Some form of darkness invades our lives, and we wonder where God is and why he is silent.

David prayed and discovered that the Lord provides strength to stand against the assaults of the evil one and a shield to protect the mind and heart. We need both—the shield and the strength to hold it up. The shield protects from the poison arrows shot by the one who battles against us and against all we want to be and do for the Lord. The shield only works when we have it in our hands and are prepared as soon as the arrows start to fly. When we get discouraged with God or when we refuse to rely on his strength, we drop the shield, and the arrows hit their mark—arrows of doubt, fear, discouragement, depression, anger, whatever your particular poison may be.

However, when our hearts trust him, we are helped. It all comes down to trust. Do we really believe that God can do a miracle? Do we really believe that he will do what he promises? Do we really trust his promises of provision and care?

Do you want joy this week? Gather your strength and hold your shield up high. Trust your loving Father with all your heart. And then live like it. ♦

PRAYER

This is a season of joy, Lord; help me to have it . . .

december18

PURE DELIGHT

For the LORD takes delight in his people; he crowns the humble with victory. Let his faithful people rejoice in this honor and sing for joy on their beds.

PSALM 149:4–5

We are invited to "rejoice" and "sing for joy" because God *delights* in us. Think about it—God experiences sheer delight when he thinks about you.

When was the last time you felt the emotion of sheer delight?

Picture this: Two young men from Los Angeles run into the backyard of their friend's house in Chicago—it is winter, and the snow is just starting to fall. They have never seen snow before, and the look on their faces is one of sheer delight. Their eyes sparkle; their faces are filled with wonder; their smiles are contagious. Both open their arms wide to try to take it all in. One is looking up so the snowflakes can land on his face. The other says, "Can you *believe* how awesome this is?"

Delight. When God looks at us, the delight on his face is not unlike the sheer delight on those California boys' faces. His eyes sparkle as he looks at you, his special creation. He can't help but be excited. He sees every part of you—and you are as clean to him as newly fallen snow because of what his Son did on your behalf. Isaiah wrote, "Though your sins are like scarlet, they shall be as white as snow" (Isaiah 1:18).

So God looks around at the angels, points at you, and asks, "Can you *believe* how awesome my child is?"

The God of the universe smiles at the very thought of you and takes delight in who you are, who he created you to be. Is that not reason enough to sing for joy today? ♦

PRAYER

I can't believe that you delight in me, Lord...

december19

IN GOOD HANDS

"For I know the plans I have for you," declares the LORD, "plans to prosper you and not to harm you, plans to give you hope and a future."

JEREMIAH 29:11

You may have heard the expression, "Everyone's talking about the weather, but no one can do anything about it." So we watch the forecasts before heading out and try to prepare accordingly. However, despite advances in modern technology—enhanced radar technology, computer models, statistical analyses—no meteorologist can accurately predict the weather.

Also, regardless of tireless efforts of sport statisticians, analysts, and experts, no one can know for sure the outcome of a specific contest. In spite of their insight and savvy, no politician or scholar can predict international events. Even highly trained economic experts struggle with trying to predict the next boom or recession. And no amount of intelligence and education accumulated by an individual, group, or institution can ensure the knowledge of how human beings will act.

The point is that no one knows the future. No one except God, that is. Not limited by time, God sees the end, the beginning, and the in-between. He knows all that has happened and all that will happen. Not only does God know the future, but he also has great plans in the future for those who belong to him.

When you feel apprehensive or anxious, fearing what might happen during the next year, the next month, the next day, or the next moment, think of these hopeful words in Jeremiah. God has good plans for your life. Your future is secure in God's hands. ♦

PRAYER

Lord, my hope is in you ...

GOOD NEWS OF GREAT JOY

The angel said to them, "Do not be afraid. I bring you good news that will cause great joy for all the people. Today in the town of David a Savior has been born to you; he is the Messiah, the Lord."

LUKE 2:10–11

The angel brought the shepherds "good news that will cause great joy." And where did the angel direct the shepherds? To a baby.

Surely that came as a surprise to the shepherds. A baby Savior? Was there a moment of concern as they breathed heavily in the night air after their dash from the fields? Did they gaze on this child and realize that, while this may be the promised Savior (hadn't the angel just said so?), salvation was not arriving quite as they expected? And the timetable would be quite different from what they (and indeed all of their fellow citizens) desired? In any case, the text tells us that the shepherds "spread the word" and "returned, glorifying and praising God" (Luke 2:17, 20).

What about us today? We can look in the rearview mirror of history and know what the shepherds did not know that first Christmas—how this salvation played out three decades later. Like the shepherds, we look into our Savior's face and know that God will do as he promises. But also, like them, we do not know how or when those promises will be fulfilled. So we go back to our fields and our sheep in our Roman-occupied territory … and we wait.

Isn't that the hardest part? Doesn't the waiting rob us of our joy? We focus on the *way* we want life to happen and the *timing* in which we want things to happen. God decides instead to answer with timing that only he understands as perfect. In the meantime, we can take a lesson from the shepherds: spread the word, glorifying and praising God. In short, even as we wait, we rejoice in this good news of great joy! ♦

PRAYER

With the angels, I glorify and praise you, Lord …

december**21**

GOOD NEWS

For to us a child is born, to us a son is given, and the government will be on his shoulders. And he will be called Wonderful Counselor, Mighty God, Everlasting Father, Prince of Peace.

ISAIAH 9:6

When we hear the word *prophecy*, we tend to think of people who claim they can foretell the future. People in strange garb, sitting in dimly lit rooms at the back of used bookstores with a sign out front featuring a crystal ball.

But in the Bible, the word *prophet* doesn't mean that. It simply means someone who speaks on behalf of God to his people. Sometimes the message is simply for one individual. Sometimes the message is for an entire nation. Sometimes the message is about what's going to happen in the near future. And sometimes (as in this verse) it really is about the future. God assures his people that a Messiah—a Savior—is coming.

Look at the promises God makes. No more crooked governments. Only justice, righteousness, and, most of all, peace. Forever.

This is good news because it's what all of us yearn for in our hearts. We know this world isn't right. We know there has to be something better.

But the most amazing part of all is that, although we do have to wait to see God make the whole world perfect, we don't have to wait to have heaven come down to earth. It's possible in our life to be connected to God and to live in such a way as to make heaven a reality in our life, in our world. Right now.

Take a moment to connect with God, thanking him for the ways he makes heaven a reality. ♦

PRAYER

Heavenly Father, thank you for ...

december22

TRUST IN UNCERTAIN TIMES

"I am the Lord's servant," Mary answered. "May your word to me be fulfilled."

LUKE 1:38

Have you ever had great hope in the plans for the future—a prosperous career or endeavor—but something changed? Suddenly, instead of looking at the future with excitement, you look in fear of what it might hold.

Many times when the Holy Spirit speaks, we react with fear or hesitation. We get nervous and don't want to accept an uncertain future. We get caught up in the noise and confusion of circumstances. We need cold, hard facts and a solution, and we need it *right now*—but our questions are met with silence.

We have a great example in Mary's response to the angel in Luke 1:38: "May your word to me be fulfilled." How about the trouble she is facing? Here she is, a teenage girl engaged to be married, and suddenly she is hit with the news that she is going to bear a child who is not the child of her fiancé. What will Joseph say? What will others say? Her future looks uncertain! Yet she responds with complete faith and trust in God.

When God calls, he doesn't say you'll never face troubles, but he does say, "Do not be afraid." God will give you strength to bear the call. Are you willing to trust him as you face an uncertain future? ♦

> **PRAYER**

Lord, I know you have the future all mapped out ...

december23

LISTEN FIRST

The angel said to [the shepherds], "Do not be afraid. I bring you good news that will cause great joy for all the people. Today in the town of David a Savior has been born to you; he is the Messiah, the Lord."

LUKE 2:10–11

Whether driving the car or at home or even in the office, our thoughts can become saturated with the pressures and chores of life and work. If we let the stress become too loud, it drowns out our Savior's voice. All of that noise shuts down our ability to tune in to what God is telling us.

Two thousand years ago, others like us felt pressure while at work. While they kept watch over their flocks, protecting the animals from danger while providing for their families, a group of first-century shepherds heard from heaven. As the Lord's glory surrounded them, they were terrified! But they were told, "Do not be afraid"—and with that reassurance, they listened to the message.

In today's world we sometimes need to hear the words "do not be afraid" and allow the Holy Spirit to remind us about the child who is our Savior. Don't allow the noises of the world to drown out the message of the birth of God's Son. As God's messengers said to Mary and the shepherds, "Do not be afraid."

The angel continued, "You will find a baby wrapped in cloths and lying in a manger" (2:12). Immediately a multitude of angels joyfully worshiped after hearing the birth announcement.

Their fear having turned to joy, the shepherds went directly to see the newborn Messiah.

During this season of rushing around and confusion, we need to be listening first and going second. Go to the Savior—the one the angel spoke of to the shepherds—and find rest, peace, and new life through Jesus. ♦

PRAYER

Lord, help me hear your voice above the noise of life ...

december24

ACCEPT HIS GIFT

The shepherds returned, glorifying and praising God for all the things they had heard and seen, which were just as they had been told.

LUKE 2:20

Sales flyers announce a great deal on the latest—the ultimate gift under the tree. The word is out, and you must *get it now* if you want to give the most treasured gift-unwrapping experience ever! But is that really the most important thing about Christmas?

The shepherds recounted the events that took place under the stars with the messengers from heaven. Those who were there at the time of the birth of Jesus were amazed. Can you imagine being one of those in the streets who heard this proclamation? The shepherds not only knew that a Savior had been born, but also where, when, and to whom. Those shepherds exclaimed with such confidence that all heaven broke out in a song of praise!

People were definitely talking. No one could keep silent about this big event. The Jews had been longing for the Messiah's advent through all history.

Mary treasured all these things in her heart. She knew the truth about her special child—that he was indeed the long-awaited Messiah.

What will you treasure this season? Some amazing gadget under the tree, or the love that knows no end? Treasure the ultimate gift to man from God—his Son, Jesus. Take him into your heart this season and treasure the gift of salvation and eternal life. ♦

PRAYER

Father, thank you for your gift . . .

december25

THE CENTER OF YOUR HOPES

But you, Bethlehem Ephrathah, though you are small among the clans of Judah, out of you will come for me one who will be ruler over Israel, whose origins are from of old, from ancient times.

MICAH 5:2

In 1867, Phillips Brooks wrote the lyrics to the well-known Christmas carol "O Little Town of Bethlehem." We sing it at Christmas. Yet how often do we dwell on the message of the first verse?

O little town of Bethlehem, how still we see thee lie! No great political decisions are being made; no governmental plans are being struck by man to change the course of humanity.

Above thy deep and dreamless sleep the silent stars go by. Just another night in the life of those in the town. Yet businesses are booming, and every inn is full.

Yet in thy dark streets shineth the everlasting Light. Into the mundane world comes a light that pierces all darkness—the Light of the world. This light will reveal truth to those willing to look.

The hopes and fears of all the years are met in thee tonight. All of history is centered on one night and one child—the longings about the future; the hopes for your wife and children, your job, your life; your successes; the fears, pain, damage caused by the world; bad decisions; grief and sorrow. As the prophet Micah foretold, God was born as a child in the humble town of Bethlehem. The only way to reestablish relationship with man was for God to become a man—to go through all that man goes through, yet remain sinless, and take all of man's sins on himself. The perfect sacrifice for our sins could never have taken place had not all the hopes and fears been met in the birth of the Christ child on that one night in Bethlehem. Trust him with your hopes and fears. ♦

PRAYER

Lord, I trust you with ...

december**26**

BROKEN MOURNING

He will wipe every tear from their eyes. There will be no more death or mourning or crying or pain, for the old order of things has passed away.

REVELATION 21:4

Sometimes we cry out of frustration or anger. We may choke up during a poignant moment in a dramatic performance or a personal story. At times, we are surprised by tears, such as when we hear a special song, visit a memorable place, or reunite with a friend. But the crying times we remember most come out of personal pain.

When a toddler loses a toy, a child loses a pet, a teenager loses a love, a man loses his father, or a wife loses her lifelong partner—a flood of tears threaten to overwhelm as grief tears the soul. Yet we are not alone in our sorrow, in these desperate times. God is with us, comforting with his love, peace, and tender care, and making this promise that one day death, sorrow, dying, and pain will be abolished ... forever!

What great sorrow do you harbor? What is your private grief? No matter what you are going through, it's not the last word—God has written the final chapter, and he promises true fulfillment and eternal joy for those who love him. Eternity with God will be more wonderful than you can ever imagine. All wrongs will be made right, and all tears will be wiped away.

No sorrow can last in the presence of God's joy. ◆

PRAYER

I feel so sad, at times, Father. I miss ...

EVERYTHING NEW

He who was seated on the throne said, "I am making everything new!" Then he said, "Write this down, for these words are trustworthy and true." He said to me: "It is done. I am the Alpha and the Omega, the Beginning and the End. To the thirsty I will give water without cost from the spring of the water of life.

REVELATION 21:5–6

"I am making everything new!" God the Creator is also God the Re-creator. At the beginning of the Bible, in Genesis, we are told that God created the world and all living creatures, climaxing with the unique creation of human beings in his image. Here, in the last book of God's Word, we read his promise to start over, creating anew the heavens and the new earth — a perfect environment for his people, his new creations.

Before the beginning and in the beginning was God, the Creator and Sustainer of all there is. And after everything has passed away, God will be there as well. He is "the Beginning and the End."

Clearly civilization is in decline. Our sinful world is rushing toward destruction. We see evidence at every turn — hatred, violence, greed, lust, corruption, pride. But what we see is not what always will be. God will have the final word, and he will make "everything new." As his children, we can look forward to a new heaven and new earth and to eternal fellowship with our Father and with his Son, our Lord Jesus.

When you are thirsty, come to the Spring. When you are discouraged, remember God's promise. When you see no escape, look to your Lord. ♦

PRAYER

Create in me a new, clean heart, Lord! Thank you for your work in me and for your promise of heaven with you . . .

SOON!

Look, I am coming soon! My reward is with me, and I will give to each person according to what they have done.

REVELATION 22:12

Waiting can be difficult, especially in the middle of a struggle or when an anticipated event brings great pleasure and joy. Little children often exclaim, "I can hardly wait!" as they wait for a birthday celebration, Christmas Day, or a family trip. We know what they mean, especially as we await the arrival of a much missed loved one. The days and hours seem to creep by—the event can't get here soon enough.

When Jesus ascended into heaven, the angel explained to onlookers that eventually Jesus would return—and they could hardly wait. Here in John's vision of the future, he sees and hears Jesus speak his promise to come soon. When Jesus came the first time, he came as a baby and as the suffering Servant. When Christ returns, he will come as the conquering King and righteous Judge.

Because Christ will reward everyone according to what they have done, his second coming is bad news for those who have spurned him. But it is glorious news for those who love God and have committed their lives to Christ—and it can't come soon enough. Wounds will be healed, wrongs made right, families reunited, bodies made whole, and justice served. No wonder John could exclaim, "Amen. Come, Lord Jesus!" (22:20).

Jesus will be returning soon. Be prepared. Spread the news. Get excited! ♦

PRAYER

Come, Lord Jesus . . .

december**29**

ALWAYS

Therefore go and make disciples of all nations, baptizing them in the name of the Father and of the Son and of the Holy Spirit, and teaching them to obey everything I have commanded you. And surely I am with you always, to the very end of the age.

MATTHEW 28:19–20

"I don't think I can do it."
   "You can—and I'll catch you if you happen to slip."

"I'm afraid, Dad. I don't want to go!"
   "Don't worry, son. I'll be with you."

"Mommy! Mommy! I had a terrible dream."
   "I'm right here, honey. It's OK. You'll be fine."

Remember being encouraged or comforted by your mom or dad? Your loving parents assured you of their presence—in the room, in the house, or just a phone call away. Secure in that knowledge, you gained the courage and peace to go on. You knew that everything would be all right.

Now you are all grown up, an adult, a man. But you still get scared to death at times and have anxiety-riddled nightmares, worrying about the future, your finances, and your family. You may even long desperately for the assurance of Mom's or Dad's strong hand and loving word. You feel burdened and alone.

But you're not alone. God is there with you wherever you are. The promise that Jesus gave the disciples as he sent them into the world is also for you: "I am with you always."

Take heart! Have hope! Be encouraged! Move out in faith!

Christ is with you. ♦

PRAYER

Father, I need you always . . .

december**30**

THE FRUIT OF JOY

The fruit of the Spirit is love, joy, peace, forbearance, kindness, goodness, faithfulness, gentleness and self-control.

GALATIANS 5:22–23

When the clouds come in and life weighs heavy around us, it's difficult to feel joy, much less to act joyful. As the new year approaches, you may feel a bit of melancholy. Perhaps the finances are tighter this year. Maybe life has dealt some difficult blows in the past year. Or as the year winds down, you're just not feeling a whole lot of hope for the future.

Life *is* tough, and if you've been facing great difficulty, you need not berate yourself for not being in a joyful mood. But you can reach deep down into your soul and discover that you already have a dose of joy there, for if you are a Christian, you have the Holy Spirit, who promises that "the fruit of the Spirit is ... joy." Joy is already there, deep in your heart. So whether you *feel* joyful is not the starting point; the starting point is to quietly sit before God and express your deepest hurts and concerns and ask him to grow in you his fruit of joy.

If you do that today, you'll find that your spirit will lift and your mood will lighten. Why? Because by seeking God and taking him at his word, you are trusting in his promises. And the more you trust, the more you comprehend that whatever is happening in your life is indeed part of his plan. It will result in good; it will give you a hope and a future. The promises, far from being stale or pat answers, are instead living and breathing promises that are true for *you* today.

Then say "Happy New Year" at the top of your lungs—and mean it! ♦

PRAYER

Lord, give me a sense of your joy ...

december31

CELEBRATION TIME!

I will sing of the LORD's great love forever; with my mouth I will make your faithfulness known through all generations. I will declare that your love stands firm forever, that you have established your faithfulness in heaven itself.

PSALM 89:1–2

Shout out with a happy yell as the clock ticks to a new year. Sing and blow out the candles. Renew your wedding vows. Cheer until you're hoarse as your team wins the championship.

We love fond memories, significant milestones, and great victories. But have you ever celebrated a future event? In effect, this is what Ethan is doing in Psalm 89.

Ethan was one of the head musicians in the temple. He wrote this song to celebrate God's promise to keep David's descendants on the throne forever. Years after this psalm was written, Jerusalem was destroyed, and today kings no longer rule over Israel. Yet God's promise was fulfilled through David's greatest descendant, Jesus.

Ethan couldn't know the future, but he knew God—the maker of the future—and so he could confidently assert, "Your love stands firm forever."

God always keeps his promises. Even when the future looks bleak and the situation is perplexing, we can count on him.

Reflect on what God has done in your life—how he led you to himself and has cared for you over the years. Remember his faithfulness and trust in his promises. Then praise God for who he is, for what he has done, and for what he will do. You may even want to break into song and celebrate! God keeps his promises. ♦

PRAYER

I praise you, Lord, for . . .

scripture index

Psalm 99:5	November 6	Experiencing God's Presence in Worship
Psalm 100:1–4	March 20	It Makes Me Want to Shout!
Psalm 100:4–5	February 7	Gates and Courts
Psalm 103:7–8	June 8	Made Known His Ways
Psalm 118:24	September 10	Dealing with Change
Psalm 121:1–2	December 9	Help!
Psalm 121:5–8	August 11	Your Shade
Psalm 127:1–2	November 27	Finding Time to Connect with the Family
Psalm 130:3–4	October 24	When Sin Seems Victorious
Psalm 139:1–3	March 26	Known and Loved
Psalm 139:8–10	February 8	Hide-and-Seek
Psalm 139:17–18	July 6	Precious Thoughts about You
Psalm 139:23–24	March 23	The Test of Time
Psalm 145:8–9	June 9	Homecoming
Psalm 145:14–16	July 7	On the Trail
Psalm 146:5	November 7	The Gift of Hope
Psalm 149:4–5	December 18	Pure Delight
Proverbs 3:5–6	August 12	Asking for Directions
Proverbs 3:9–10	August 26	What Money Can't Buy
Proverbs 3:11–12	August 27	But It Hurts
Proverbs 3:28	July 20	Putting It Off
Proverbs 4:5	August 31	Wise Up
Proverbs 6:6	May 21	Get in the Game
Proverbs 6:27–29	August 30	Consider This — First
Proverbs 10:9	July 23	We Are Being Watched
Proverbs 13:4	May 21	Get in the Game
Proverbs 14:8	November 3	Looking Ahead
Proverbs 15:4	July 16	Word Choice
Proverbs 15:15	December 16	A Continual Feast
Proverbs 16:32	February 10	One of Your Best Friends
Proverbs 17:22	December 16	A Continual Feast
Proverbs 18:24	February 16	Sticking Close
Proverbs 22:6	July 29	How to Have Perfect Children
Proverbs 22:7	July 26	Breaking the Chains of Debt
Proverbs 23:2	October 12	What Makes Gluttony Deadly?
Proverbs 24:16	March 4	When Life Hits Hard
Proverbs 25:28	November 29	The Freedom of Self-Control
Proverbs 27:17	January 16	A Faithful Friend
Proverbs 29:11	February 25	You Can't Bury Your Anger
Proverbs 29:25	January 21	What If?
Ecclesiastes 12:1	April 24	No Alibis, No Regrets
Isaiah 1:11, 13	December 12	The Giving
Isaiah 1:17	June 22	The Heart of Justice
Isaiah 1:18	December 10	Clean!
Isaiah 1:18	December 18	Pure Delight
Isaiah 9:6	December 21	Good News
Isaiah 26:3	December 8	Give Peace a Chance
Isaiah 30:18	July 8	Justice I Am
Isaiah 40:30–31	April 19	Soaring
Isaiah 44:13	July 11	What Are You Building?
Isaiah 50:4	April 8	Listen

topical index

NIV Once-A-Day Bible

The *NIV Once-A-Day Bible* organizes the New International Version—the world's most popular modern-English Bible—into 365 daily readings. This softcover edition includes a daily Scripture reading from both the Old and New Testaments, plus a psalm or a proverb, followed by a short devotional thought written by the staff at the trusted ministry Walk Thru the Bible.

Softcover: 978-0-310-95092-9
Ebook: 978-0-310-41349-3

NIV Once-A-Day Bible: Chronological Edition

The *NIV Once-A-Day Bible: Chronological Edition* organizes the New International Version—the world's most popular modern-English Bible—into 365 daily readings placed in chronological order. This softcover edition includes a daily Scripture reading, followed by a short devotional thought written by the staff at the trusted ministry Walk Thru the Bible.

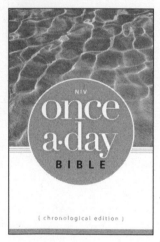

Softcover: 978-0-310-95095-0
Ebook: 978-0-310-41348-6